YOU GOTTA DEAL
WITH IT

YOU GOTTA DEAL WITH IT

*Black Family Relations
in a Southern Community*

THEODORE R. KENNEDY

New York   Oxford
Oxford University Press
1980

To Mama
and Daddy, Alvera, Saundra, Sonny, Billy, Clint,
Gene, Terry, Richard, and Baby Dean

Library of Congress Cataloging in Publication Data

Kennedy, Theodore R   1936-
  You gotta deal with it.

  Bibliography: p.
  Includes index.
  1.   Afro-American families—Southern States.
2.   Southern States—Rural conditions.   I.   Title.
E185.92.K4   301.42'1'0975   79-14476
ISBN 0-19-502591-1
ISBN 0-19-502592-X pbk.

This reprint, 1981

Printed in the United States of America

THE black family has long been a subject matter for social scientists and there are almost as many interpretations of the black family as there are writers on the subject. One reason for so many different accounts is that every author on the subject attempts to reify the concept of family. Lately, social scientists have recognized that this concept may not be applicable for a discussion of the black family. However, these later writers have had to contend with already established constructs concerning family and feel they are bound to follow preconceived ideas for representing family structure. As a result, the representations of the black family have become so analytical that one has problems recognizing the people being discussed.

The main reason for my writing this book is to indicate a departure from these preconceived ideas that force reification of the concept of family, as well as from the use of conventional ways of reporting data. In a way, I have taken the attitude that the members of the black family are better equipped to speak for themselves. And only when it becomes absolutely necessary do I try to provide an explanation instead of an interpretation of the data. Consequently, I have chosen to include actual dialogue between members of the families and myself, along with

dialogue between members of these families. The book is therefore not limited to the academic world, but its contents can be
shared with everyone who is concerned with family life among
blacks in a small southern town in the United States.

Obtaining actual dialogue required the extensive use of the
tape recorder, accurate notes, and a good memory. In some cases
using the tape recorder was not possible and I had to take notes.
Sometimes even note-taking proved difficult. In this case, I had
to rely on memory until I had time to make notes. I used both
my memory and notes and then set up an interview to verify
my data. During the interviews I was able to use the tape
recorder.

Within two months of my stay in Vera Ridge I could use my
tape recorder almost everywhere I went, in public places and
social functions. However, in the few instances where the tape
recorder was not possible I relied on my method of note-taking.
As a result, the dialogue in this book is accurate. The only
change made was to protect people from being recognized; I
have replaced real names, places, and events that would make
it obvious whom, where, and what I actually recorded.

The study presented here could not have been accomplished
if it were not for the following people and organizations to
whom I am sincerely grateful: Professors Barnett, Carroll,
Lieber, Silverman; Szwed, director of The Center for Urban
Ethnography, University of Pennsylvania; Taylor, director of
Afro-American Studies at Princeton University; The Ford
Foundation, Division of Administration, Manpower Service and
The Department of Health, Education and Welfare. I wish to
express a very special gratitude to the people of the community
I refer to as Vera Ridge. Without their understanding and as-
sistance I would not have been able to accomplish the task I set
out to do.

T. R. K.

Port Jefferson, N.Y.
March 1979

CONTENTS

YOU GOTTA DEAL WITH IT

*T*HIS ethnography is a result of a year's study in a small town in the southern United States. For reasons of privacy I have changed the names of the town and the individuals in it. I have tried to enliven the narration with many of my personal encounters with the people of the town.

The town I call Vera Ridge has a population of approximately thirty thousand—of which one-third is black. Vera Ridge is a typical southern town. This is especially true in terms of the disparity between the black and white population. One characteristic that makes Vera Ridge a typical southern town is its clear line of demarcation, or, in this instance, the railroad tracks. There are other characteristics: the vast differences between the white and black standard of living. Poverty, unemployment, under-employment, low wages, inadequate housing, medical, educational, and recreational facilities—all signify problems in the black community.

The white community varies economically from a small exclusive wealthy section to project housing for welfare recipients. The exclusive part of the white section is divided into two areas: One is Pine Crest, where the Culpeppers, Ropers, Golfs, Orrs, and other well-established southern families reside. The other section is referred to as "Jew Hill." This is where the Jewish population live. Pine Crest is adjacent to a golf course. Amidst the golf course is Vera Ridge's Country Club that excludes blacks, Jews, and "foreigners."

To the black population, all the people who lived on the other side of the tracks were white. Black people did not distinguish between Jews, foreigners, and other whites. However, on two occasions I was able to gain some insight into how whites felt about other whites in Vera Ridge. Once when I was shopping at a drug store buying film and other camera equipment, the owner and I got into a conversation. He did not have the right equipment for my camera, but he said, "I think that Jew boy has it over there at Goodman's Supplies."

I asked for directions and he said, "It's right down the street. You can't miss it."

I didn't feel comfortable asking him what he had meant by "Jew boy" at that time. Later, after I had been purchasing items from his store for about a month I decided to find out what he did mean. I walked into his store and when he saw me coming, he said in his customary way, "How are you doing today, Reggie. What can I do for you?"

He had become very friendly toward me, but I am sure it was only because I spent as much as a hundred dollars a month in his store. So, I decided I would ask him about his remark. He replied, "Now let me get this straight. I don't have nothing against anybody so long as they stay in their place. But, we've been calling them Jew boys ever since I can remember."

"Is Mr. Goodman Jewish?"

"They all are. All of them up and down that street. It used to be one old boy there. He owned a hardware store. Now half the town's business is owned by them."

I knew that wasn't true, although I didn't know how many Jewish-owned businesses were in Vera Ridge. So I asked, "Are there that many Jewish people in Vera Ridge?"

"More than otta be here . . . I mean, if we're not careful, they are gonna take over all the businesses."

"Where did they come from and what would make them want to come to a small town like this?"

"That furniture factory. They brought it down here. Ain't nobody said too much about it because it gave jobs to so many of our people, even your people got jobs there. But it didn't stop there. They brought this discount house here, ran some white people outta business, then came a doctor and now there's two lawyers. There may be more, you never can tell."

"Who uses the doctor and lawyers?"

"The Jew People, your people go to them too, and some poor white trash who don't know no better. None of us would ever think of using them—at least I wouldn't. I think them lawyers came down here when we had all that trouble from them people up North coming down here trying to tell us how to live our lives."

"Where do they all live?"

"They all live over there next to that wooded area just as you come in to town from the North. Up there on the hill. We call it Jew Hill. They built these fancy houses. Every one of them is rich. Of course I never been up there myself, but they say those houses are big and expensive and that in front of every one of them sits a big new car. You gotta give them credit. If they are poor, they get rich. If they are rich they get richer. They tell me they'd sell their own mama if there was money to be made. 'Course I don't know nothing about that. That's what they say."

"Who are they?"

"Oh, people around town. People who ought to know what they are talking about."

"What do they do besides work? I mean what kind of community activities are they into?"

"They stick pretty much to themselves for the most part. I think they go out of town, to "The City," when they want to have some fun. We had some trouble with them a while back. Them lawyers that came down here, they tried to join our country club. That's when we put our foot down. We don't want them there. That is one thing I could never figure out about people, why do somebody want to be where they ain't wanted. If you let one of them come in, pretty soon the Jews would take over the place. They didn't get in though."

Although I would have liked to continue my conversation with him I didn't feel that comfortable in talking with a white man. During our conversation he would come very close to revealing his position about black people and I felt it would be unwise for me to respond to him. There were times when he would become emotional about his position on the Jewish population, while at the same time he would be saying that he did not have anything against them. He would turn red and pound his hand to emphasize a point he was trying to make. I learned that there were approximately three hundred Jewish people living in Vera Ridge. I wanted to talk with some of them, but felt it was unwise because, for me, there was no way to distinguish people who were Jewish from any other white person.

I was able to obtain a further distinction made by the white community between "us" and "them." A banquet was being held at the Vera Ridge Country Club honoring some politicians. The regular staff of blacks who serviced the club wasn't enough and additional help was needed. A member of one of the families I studied told me about the event and asked if I wanted to work. I agreed and he said I would have to wear a uniform. I told him I didn't mind because I wanted the opportunity to observe blacks working in an environment among white people. I also wanted to see the white "society" people of Vera Ridge. Of course I had never waited tables before and didn't know if I'd last through the event.

I learned two things. One, how much the white community hated the blacks, especially "trouble makers," and, two, their contempt for the Jews and "those foreigners." I never quite understood who constituted the foreigners. At one point, Italians were referred to as foreigners, and at another point the foreigners were "them white northerners." At any rate, if you were not a Culpepper, Roper, Golf, or Orr, and you were white you were in trouble.

I had a difficult time keeping my composure when serving these people and listening to their conversations, which they did not try to disguise. Once I was approaching a table with drinks and the conversation was about "that nigger who was running for mayor." I thought they would at least lower their voices or postpone their discussion until I had served the drinks but, as if I were not there, one of them said, "Them niggers are getting too smart for their own good. We're going to have to do something about them."

They went on to indicate that a visit from the Ku Klux Klan would do the job. I shook as I placed the drinks in front of them. One man said, "A nigger had the nerves to ask me to call him Mister. I looked him dead in the eye, then I spat at his feet, turned and walked away. I should have spat in his face."

At another table people were talking about how the black population of Vera Ridge was growing and that they would have to redistrict the population so that no part of the black section would constitute half the number of people in any given section. What I later learned was that Vera Ridge was redistricted into a pie-shaped section. The center of the pie was the black sections, so that the closer you are to the center, the fewer people (black, that is) represented a part of each section. The farther from the center, the greater number of people represented each section. Therefore, no matter what district, there would always be a majority of whites over blacks.

Most of the men's conversations that I heard dealt with politics and had black overtones. While serving a table where mostly women sat I overheard one say, "I'll go to my grave before I ever let any nigger or Jew join this club."

She indicated that it was all right for niggers to work there because they could be controlled; however, "If you let a Jew in here, he'll own the place before you know it."

The others at the table seemed to agree. One of them mentioned something about Italians. She said, "Out yonder them Italians keep to their farming and they don't try to come where they ain't wanted."

Another woman remarked, "But you have to watch out for them foreigners. You can never tell what they're up to. They have funny eyes and when they look at you they seem to stare right through you."

In a way I felt a sense of relief. It was good to know that blacks weren't the only hated people in Vera Ridge. On the other hand, I felt hostile toward the Jews because I felt they were strong people. They are intelligent and powerful enough to establish themselves anywhere in the United States because they had judges, doctors, lawyers, and money to fortify their position. I thought to myself, "Why do they have to put up with this shit?"

I felt hostile toward the Italians because they had the power of one of the most powerful organizations in the world at their hand. They should be able to move freely anywhere they wanted to go. They didn't have to be dirt farmers living on the outskirts of any town. I realized that my hostility really wasn't directed at the Jews or the Italians, it wasn't even directed toward the blacks. I was angry with myself for being there in the first place. I rushed to the kitchen, put down my tray, and told the black man in charge I was quitting. I asked how he could take the things that those people were saying right to his face, and he said, "Now don't you go starting no trouble. I have to work here. I live in this town, you don't. It's always been this way, so long as I get my pay I don't care what they say."

"Well, I'm leaving. You can have whatever money I have coming to me. I don't live here and I don't have to work here and I won't take their shit. I'm changing my clothes and getting out of here before I do or say something that may get me into trouble."

"You're doing the right thing then. That's the trouble with you young people, you don't have no patience. Things don't come right over night."

I didn't even want to respond to that statement. I got into my car with the intention of driving home. However, when I reached the exit gate I decided to go by the residential areas of

Pine Crest and "Jew Hill." Just after leaving the golf course you come to a main street that will take you to the highway leading through the center of Vera Ridge. If you turned left on this main street you could approach the periphery of Pine Crest. I felt safe entering this area because the street that leads you there is the same one that leads to the freeway leaving Vera Ridge.

I didn't stray from the main road while driving through Pine Crest. This was the wealthy area of Vera Ridge. People living here were said to be families with "old money." On both sides of the road you could see old, large two- and three-storied houses. All were painted white or near white. Each home had a large, fenced yard. The lawns were well kept and hedges making different patterns stood neatly trimmed. There were large oak and pine trees—some of them clustered, others spaced apart. Every home had a black cast iron figure with a hat and lips painted red. Most of them were holding some kind of light fixture. Some homes seemed very old and looked more like plantation mansions, while others seemed to copy early post Civil War architecture. I traveled almost a mile before I came to the end of Pine Crest.

In order to get to the Jewish section, I had to retrace my drive to the golf course entrance. Once I reached the street that takes you downtown Vera Ridge, I had to turn right and travel approximately a mile. I then turned off the main road toward a wooded area. I had a story in case I ran into trouble for being there: I'd simply tell anyone who stopped me that I had gotten lost. I drove on a narrow road that wound its way up a hill and came to a fenced area, only there was no gate where a gate would normally be. I drove through the opening in the fence. A short way into the enclosed area you have a choice of three possible directions. I could see some homes through the wooded area and I didn't feel apprehensive because I was in a Jewish section. They couldn't be too bad—I thought.

I chose the extreme right turn; however, that led directly into someone's driveway. Before I could turn around and head out, I was stopped by a man carrying a shotgun. He came over to the window of my car with the gun pointed at me. I didn't know what to do. I thought of taking off, but I figured he would probably shoot at me. He said that I was on his property and wanted to know what I was doing there. He told me I had better be careful driving into this area because they had had some trouble "a while back and people living here are pretty uptight about strangers."

I wanted to ask him why he carried the gun, but I thought better and decided to tell him I had gotten lost. Having checked my car, especially my license plates, which were out of state, he must have believed me. He gave me directions to downtown Vera Ridge and told me that it was not safe for me to be in the area. He said I could have gotten shot.

I didn't wait for any further explanations or ask any further questions. I followed the road he had suggested until I had reached the exit from which I had come. I did not see much of the so-called Jewish area, but what I did observe led me to believe that the homes were large and occupied large areas of land. Had I known the area better I could have approached it from the front side where I could have gotten a better view. Nevertheless, the homes were expensive and the economic status of those living there was upper middle class and above. I later learned that Jews with lesser wealth also lived in the area but I didn't revisit this section of Vera Ridge.

Those blacks who worked as domestic servants were mostly employed in these two areas. The majority of the whites, however, lived in or near the downtown sections of Vera Ridge. They are mostly white and blue collar workers and live in single dwellings. There were some apartments, but they were few. The sugar factory employed over half the white people living in this section of Vera Ridge. Vera Ridge, like most small southern towns, had its poor whites.

Most of the poor whites lived in the project housing and were on some kind of welfare. The project housing was set close to the railroad tracks, only it was in the white section of Vera Ridge. It covered four blocks and looked very much like the project housing in the black section of Vera Ridge. Any time during the day, if you drove by, you could see lines of clothes, people sitting on porches, and children playing in the yards and in the streets. The project housing was just as dilapidated as the one in the black section. There were abandoned cars in yards and on the streets. Tobacco spits had turned the grass and sidewalks brown. A sort of stench pervaded this area. The people in this project who work hold the unskilled jobs at the sugar factory and other places of business in Vera Ridge.*

On the outskirts of Vera Ridge, away from the Jewish section, there are scattered houses occupied by whites who are as poor as the whites living in the project housing. The houses are old and run-down and are badly in need of repair. They approximate the conditions of most of the houses in the black section of Vera Ridge. There are broken-down cars in the yards—some being repaired, others sitting abandoned. Some yards have chickens, pigs, and cows in a fenced area. Often you can see old people swinging on the porches, or very young children playing in yards. Some of these homes are still without modern conveniences and the toilets are on the outside. You do not have to go into the houses to see their internal conditions, often doors hang open and flies and other insects are very noticeable.

In contrast to the white section of Vera Ridge, the black section is even more bleak. What industrial unit there is, is located in the black section. So are the sewage processing plant and the garbage dump. On the other hand, the central business district, with all its public services, is in the white section of Vera Ridge. Only three small white businesses are located in the black section. These are food and dry goods stores, and a liquor store.

A further characteristic of Vera Ridge that makes it a typical southern town is its organization of the Ku Klux Klan (KKK).

---

* The sugar factory is the major place of employment for blacks. The furniture factory is small and only employs a small number of blacks.

Some people say Vera Ridge is the original home of the KKK. I have heard whites boast of having hung more "niggers" in Vera Ridge than in any other southern town of its size. Blacks still talk about the executions they witnessed. One man told me, "They did it two ways. If they wanna git you right away, they hang you. The tree's still up there. Right over them tracks. They got a sign nailed on it so people can see it. I would be 'shamed to let somebody see something like that. Then they had the chair. 'Least you didn't get it right away. 'Course I don't know which one was worse, hanging to death, or waiting for the chair. They had to wait 'til the man made his rounds before they could 'lectricute you."

"And you still remember all of that?"

" 'Member it! I 'member it all right. I can still see it now. Just as it was happenin' right here today. I had to be there."

"I don't understand. You said you had to be there."

"Yeh! I had to be there 'cause my daddy made me."

"He made you watch people being electrocuted? They let anyone watch?"

"No! Not just anyone. My daddy was the undertaker for the black people and he had to take the body once they got through with it."

"And he made you watch?"

"Yes! I had to watch so I'd know what to do when it came my time. You see, he wanted me to be a undertaker just like him. He wanted me to take over the business when he got too old."

"How old were you during all of this?"

"I guess I saw my first one when I was around nine. I was scared. I told him I didn't wanna watch, I didn't wanna go, but he made me go, and he made me watch—all of it—everything."

"Why aren't you running the business today?"

" 'Cause I couldn't take it. Oh, I went to school for it and I got my license and everything, but I just don't wanna practice it."

"What? Don't they make good money?"

"Let me tell you somethin'. And after I tell you, you tell me if you was me, would you be practicing. I want you to tell me that."

"Was it that bad?"

"Bad! It was worse than that. Have you ever seen anybody after they been 'lectricuted? I mean before he's all made up, if you can make him up and lay him out after they get through with him."

"No, I haven't and I don't think I want to."

"Well, once you do, you'll never forget it 'til your dying days. You'll never forget that look on his face and the screaming while he's being strapped in that chair. They tie you up tight, so tight that the straps seem like they will snatch the raw flesh off of you. And then they do it. That man start sending the juice through his whole body. Nothing sound worse than hearing that juice being turned on and going through your body. And they just keep pumping that juice into you—long after you're already dead, they keep giving it to you. Many times I stood there crying and holding my hands over my eyes. But my daddy would snatch my hands from my face. He'd tell me to 'shut up and look.' I didn't know what I feared the most, my daddy or seeing that man 'lectricuted."

"No wonder you don't want to practice undertaking."

"That's not all of it. The worst of it was smelling flesh frying —just like you was cooking somebody over a open fire. You never smell nothin' 'til you smell burning flesh from a man. After they got finished with him, me and my daddy had to take over. Sometimes we had to scrape the flesh from the chair— 'cause they done cooked him so much. What do you think it's like, seeing a man alive one minute and a few minutes later you're scraping his burned up flesh from that chair and trying to piece him together? I had to do that. Now you see why I drink so much? Now you see why I can't hold my hands steady? Now you see why I can't practice that? Now can you see!"

"Yeh! That must have been something. I feel bad enough just hearing about these kind of things, but to have seen them. I'm telling you, I don't know what I would have done. Maybe your daddy was also showing you how terrible the white man can be in hopes that you would never become a victim to the electric chair."

These experiences exhibit just some of the characteristics that make Vera Ridge a typical southern town. Another is the hate and fear that exist between the black and the white people. For the most part, the whites hate the blacks and the black people fear the white people. The blacks of Vera Ridge still fear the vengeful whites. There were recent instances of bombings, with groups of blacks jailed for demonstrating, a woman dragged by her legs, and a young man hanged while in jail. It is this latter incident that created the widest despair between the races. Most of the blacks feel they will never get "true" justice from the people of Vera Ridge.

As one woman told me, "Day after day you see things happen to your children, you see things happen to you and you are helpless to do anything about them. Who can you go to for help—no one. If you try to show when you've been mistreated if they don't laugh at you, they're telling you 'If you don't watch out you'll be next.' It ain't been over two months since Mr. Laddy and his grandson went for a walk and nobody have seen or heard from them since. If you try to call your people together, you may get a few soon after something like that happen to us. Take this young man who they said hanged himself in jail. We called for a meeting, but the fighting and arguing between ourselves didn't produce nothing much. If we boycott the white people's stores it ain't long before some of us are bought off and the whole thing fails."

"With the kind of problems you are having down here how can someone let himself be bought off, and what do you do about it?"

"Money! Honey! Money! All you have to do is wave some of that green stuff in some of these black faces and they'd snap at it in a minute. In one way I can't blame my people. Any time you stand up for what you believe in you never know what day will be your last one on this earth. They got us either way. If we try to do something for ourselves you may wake up dead. If you don't do nothing for yourself, you may never wake up. Now just like that poor boy who they said hung himself in jail. No black person in his right mind would believe that story. I know only too well when they take you to jail they take everything away from you before they lock you up. Now how was that poor boy able to get his belt and hang himself in jail? I know our people, even if he had a belt, we don't like dying—especially if it means killing ourself, no way—they did it as sure as I'm standing here talking to you. I know in my lifetime I ain't never gonna see any change; maybe for our young people—if they don't kill them off—they will."

The hanging of the young man in jail stirred up the black community for a little while. No one knew that he had hung himself until the next day, in the afternoon. His mother was told by the authorities that he had apparently committed suicide. When she received the notification the young man had been removed from the jail, taken to a local hospital where an autopsy was performed, and then brought to the funeral home where he had already been placed in a coffin. There was a sign on the coffin, DO NOT OPEN. All of this had taken place before the mother learned of her son's death.

Many questions were raised, but never answered to my knowledge. The mother at first denied that she had told the authorities (police) her son was on drugs and fighting with his sisters and brothers. However, before anyone else could corroborate her story it was alleged that a black member who proclaimed himself to be the spokesman for the black community had told her not to talk to anyone. A lawyer representing the National Association for the Advancement of Colored People (NAACP) was persuaded to come down to Vera Ridge to investigate the situation. He agreed to render his services only if the community could come up with a certain amount of money as his fee. The people of the community were not able to raise the amount needed so I provided them with the balance.

The lawyer came several days later. However, he said that he could do nothing about the situation unless he was provided with evidence that the young man's civil rights had been violated. One woman at the meeting told me, "Well, there goes another one of our young men. They're killing us like dogs and we can't do nothing about it."

The check I had given them to make up the balance of the lawyer's fee was to produce a final warning to me that I was next on the list of the white man. I was seen as a trouble maker and was told that if I knew what was good for me I had better get out of town. I received a call from the black member who proclaimed himself the spokesman for the black community. He told me that he had heard from the authorities downtown that I had better watch my step because I was heading for serious trouble.

The mother of the young man was under extreme pressure. She and her nine children (now eight) had been persuaded to move into the white projects by the proclaimed spokesman of the black community because the court had ordered that government housing be integrated. Hers was the second family to try living in the white project housing. The first family, after only a few weeks, decided to return to the black section of Vera Ridge because it could not take the harassment it received from the white people, not only of the project housing, but in the community itself.

Therefore, the death of this young man was seen as a warning to his family to move out of the white project housing. And the bitterness between the races continued. Where legal separation has been abolished, actual separation and reprisals against legal action in favor of blacks have caused even more hatred among the whites and equal fear among the blacks. Vera Ridge is a typical southern town because its problems are shared with many southern towns throughout the United States.

Blacks, especially the younger ones, are afraid to seek medical attention from the white clinics and hospitals. Young blacks are seen as the source of the trouble coming from the black community—and this is reflected in the way they are treated. A member from one of the families I studied had a toothache. I told him he should see a dentist and have it pulled. The tooth had been broken off at the root, and the root had rotted and become infected. The entire left side of his face was swollen. He was in constant pain. He carried a bottle of whiskey around with him and used it to deaden the pain. I asked him why he didn't see a dentist, and he said he didn't trust any white man— especially one with a needle. I told him I would go with him, but he said that he would have to think about it.

Every day I would go by his home to see him. He would be lying in bed, groaning. Each time I suggested taking him to the dentist he refused. He had not worked for over a week, and he and his wife argued daily. She said she would throw him out of the house if he didn't go to work. How could he work with an infected tooth? He stayed drunk. The more his tooth hurt, the more he drank. The more he drank, the drunker he became— thus the more he and his wife argued. Finally, I convinced him to go to the dentist by assuring him that the dentist wouldn't hurt him. He became even more convinced to go once I told him that he wouldn't have to worry about the pains anymore.

The next morning, I called for him and drove him to the dentist. He didn't have any appointment, but I thought he would be given something to get rid of the infection and after the swelling had gone down he could return to have the tooth removed. The receptionist took his name, and asked him if he could pay. I said I would pay for it. She told us to be seated. In a few minutes he was called and the dentist's assistant asked him to enter a room. He wanted me to come with him but I said I didn't think they would allow me. He hesitated, but I gave him a nudge and he went in. In less than five minutes, I heard him scream—he was yelling very loud. He yelled so loud I wanted to go in and see what was happening. I thought perhaps the dentist was lancing his gums to drain the tooth. He continued to yell for more than fifteen minutes. About a half hour later, he came out. There were tears in his eyes, and he was holding the swollen side of his face. I first joked with him, and told him he was acting like a baby. He said nothing—just held his face and the gauze that was in his mouth. Blood began to drip from his mouth. I asked him what had happened, but he said nothing, just nervously stood on one foot and then the other while motioning me to take him home; he was in pain.

I went over to the receptionist and asked when he was to return. She said he didn't have to return unless something went wrong. She then said I owed thirty dollars. I asked her why I owed her that much. She said the dentist had extracted three teeth. No wonder he was yelling as loud as he did. Later I learned from him that he had no X rays, no Novocain— nothing! "He just open my mouth, looked in it, took some pliers and started pulling," Billy told me. Now I knew why he feared going to the dentist.

Approaching Vera Ridge from the south, you can see a forest of pine trees. The earth is painted with red clay. A creek flows under the road, a meadow breaks the forest of pines, and a golf course can be seen in the distance. But you must keep going. You have five more miles before you reach the tracks—cross them and you enter the black section of Vera Ridge. If you stand on the other side of the tracks, where the white people live, and look north, you cannot see the black section because a row of very tall trees borders the tracks. Further down the tracks, where the row of trees ends, the business section begins on the white side of the town.

There are only two asphalt-paved streets with sidewalks in the black section of Vera Ridge. Most of the streets are clay-paved or simply dirt roads. There is no drainage system; therefore, when it rains, the streets and yards are flooded. Most of the houses are built on brick blocks and escape the onrushing water. In some cases, where the houses are built close to the ground, the floors are often inundated with water. Except for recently built houses and apartments, the houses owned by some well-to-do blacks, most of the buildings are dilapidated— some more so than others. These dilapidated houses are con-

structed from wood and have corrugated iron roofs that are rusted and, in some cases, with pieces missing. Almost all the roofs leak; and it is common, on a rainy day, to see containers sitting in different locations of these houses trapping the water from the leaking roofs.

Only one school is located in the black section of Vera Ridge. It provides education for students in grades one through six. To get an education beyond the sixth grade, blacks have to go into the white section or to a high school several miles west of Vera Ridge. This school was originally all white, but it is now over ninety percent black because the white children were placed in private academies after the Court ordered integration in 1954. Actual integration in Vera Ridge did not begin until 1965.

Some of the young people attend a nearby community college that had been only recently integrated two years ago. Except quarters for the athletes, there is no housing available at this college. Many problems have arisen as a result of the integration. One is the racial clash between black and white students. This conflict at the community college spilled over into the black community. I was told, "It was brought home because some black guys started messing 'round with white girls." One incident, as a consequence of this activity, was the bombing of a black home. Melvin, who had told me about the black man–white woman incident, went on to say, "A few years ago a black man wouldn't be caught dead looking at a white woman. Now he's so bold to bring them right down here. If you don't believe me go 'round to Jake's place. They come in there every night."

Because of the distance between Vera Ridge and where the community college is located, most of the black students attending the college did not have their own transportation and there was no public transportation provided, so they formed carpools. However, this form of transportation was not always reliable, and as a result students often missed their classes. This, coupled with their inability to cope and adjust to the college environment, was responsible for the great drop-out rate of the black students, so I was told. As a result, most incoming students usually failed their classes or dropped out of college by the end of the first year.

There are very few activities in Vera Ridge for young people. There is a Community Club House that serves as a social gathering place. Its major function is to provide the young people with planning basketball tournaments that continue year round. On a few occasions, social events such as parties and dances take place in the Community Club House. It was also used for members of the community to discuss problems that concerned blacks as participants in the overall community of Vera Ridge. Some church groups and organizations such as the National Association for the Advancement of Colored People also use the Club House. There is an Elk Club; however, it is used only by its members, except on Sundays, when a church group holds its services there.

Many churches and cafe-restaurants are located in the black section of Vera Ridge. Of the thirty-five or so churches, over two-thirds are Baptist. These churches are not all single structures built for the purpose of worship. Some of them were originally homes later converted into churches. Others looked as if they were once structures used as garages or for storage. Some of them are simply a large room in a home or the chapel in the funeral home. There are eleven large churches—large in that they have three to five hundred members, although all the members are never there at any one time. On the other hand, the smaller churches may only have twenty to thirty members. The largest membership, of course, belongs to the Second Baptist Church. On Sunday, you can see people darting across vacant lots, scurrying down dirt roads, driving in from nearby communities, or simply walking from their homes next door or across the street—all on their way to church. These churches are the major places where people come together collectively as a group for the express purpose of socializing.

The number of cafe-restaurants approximates that of the churches. None of them are very large, and only a few of them are open to serve breakfast, lunch, and dinner. Vera Ridge has some twenty to thirty men who live there temporarily because they work in the sugar refinery. On the weekends they return to their families in nearby communities. The closest community is River Rock, and it is twenty miles away. These men, as well as the single men and women of Vera Ridge, patronize these cafe-restaurants in the morning and at lunch time. The cafe-restaurants are usually family-owned operations. Whichever member (or members) of the family is available at a given time lends the services necessary for running the cafe-restaurant. For the most part, these cafe-restaurants do not provide the sole income for any of the families operating them. Some family members have regular jobs, while others have part-time jobs or attend school. However, all of them who are capable will spend some time each day in the establishment. You should not be surprised by the number of cafe-restaurants and churches located in the black area once you learn that they are the major places for people to "get together" and spend much of their time (and for some, most of their time) away from home.

The income for most blacks is below the poverty line established by the federal government. One-third of the blacks of Vera Ridge receive some form of welfare. More of them are eligible. However, for reasons beyond their control they cannot receive it. Eligibility in this state refers to guidelines set by the state. The federal guidelines are often ignored. For example, to get food stamps you have to buy one hundred and twenty-five dollars' worth in a single purchase. For the one hundred and twenty-five dollars' worth of food stamps, you have to pay seventy dollars. But those people who are eligible for food stamps don't make seventy dollars a week. Therefore, most of the eligible people cannot afford to purchase food stamps. Another reason eligible people do not receive welfare is because they are trouble makers. Trouble makers is the term for those blacks who demonstrate or protest for a change in the current social policies toward blacks—either at their jobs, at school, or at the courthouse.

The major source of employment in Vera Ridge is the sugar-cane refinery. It employs half the black population that is eligible to work. Vera Ridge also has several other types of businesses: a garment factory, a furniture factory, two department stores, the telephone company, and other small businesses that employ blacks. Blacks also work as maids, servants, janitors, and other domestic employees. Still, jobs for blacks, especially young blacks, are scarce. The situation has been aggravated by the companies that aim to discourage any signs of "militancy" that this age group is said to demonstrate. Any young black who appears to be "militant" will not be hired.

Most black people who are unskilled laborers make between three and four thousand dollars a year. There are some who make less than three thousand; however, their jobs do not require full-time employment. People with jobs requiring some skill only average between five and six thousand dollars a year. For example, Toby and Charlette are disc-jockeys for a white-owned, black-operated radio station. Whereas Toby has four years of college education and Charlette only a high school diploma, both earn the same amount of money: two dollars and fifty cents an hour. The telephone company has two blacks working for it: a linesman and an operator. The linesman receives approximately six thousand dollars a year—so he says—the operator receives approximately five thousand a year. Cynthia, the telephone operator, told me that she had been working at the telephone company over five years; however, she takes home less than a hundred dollars a week. Melvin, the linesman, said he had only been working for the telephone company for two months. He had just come into the area because they had promised him six thousand dollars a year. Dotty, Jean, and Eula work for the two department stores. Dotty said that she had been working there over seven years, but she only receives ninety-five dollars a week. Thus, the majority of the black population is either on welfare and/or performs manual labor.

Blacks who earn eight thousand or more dollars are the ones

who own their businesses or are teachers. I do not have any exact earning figures because they refused to reveal them; however, they indicated that they made eight thousand dollars and over. Those owning their businesses include a mortician, a dry cleaner, and a doctor. Blacks also own a number of cafe-restaurants, which are always used to supplement their income. Most of them barely make enough money to operate. One other type of black-owned business is rental—usually a room in a person's home or an addition put on the cafe-restaurant. There are also two barber shops. They too have additions that are rented out. One of the barber shops has a four-apartment complex attached to it.

In addition to the previously mentioned black-owned businesses, there are two beauty parlors. They are located in the homes of the operators, and are only open on the weekends. There is a curbside market, a general food store, and a barbecue stand. The food store can handle only items that do not require long refrigeration. One of these food stores is a very small curbside market, and the other does not have the capital to stock many items. As a consequence, they do not get much of the black business. The two white-owned food stores located in the black section get most of the black trade.

The white-owned businesses located in the black section of Vera Ridge are very profitable because they provide blacks with a needed service: letting them buy goods on credit—specifically, for foodstuff, clothing, and oil to keep the stoves burning. The people who rely on this kind of purchasing are caught in a vicious circle of entrapment. On the one hand, it provides a means whereby the basic things a person needs can be obtained without having to dole out immediate cash. On the other hand, the prices charged for these items are twice, and sometimes more, as much as they would cost if they were purchased downtown. As a consequence, the blacks who must rely on buying at the local white-owned businesses maintain a running account on which the balance is never paid off. The necessity to patronize these stores takes away an effective weapon "we could use against the white man if we didn't have to depend on him the way we do," Linda so often told me. For example, the owners of the businesses made it clear that any black "making trouble" would be denied benefit of credit in their stores.

Therefore, it becomes difficult for blacks who depend on the credit they receive from these stores to engage in any activity for the purpose of protesting against the status quo. The threats of the white owners of these businesses have gone so far as to make conditions on the parents whose children "make trouble," or have a "militant" attitude. One white owner said he would "blow the head off any damned nigger I catch gettin' smart with me. And, if one even think of puttin' his hand on my daughter—I'll hang him maself." I stood there in amazement, while other black shoppers continued to collect their groceries as if nothing had been said. I dropped the items I had in my hand on the floor. An old woman walked over to me and began picking up the things I had dropped. As she did, she said, "Honey, ain't no use. You'd jest be gittin' yourself in trouble. I know what's goin' on in your mind—it crossed my mind a many times—but we gotta eat. You jest go on now. I'll put these here things back."

At first, I was angry with her—then just as quickly as I became angry, I became sad for her. She looked just like my own grandmama, whom I loved very much. How could I be angry with her? Of course, my grandmama didn't take anything from any white man; she told him just what she thought of him, no matter who he was, and he never bothered her. Then I thought to myself, some black people are scared of white people; and in a way, I guess they have their own reasons. So I turned and walked out of the store—a place I would never patronize again.

Because there are three distinct sections in Vera Ridge, I have labeled them A, B, and C. Section A is a residential area that consists mostly of new project housing and homes; therefore it is the most recently developed section. Except for the planting of lawn grass, there isn't much landscaping. The area was originally a forest of pine trees, but where the buildings stand, all

the trees were removed. The project housing sits close to the
railroad tracks. Only a small cluster of trees separates the housing from the tracks. To the side of the project housing is a structure, built at the same time as the project housing, that contains
a laundromat, a cafe-restaurant, and a liquor store. It is the only
legitimate liquor store in the black section of Vera Ridge. Liquor
is sold in many of the cafe-restaurants; however, the sales are
under the counter. The area around the liquor store is a popular
place for people to socialize. There is drinking, card-playing,
gambling, and dice-shooting—all going on simultaneously.
These activities go on from the time the liquor store opens until
it closes. The area is especially popular with the young people,
and parents constantly patrol it to make sure their children are
not there.

The people living in the project housing are mostly unskilled
laborers. Many of the families are on welfare. The rent for these
housing projects is determined on the basis of one's income and
the number of children in the family. The people who live in
the homes in this area have recently built them. The oldest
house in this area is no older than five years. The costs of these
homes range from ten to fifteen thousand dollars. People whose
homes cost ten thousand dollars have to pay a mortgage note of
one hundred and fifty dollars a month. This is approximately
two-thirds of their monthly income from their regular employment. People with homes that cost fifteen thousand dollars pay
a mortgage note of one hundred and seventy-five dollars a
month. This is over half of their monthly income from their
regular jobs. However, most of these people own cafe-restaurants, beauty parlors, barber shops, or they rent rooms.

These houses are small ranch-type homes. The only difference
between the ten-thousand- and fifteen-thousand-dollar ones is
that the latter has an additional bedroom, a fireplace, and an
enclosed garage and porch. Some of the people who have ten-
thousand-dollar homes enclosed their own garages and porches
themselves. All the homeowners seem to have pride in their
ownership. This pride is expressed in the fact that they "owned"

their homes, rather than renting. Most of the homes were still largely unfurnished. The people, for the most part, bought furnishings when they had saved enough money—they did not want to buy "on credit." You can walk into most of these homes, with few exceptions, and see rooms only partially furnished. Unlike the people who live in the project housing—who purchase a complete four-room package for six hundred and ninety-five dollars—the people in the homes stressed quality and ownership. For example, in the project housing, people talked about the furniture and other household items as belonging to "the white man."

The furniture they bought came from the furniture factory. It was poorly built and mass-produced to keep the prices down. Speaking of the furniture in her living room, one woman told me, "It will be no good, thrown out and replaced by more stuff I get from him 'fore I even pay for this." On the other hand, the people who live in the homes have an attitude of pride: "This is mine. I paid for it with cash. I don't owe nobody a dime for anything you see in this house." In other words, they only purchase items for their homes when they can afford to pay cash for them.

A big fight broke out between a woman and her husband because he had discovered the hiding place where she kept her money, and spent most of it. The argument started in their home, but as he tried to leave, she followed him outside, and continued to yell and scream. I heard her say, "I've been saving for months to buy my dining-room set and you went in there and stole my money. That was my money. I worked hard for it. I saved it up. I went without—and my children went without— just so I could save up to buy my dining-room set, and now it's all gone. I'm warning you, if you don't put it all back, I'm going to break up your car, and I'll do it, you know that."

One evening, when I was returning to my house, I heard a child yell, "Leave my mama 'lone." As I looked over where the noise was coming from, I saw this woman using a hammer and breaking the windows of her husband's car. He tried to take the hammer from her, and she swung at him. He grabbed the hammer, but not before she hit him on the hand. He got angry and began fighting with her. People came from all around. Someone must have called the police, for they came to the scene. When the man saw them coming, he ran. The car looked as if it had been through a wrecking-yard. She explained to the police that her husband had stolen her money. The police asked if she wanted to make a complaint, and she said, "No! I'll take care of this myself."

She had six children. The young ones—two girls and a boy—were crying and holding onto their mother. The oldest boy—about thirteen—said, "Mama, don't worry, I'll get him for that." She turned to him and said, "Sylvester, I don't want to hear you talk like that—you hear me! You ain't gonna do nothing. Now you take the children in the house—right this minute."

A common feature of both the homes and the project housing is the use of slipcovers draping their sofas and chairs. In some homes, the sofas and chairs are custom-covered with plastic slipcovers. This is done to protect the furniture from abuse by their children. Often, children are not allowed to sit in the living room, and in most cases the back and side doors are used to enter the homes. "Only company comes through the front door." Some of the people remove the slipcovers when they have company, and replace them once the company leaves.

In section A, all the roads are paved with clay. When it is dry and the wind blows, everything is covered with a coat of clay dust. The people living in their homes have tried to landscape their yards, but the only thing that seems to grow well is Bermuda grass for their lawns and pine trees. Where the soil is not clay, it is very sandy. Where there is grass, people keep it cut. Where the grass cannot grow, people keep it raked.

Section B is the original black area of Vera Ridge before it expanded. Most of the homes in this section are old and dilapidated. There are four well-kept homes in this area. They belong to Peggy (the entertainer), Mr. Smith (the dry cleaner), Mr.

Pierce (the doctor), and a man whose father used to own a funeral home. The largest project housing in the black section is located in section B. There are also two four-unit apartments and the Community Club House. The only school in the black section is located in this area. On the border of sections of B and A, the sugar refinery is located. However, the majority of the structures in this area are churches, cafe-restaurants, and dwellings. Most of the "well-to-do" blacks live in this section. Their homes are not located in one area; instead, they are dispersed within section B. For example, the undertaker's home sits on a corner. It occupies a lot approximately one hundred feet deep and fifty feet wide. Directly behind it are some of the units making up the project housing. Across the street from the undertaker's home is one of the cafe-restaurants. Next to it sits one of the large churches in the area. In no single block of this section do you find houses or structures that are not dilapidated.

A recently built freeway cuts through the center of section B. It has isolated some of the residences from the rest of the community. One homeowner, bitter because of the freeway, is the son of the man who owned the first funeral home. One of the giant pillars that raise the freeway so that it goes over this section is only a few feet from his home. He says that the roar of the traffic creates so much noise it is difficult to sleep at night. The carport that houses the hearse and the pillar that elevates the freeway make his home and the immediate area seem rundown. But inside his home, it is well kept.

Most of the cafe-restaurants and churches are also located in section B. There is one of the white-owned grocery stores, the curbside market, and the grocery store owned by a black man. The project housing occupies two blocks. It was built in the late Forties, and the brick-faced facades are falling from the mortar. The grounds around the project housing are bare of grass. Clotheslines—some rusted, some broken and in need of repair—crisscross every backyard. Windows are broken, and are stuffed with cardboard. Very few screens are still on the windows. Steps sag, and in some cases they are missing. The project housing is divided into quadri-plexes. There are two apartments on the ground level and two above; each quadri-plex sits close to its neighbor.

Inside the apartments, deterioration is even more apparent. Fixtures in the bathrooms are broken, and some do not work. Appliances in the kitchen (stoves, refrigerators, and ovens) do not operate. The linoleums on the floors are worn smooth, and some of them have holes. The faucets leak, and some have a continual drip. The water coming from them tastes of rust. Oven doors are falling off their hinges, and various objects are used to keep the door closed. In many of the rooms, the ceiling and walls are losing plaster, and the flakes of the plaster keep falling on the floor. There are cracks in the ceiling and walls. Some of the light fixtures do not work. There are not enough electrical outlets in the different rooms, so people use extension cords. These run across the floor, attaching television, radios, and lamps. In most of these apartments, the furniture is worn and broken. The sofas and chairs have holes in them so large that the bare springs show. Legs on the wooden chairs are broken, and in some cases missing. The curtains and window-shades are falling off their rods, some torn and others pinned. Although most of the apartments are deteriorating, some are kept clean and tidy—these are the ones that no longer have children in the family. These have two and three bedrooms. Even so, some members have to sleep on the sofa in the living room, because of the size of the family. There are no fewer than four children in each apartment, and in some as many as nine. Most of the people living in project housing are on welfare.

Near the sugar refinery are blocks of small houses, all owned by the refinery. They are rented to people who work there. The rent is only fifty dollars a month. Some of these houses do not have inside toilets. The houses are built very close to each other—so close you cannot walk between them. There is only an outside wall, and no ceiling attached to the roof. The roofs are constructed of corrugated iron, and the houses sit on cement blocks. There are only two dividers in each house: one separates the living room from the bedroom, and the other separates the bedroom from the kitchen. The houses have a front and a back door. Space-heaters are still used for heat, and some of these houses still have wood stoves used to cook on. The one-string electric light hangs from the ceiling in each of the three rooms. The people living in these houses are poorer than the ones who live in the project housing. They pay most of their wages to the sugar refinery where they work, in rent. They are all on welfare. However, because they have a job, they do not get much aid. The welfare agency is very strict, and constantly monitors the income received by each family. If they get a raise, it has to be reported. If additional people move in, they have to be reported. When work is slack at the refinery, these are the first people to be temporarily laid off. Sometimes that is as long as a year. Therefore, many have jobs other than those at the refinery. However, they attempt to shield this from the welfare agency. In one of these houses, there are twelve people. At least three generations of people occupy these houses; however, there are few male adults permanently (for welfare information) living there. Only daily observation will reveal the exact number of adult males in each home.

In every block of section B, there is at least one cafe-restaurant and one church. Originally, there were no restrictions on the type of structure you could build in the black residential areas of Vera Ridge. A stricter building code is now being enforced. Cafe-restaurants currently in areas where re-zoning prohibits them are not allowed to repair. Once they become "unsafe," they are condemned, and must be torn down. The town's government is quick to condemn structures owned by blacks it considers trouble makers. Church members are pleased with this new ordinance, because churches often share space with these cafe-restaurants; on Sundays, as one woman told me, "You don't know whether to pray or dance." She was referring to the music coming from the juke box of the cafe-restaurant. The majority of the homes in section B have two and three bedrooms. These homes are owned by the people who live there. There are five old families living in section B—old in the sense that they or members of their families have always lived in Vera Ridge and in section B. Such families as the Plummers, Greens, Walkers, Cunninghams, Reddicks, and Smiths own much of the land, and have more members as representatives of section B's population. Often areas of this section are designated by any one of these family names. Hence such expressions as 'in the Greens' area,' 'over at the Plummers,' or 'in the Cunningham section,' are used to direct people in the community.

Section C is separated from B basically because it is an area that was once occupied by poor whites. There are still a few poor white families that lived on June Street, the street that separates section B and C. Blacks seem to take pride in saying, "It's the worst section in the area." These houses where the poor whites still live are similar to the house I described near the sugar refinery in section B. However, two of them are larger, and have more yard space. In two houses live widowed women, both in their seventies. They occasionally sit on the porch and rock. There is a black woman who visits with them and she does grocery shopping for them. Another house is occupied by a woman and her daughter. They are both old. The daughter leaves the house daily, but no one seems to know where she goes. Sometimes she takes a shopping bag, and brings back groceries. The oldest of the whites who live in this section reside on the corner of June and Palm Streets. Their house has a fenced-in yard, with chickens running all over it as well as through the house. There are two pigs in the backyard. The old white couple there are often seen on the porch, rocking. If you pass by, they will talk to you, although you can't always understand what they say. If you go by five times a day, they are going to tell you, "I don't have nothin' 'gainst Colored people. I lived with 'em all ma life." The house they live in is falling apart. The steps are detached from the porch; the screen doors are falling off the hinges, and some of the corrugated-iron roof has fallen down, and lays at the side of the house. The whites who still live in this section were too poor to move when blacks started moving into the section—actually, they refused to leave because they were attached to their homes. The white authorities have tried to replace them several times, but they will not go.

The only new structure existing in section C is an apartment complex built for senior citizens. All the homes here were previously occupied by poor whites. Some of the houses have been repaired. However, the majority are dilapidated. There was a plan for a new housing development, but it has not begun. Most of the area is wooded. There are several cafe-restaurants, three large churches, and four smaller ones. The main barber shop is located in section C. It is the one most frequently used, not only for haircuts, but also for socialization. Both men and women gather there and talk about events that have taken place since they last saw each other. One major topic always discussed is the white women who come into the area. The police have come and taken them to jail; however, when they get out, they return. These are the prostitutes. Black women have tried to keep them out, but the black men who engage the prostitutes' services protect them. Black men have fought with black women who have attacked these white women.

The sandy area of section C makes it difficult to keep one's house free of grit. The farther you go into section C, the more the homes are separated from each other. People living on the outskirts of section C have larger parcels of land. They use it for growing vegetables, and some people raise hogs and chickens. Most homes in the area look as if they are temporarily situated. They are on high cement pyramidal blocks. You are reminded of homes located in areas where flooding takes place— you have to climb not less than six steps to the porch to enter any of them. These houses are more like shells, because only a few of them have insulation in the walls. Where there is insulation, it was put in by the current owners in a makeshift fashion.

Very few people in this area have furniture that isn't very old. While some have modern appliances, the majority of the homes have old-fashioned stoves that use bottled gas. In one of the homes (and this is typical of many), the living room has two old sofas with bed sheets covering them. There is a large color television, an oil heater, and a reclining chair. The floor is wooden and is covered with a hooked rug that is placed in its center. There is a lamp sitting on the television, and another standing behind the reclining chair. From the living room, you walk into a large dining room. The walls are papered. However, the wallpapers do not match. There is a large old square table sitting in the center of the room. Next to one wall stands a bed, where an old man lies sleeping. The floor is wooden, and the wood is bleached white from many scrubbings. One exit from the dining room leads to a kitchen, and the other two exits go to bedrooms. On the outside wall, between the two bedrooms, is the bathroom. It was added only recently; before, they used outside toilets. There are no sewage drains. The houses in this section have cesspools.

People who live in section C are referred to as "country people." There are many young people who are no longer in school. Some are dismissed from school because of fighting. Others never attended. Many of the homes in this area are run by single parents. Some have the father present; others have the mother. There are some where the grandmother and/or grandfather is head of the household. In a few cases, the household may be headed by an older brother and/or sister.

Randy is a fifteen-year-old male. Presently he stays with his father. He has three sisters and four brothers. His mother is "somewhere up north. She left when I was four. I only saw her once," Randy told me. He says he doesn't usually get along with his father, and when that happens he goes to live with his grandmother across the street. "When I get tired of staying with my grandmama, or when she put me out, I go to stay with my sister. Sometimes I go to my brother's house; other times to my friend's house. His mama let me stay there whenever I want to. His daddy don't like me though. He thinks I'm a bad influence on David, his son, my friend. But I try to stay outta his way. I ain't that bad. Sure I got kicked outta school, but I ain't gonna let no white folks run over me. I don't like goin' to school with them white folks anyway. I can't get along with 'em."

Most of the young men in this section who are Randy's age seem to have problems with school. They get jobs, but they only last a few weeks—if that long—before they lose them. Their favorite pastime is sitting in old abandoned cars along the roadside, talking about their manhood. Randy said he already has one child, and he thinks he has another. The parents in this section do not seem to watch over their children as parents do in other sections of the black community in Vera Ridge. Randy said he could take his girl out and keep her out all hours of the night. He said her folks would get angry with both of them, but that wouldn't stop them from letting her go out with him again. I asked him if I could talk with his girlfriend, and he said it was all right with him if she didn't mind. He arranged a meeting for us. He told me to meet him by the abandoned cars the next day. I was supposed to be there at one o'clock, but I arrived early.

I walked up to one of the cars. Two young men sitting in another car called me over. I recognized one of them as David as I walked to the front seat of the car. There were two young women sitting slumped in the back seat. David said to me, "My girl wants to meet you," and he pointed to one of them in the back. She said, "Hi!," and then asked me if I really came from California. They wanted to know all about California, and asked me if I would take them when I returned. I asked them what they were doing there, why they weren't in school. They laughed and the young man next to David said there were better things to do than sitting in a classroom. I asked them whether their parents knew where they were. One of the young women (only thirteen) said her mama didn't care. The other one said she didn't know "where her mama was." The young man sitting next to David looked at me and laughed. I told them they could get themselves into trouble if they weren't careful. The young man sitting next to David said, "Tell us somethin' new."

While we were talking, Randy came up. There was a young lady with him and she was carrying a baby on her hip. I looked at Randy and he said, "No! That's her brother. It ain't mine." I asked her name; she told me. I asked her age; she told me. I asked her address; she told me. She responded only when I asked a question. It was as if she was afraid to talk to me. Then Randy said, "Tell her, Reg; tell her I was with you yesterday. She don't believe me." I told her he was with me. Then she asked what time, and for how long. I asked her why she wanted to know this, and she said, " 'Cause I don't think he was. I know where he was. He was over to Ora Lee." I assured her that he was with me; and I think she believed me. I asked her why she wasn't in school; and she said she had to stay home and take care of her baby brother. And this is the way of life for many of the young people in section C.

The young people here only go over to sections A and B when they are going to a job or visiting with other relatives. Even then, they may be confronted by young people of sections A and B. Each section's youth are territorial-minded; and when any member from section C invades the territory of sections A or B, there is usually a fight. There is no conflict between youths from sections A and B. At first I did not understand why Randy didn't want to come to my house. Later when I saw him, it was apparent he had been in a fight. He told me he had gone to see his aunt, who lived in section A, and "Two guys jumped me, but I didn't run from 'em. They got in some good licks on me, but I got some good licks on them too."

I asked Randy why there were problems between the different young people; and he said, " 'Cause they think they's better than anybody else." I had a difficult time getting him to come over to where I lived, and even when he consented to come, it was on the condition that two of his friends accompany him. They wanted to bring knives with them, but I persuaded them not to. I had to pick them up in my car at night, take a specific route they pointed out, and return them by car, before they agreed to visit.

Whereas some of the people in sections A and B were poor and on welfare, most of the people in section C were poor and on, or should have been on, welfare. Only a few worked at the sugar refinery. Some worked at the furniture factory; but most of them did days' work or janitorial services. They didn't have many clothes, and, for some, the clothes they had were old and worn. Many of the young girls had babies by the time they were fifteen. During the day, you could see them walking down dirt roads, across a sandy field, or sitting on steps, nursing their babies. There were very few activities in section C for young men and women. They didn't participate in the few activities that occurred in sections A and B, and there were no forms of recreation in section C.

The one thing they seemed to take pride in was the fact that they were 'mamas' or 'daddys' to children. Once, while visiting the place where the abandoned cars were, and interviewing some of the young men and women, I was invited to participate in a game they played. One young lady said to me, "Why are you asking so many questions?" I explained to her about my study. She said, "You're asking a lot of personal questions. You wanna do our thing?" I asked her what was their thing, and she said, "You'll find out."

I told her I couldn't unless I knew what it was. She said, "You keep on talking about being a man and being a woman, well you can find out better if you do this thing with us." I told her I didn't think I should; and then the other two girls joined in with her to persuade me. I continued to refuse. Finally, Randy called me to the side and said, "Come on, man, if you don't wanna do nothin' you don't have to, in a way. But if you don't come they won't talk to you no more." So, I decided I would go.

We went to the area where the bushes were high and thick. Once inside the area, you couldn't see out and no one could see in. I called Randy aside, and asked him what was supposed to happen. He said, "You'll see." I told him I wouldn't do anything "nasty," and he said, "It's up to you, but if you don't the girls may think you're funny." I got nervous. I wanted to continue my communication with this group, but I suspected they were going to indulge in sexual activities. I didn't wish to take part, not only because the young ladies weren't old enough, but also because of my position in the community. The young men were ordered to line up straight across and the young women stood in front of them. There were four girls and six boys. I stood to the side. The girls urged me to join the rank, but I refused. Then the girl who initiated the game said, "Forget about him, I want to see you do it. The one who wins get what I got."

The young men unzipped their pants and exposed themselves. They then began walking toward the community—with the young ladies urging them on. I didn't know how far this would go. At first I followed a good distance behind them, but as they seemed to be aiming for the opening in the bushes, still exposed, I thought it better for me to leave by the back way. I hurried to my car, and sped away. A few days later, I saw Randy. I asked him what had happened. He said that he had won, that all the other males had rezipped their pants and he was the only one "with it still hanging out." Of course, he didn't reach the opening into the community; nevertheless he held out to the last, and therefore was declared the winner. He told me that the girls made unfavorable remarks about me, but that he had smoothed it over.

And this is the lifestyle of the young people in section C. Achieving manhood and womanhood was the most important thing for them. In contrast, the project housing that catered to senior citizens presented the other extreme of the picture of section C. Most of them were waiting to die, while the youth were plotting how best to survive in a world they saw as hostile and unfriendly toward them. The key to survival was the ability to become a man or woman.

My brief communication with one of Vera Ridge's black community members led me to believe that it was exactly the kind of community I would like for the kind of research I wanted to do. I had no idea of the problems I would face before my research would be completed. I had pictured the small black section of a southern town as being warm, friendly, and receptive to an outsider interested in doing research within their community. I believed that the exchange between myself and the people of the black community would be equally rewarding once we got to know each other. However, from the first day I set out for Vera Ridge I began to feel uneasy. The feeling was to last, to some extent, until I left. My troubles began almost immediately upon arrival in Vera Ridge.

A FEELING
OF ENTRAPMENT

*T*HE feeling that gripped me when I first drove across the Mason-Dixon line became stronger as I continued deeper into the South. It made me think about my own experiences as a boy growing up in a southern town and I felt as though I were entering a strange country and could imagine an iron gate falling closed behind me. I felt trapped, as though everything before me was hostile. I could see myself as the black man being dragged behind a speeding car. I visualized myself as a young black male being burned alive while my mother, father, sisters, and brothers watched, crying and screaming and begging for my life. I could hear the screams of a dying young man as the flames engulfed and consumed his entire body. I could see myself being dragged out of my house by white men who were searching for a black man who allegedly raped a white woman. Or trying to defend my sister as three white males tore off her clothing and began raping her. Yes, I could picture all these things as I crossed the Mason-Dixon line into the deep South to conduct my first year-long anthropological fieldwork.

I tried to time my entrance into the South so that I could

drive all the way to Vera Ridge without having to stop (except for gas) once I crossed the Mason-Dixon line. It was late in the evening when I reached the Vera Ridge city limits. There were two freeway exits marked Vera Ridge, and I was not sure of the one to take. I decided on the second exit. As I left the off-ramp, I saw a black woman emptying a garbage bag into a big trash container. I pulled over and asked her for directions. She asked the number of my house and said, "Used to be, all folks had to do was go straight this way or straight that way and you could almost get anywhere you wanted in no time. Ever since that there highway been here, people just got cut off from each other."

She told me that I was only a few blocks from where I wanted to go. "But, you gotta go all the way 'round yonder way to get there. I don't remember seeing you 'round here before. You must be new here?"

"Yes, I am. I'm a student back East and I came here to do a study on the black family."

"What sort of a study?"

"Well, I have my own ideas how we live and get along and I want to do a study to see how much of my own ideas are right."

"If you have your own ideas, why do you need to do this study?"

"Because, I could be wrong about some things."

"You consider yourself to be black, don't you?"

"Yes."

"Then if you be black, you gotta know how we live, right? You don't need no study to find out that. We black folks all like the same. . . . Just that some of us have to work harder to get somewhere and some of us don't have to work so hard."

"Well, that's what I want to find out. I want to know why some of us get somewhere, why some of us want to get some-where, and why some of us don't want to get somewhere."

"I can tell you that. Greedy! That's what it's all about—that's what it all amounts to. Greedy or Uncle Tomming it. If you kiss-up to these white folks, you can do better; if you don't, you might not do at all."

"After I get settled down, do you think I can come back and talk with you sometimes?"

"I don't know—you may be anybody, trying to find out things about me and other folks 'round here. You can't go 'round trusting just anybody. I will think about it. You can always find me right here six days a week, from eight o'clock to five."

"Thank you."

"Ain't nothin'. You know what? You talk funny. How come you come to talk that way?"

"I don't know. I guess it's because I have been so many places, and people talk different wherever you go. I guess I picked up many different kinds of ways people talk."

"It sounds nice; I think I like it. Maybe I'll have you come 'round to talk to me just so I can listen to you talk."

"Are you making fun of the way I talk?"

"No! It's nice. I wish more of our people talk the way you do. Well, I best be gittin' back to my work 'fore I lose my job. You just go two blocks in that direction and . . ."

I thanked her for the directions and bade her good-bye. I got into my car and drove off. All of a sudden I began to be frightened, scared, and nervous. I just wanted to turn around and head back to the East. It was so depressing as I drove down the streets. I saw houses that looked as if they were going to topple over in the slightest breeze. I saw children playing in the street with clothing that seemed more torn off of their bodies than on. I saw people standing on the corners talking, people sitting on porches talking, people walking down the dirt roads. They all seemed to stare at me as I passed. I told myself that it was because I had an out-of-state license plate and was driving slowly. They looked hostile, as if they were telling me I had better get out of town. Still I drove on.

When I found the house, I parked the car on the street, got

out, went to the door, and rang the bell. A middle-aged woman
came to the door. I told her that my name was Reg and
that I . . .

"Oh! I've been expecting you. My name is Mrs. Walker. I
didn't know which airport you would arrive at. So I had Mary
go to the airport here in Vera Ridge, and I told my daughter to
go the airport in Livingston, just in case you showed up there.
Well, don't stand out here, come on in, you must be tired from
all that driving. I thought you was flying here."

"I'm sorry that I caused you so much confusion, but . . ."

"Oh, that's all right. I just wanted to make sure that you got
here all right. Would you like for me to fix you something to
eat?

"I'm not hungry. I ate on the road, but I would like something cold to drink."

"I expected you to come in later. Mrs. Jones, the lady who
said you could live with her if you wanted to (after seeing the
room of course), will not have it ready for you until later this
evening. I'll take you over there when it's ready if that suits
you."

"If you don't mind, I would like to rest for a little while. The
drive here was a long one and if it's all right, I would like to
unwind a bit."

"I know what you mean. I can't drive long places myself. I
get carsick. It's perfectly all right with me whatever you decide
to do. If you don't like the room where I'm taking you, you can
stay with us 'til you do find a place that suits you. My two sons
each have a room and I can bunk them up together. The rest of
my children are away now. Some of them are in school, some
of them married and have their own homes and the others are
out of the country."

I sat there on the sofa, looking around the living room. Many
photographs of people crowded every spot a photograph could
be placed. I noticed a piano, and decided to go over and play it.
I asked Mrs. Walker if I could and she said, "Go right ahead, I
love to hear church music."

I thought to myself that she had given me a cue to the kind of music I should play. I told her I didn't know many church songs, but would try to play the ones I knew. She is the undertaker's wife. I wanted to smoke, but was hesitant to ask her permission. I did see ashtrays, though. So I decided it was safe to ask her; after all, the only thing she could say was, "No!"

"Mrs. Walker, do you mind if I smoke a cigarette?"

"No, I don't mind. It's perfectly all right with me. Go right ahead. None of us smoke here, but I'm not like some people I know, just cause they don't do certain things they don't want you to do them. That's the trouble with this world, people all the time trying to make you live like them, and God knows I would never live the way some people I know live."

She brought me a glass of iced tea and said, "I'll call Mrs. Jones, maybe she has the place for you ready earlier than she said. Anyway, I will let her know that you are here."

After the telephone call, Mrs. Walker came back into the living room. I was trying to play "Go Tell It On The Mountain" (a religious song I remembered from my childhood), but was not playing well. She knew the hymn and started to sing along. I played it so badly that she stopped and decided to tell me what she and Mrs. Jones had discussed over the telephone.

"Mrs. Jones said to give her an hour and she would have the room ready. As you can see, 'um doing my ironing and watching my stories on television. I'm going back to my work, you feel at home, you're at home here."

She went back to her ironing board and began ironing. I decided I should give up on the piano. I went back to the sofa and began drinking the iced tea. After sitting there for a while, I felt rested and decided I wanted to walk around outside. I asked her if it would be safe for me to leave my things in the car because I did not feel like unpacking them and repacking them when we were ready to go to Mrs. Jones' house. She laughed and said, "You ain't in the big city now. As long as your car is locked it will be all right. There's usually someone looking over here from their home and they will take notice of anything that happen—especially if it is a stranger. They know you are here already and I bet half the town knows it. Things don't stay a secret around here very long. I can hear them now, Oh! Mrs. Walker has a visitor and he's a nice young man and her husband is away—out of town. It wouldn't surprise me none if Miss Cora, down the road, would drop in any minute to borrow something. She is so nosy and wants to know everything happening at this house. She isn't even a good friend."

I told her I was going out for a walk, and asked her for the general directions to downtown. She said, "Whose downtown? If you mean the main downtown, where the white folks live, it's one direction. If you want where the blacks folks hang out, it's another direction."

"I mean an area where I can go and buy some things I need, like cigarettes, and some small clothing items."

"Well, I guess you better go to the main downtown. But don't go too far 'cause we have to go over to Mrs. Jones in about an hour. If you get lost, just ask anybody and they'll tell you how to get back here. Just tell them you want to go to the Cunninghams' and that'd put you in the right direction for here."

I walked out of the door and looked around. I knew that Peggy lived in the neighborhood not far from Mrs. Walker's. I had met Peggy, a famous entertainer, in New York, but it was in passing, and I don't remember exactly how she looked. She sent a letter to the Walkers that introduced me and asked them to help me find a place to live. Since there were only two houses in the immediate area, and she was supposed to live across the street from the Walkers, I supposed that the larger of the two houses belonged to Peggy. I thought I might go and see her mother, who was very ill, but I decided against that and headed for the downtown area.

On the way I saw a young man whitewashing a fence. I stopped to ask him for directions to a place to eat. Actually, I had not eaten and I was hungry, but I did not want to trouble Mrs. Walker for any food. I did not know if it was the right thing to do. Later, I was to learn from a young man that when

someone offers you food you should accept it. He said, "If somebody offer you food, that's a good sign. It's a sign that they like
you or at least accept you at that time. The worst thing you can
do is not to take it—even if you have eaten and you ain't
hungry."

Many people were to say this to me before I left Vera Ridge.
Even if you know that the person offering the food has only
enough for himself or herself, you should accept. Nevertheless,
you must also learn how to refuse and under what circumstances you are allowed to refuse without insult. To learn how
not to accept food when it is offered is to be well on one's way
to functioning in the community. However, I was to learn all
this much later in my stay.

I asked the young man who was whitewashing the fence
where I could eat and he said, "You can eat almost any place
'round here nowadays. 'Least that's what they say. They can't
throw you out like they use to. 'Least they ain't suppose to.
Some of them white folks act funny when you come into their
place, so most black folks kinda stay out of them. There are
some black folks who go in all them places, 'specially where the
white folks don't like them to come in. Those black folks like to
make a scene, start trouble. They want to make the white folks
mad. They go in and sometimes they only order a glass of
water, then they walk out laughing. I don't know if that's the
right way to do it, but they got more nerves than I do, 'least I
can respect them for that. I do know that you can eat at Thompson's cafe without having any problems and they have pretty
good food—if you like white folks' food."

As I was talking with him, a white man came toward us.
The young man said he had to get back to work, so I thanked
him and walked toward Thompson's. As I walked, I spoke to
every black person I met, and they all seemed very friendly
and returned my greeting. Sometimes I stopped to talk with
them. An elderly man said, "I don't ever 'member seeing you
'round here before. Whose boy is you?"

"I just came to Vera Ridge today. I am a student at a university back East. I came to Vera Ridge to do anthropological field-work—a study on the black family."

He seemed concerned or puzzled. I did not know how to interpret his reaction. He scratched his head and said, "That's nice." Then he walked away.

Other people would say nothing to me at all, and there was one young black man who said, "You better watch your step down here. Some people get suspicious of strangers going 'round asking lots of questions. They don't know who you are or what you're all about, so I'd be careful if I was you."

Still, some of them had me go into detail about the nature of my work in Vera Ridge. For example, one person asked me why I was studying to become an anthropologist. Then he added, "Oh! Them's the people who study Africans. What are you doing down here? Come to think of it, some of these people 'round here do look like they just come outta the bush."

I tried to explain to him that I became interested in studying the black family because I felt that most of the studies did not represent black lifestyles fairly, and that I wanted to spend at least a year living and working with black families so that I might be able to present another view. Then he said, as others had said to me, "Don't you know what black folks are all about? Why do you have to study something that you are, that you live? Ain't you black?"

I was hard pressed to give him an answer. I felt that if I tried to explain it the way I would talk to a fellow student or a professor he would not understand, so I said, "Well, it's like this: people have ideas that because they experience something they know all about it. People who have certain degrees from universities think that they are knowledgeable about everything that goes on in life. People like truck drivers think they know all about trucks. What do you do?"

"I lay bricks. 'Um a bricker."

"Do you believe that people who lay bricks know all there is about bricks?"

"Well, if there is something else to know, there's nobody that

can tell it to me, because I've been laying bricks since I was sixteen years old—all kinds of bricks and if I can't lay them, nobody can . . . but I think I understand where you're comin'
from. I'm sure that there are people who can tell me something
about laying bricks and it will help me understand more than
I do now."

"This is the kind of thing I mean when I say that I am studying the black family. Because I am black doesn't mean I know
all that it is to be black. I can only tell you about my own black
experience. However, every black person doesn't live the same
way as I do—even more important is the fact that it is more
difficult for a person to try and explain something about himself
than it is for someone who can stand back and take a good look.
Maybe I didn't explain it the right way, but I hope you understand what I'm trying to say to you."

"I understand what you're saying, man, still it seem a waste
to me. If I was in school—going to college—I can think of much
better things to study than black folks."

With that he said good-bye, and I continued toward Thompson's. As I got to the door, I saw a black woman coming out. I
asked her if it was all right if I went in to eat, and she said, "If
you're hungry. But you won't catch me eating in that place."

I thought she had had some trouble. Perhaps it was better if I
did not eat there; but then she said, "I don't eat no white folks'
cooking, I just work here, 'specially when they don't want to
serve you in the first place. You never know what they might put
in your food. Anyway, they ain't clean. I see them scratching
everywhere on they bodies and then go right ahead and put they
hands on your food. They hair get all over everything they touch.
Anyway, I don't like the kind of food they cook. I don't like the
way they cook it. Give me some good old soul food anytime. Anyway, nobody can cook any better than me, so why should I pay
my hard earned money for what they cook?"

"Can you tell me about the food you call soul food?"

"You gots to be kiddin'. I knowed you sounded funny—the

way you talk and all that, but if you don't know what soul food is you must be one of them."

"One of what them?"

"Them niggers, oh, excuse me, them colored people who think they can act white. They try to act just like them white folks—talking all proper and acting all funny. Now you know what soul food is and if you don't I ain't got no business wasting my time talking to you in the first place. You just go right on in there and stick your belly full of them white folks' food. A good old plate of collard greens and corn bread may get you sick; you just may die."

She laughed and walked off. I knew what soul food was, but I wanted her to tell me. I went into the cafe and sat at the counter. There was a fat, white woman with a young girl sitting beside her. They were eating pie. I sat two seats from them. When I sat down, the fat woman got up, grabbed the child by the hand, put some money on the counter, and rushed off. I sat there for about five minutes, waiting for someone to take my order. Finally, a white waitress came up to me and said, "Can I help you . . . sir?"

She took my order, and while I waited for it I started to think about some of the problems I had already faced in Vera Ridge, although I had only spent a few hours there. I had thought that the people would be happy to know that someone was studying them. I thought it would be rather simple to obtain information; however, aside from the fact that people had difficulty understanding me, I had difficulty trying to explain me and my work to them. I had to ask myself: just what am I doing and how do I describe what I'm doing so that these people understand. In other words, I had to learn how to communicate before attempting to obtain any data.

The waitress brought me my food, and she all but threw it down on the counter. I ate in a hurry and paid for the food, then left. An hour ago, when I arrived in Vera Ridge, I was very tired and exhausted from the trip. In my excitement of walking through downtown Vera Ridge, I guess I had forgotten that I was tired. I felt like walking around downtown, but I happened to notice the time and realized that I had been gone over an hour. I headed back to Mrs. Walker's house. I did not have any problems finding my way back, but told myself that I would use the excuse of being lost in order to talk with people I met on the way. As I walked past a project housing, I saw four men sitting on a porch. I spoke to them in passing, and one of them called for me to come over. I walked over, and the one who had called said, "Are you new here?"

"Yes, I just got here today."

"What are you doing in Vera Ridge?"

"I came to do a study of the black community."

"We're part of the black community, you want to study us?"

"Well, after I get settled and find a place to stay, I would like to talk with as many of the people living in Vera Ridge as possible, especially if they have lived here for a long time."

"You think them honky whites goin' to talk to you?"

"I am only concerned with the black community of Vera Ridge."

"Well, then all of us, we been living here for a long time. We was born here and the way things are goin' we will probably die here. Now, what do you want to know?"

"Right now, I am trying to find a place to live."

"You mean you don't have a place to stay?"

"At present I am staying with the Walkers, the lady who lives right over there. She is taking me by a Mrs. Jones, because she is supposed to have a room I can rent. Actually, I would like to have an apartment, or a place where I can stay to myself."

"Well, don't worry, we'll find you a place for a small fee."

"You can?"

"What kind of a place you lookin' for?"

"An apartment or a house."

"Yeh! We can find it. Just lay the bread on me, man."

"Where is this place?"

"I know a hotel where you can rent rooms for almost nothin'."

"No!," one of the other men said, "he don't look like a person who want to live in a place like that."

"You just keep quiet, Billy, let me handle this," said the man who originally called me over.

I became suspicious, and decided I did not want to seek the aid of these men. I did want to talk with them later, because they seemed like people who knew a great deal about certain aspects of Vera Ridge and the black people who lived there. So I told them, "I have to get back to Mrs. Walker's house; maybe I can get in touch with you later."

"How can we get in touch with you?"

I told them Mrs. Walker would know where I was, and that they could contact her. As I walked away, I heard them laugh and say, "We got us a fish!"

When I got to Mrs. Walker's house, she was nervously pacing back and forth in the living room. I had been gone a little over an hour, and she seemed very worried. When I walked through the door, she said, "I know you couldn't get lost. I wasn't worried about that. It's just that Mrs. Jones is a funny woman. You see, she lost her husband several years ago and she lives alone. She has diabetes and she is very funny about being on time."

I thought to myself, what does having diabetes to do with being on time. Mrs. Walker said that Mrs. Jones really does not like people living with her. "But she needs the money very bad. She used to have lots of money and only 'important' people around her. Since she went broke, she's been failing in health and in spirit. She pretends she don't know how to deal with people who are 'not her equal,' so we had better get over there right away 'fore she change her mind about renting the room."

What Mrs. Walker said about Mrs. Jones was enough for me to know that I did not want to rent the room, but I decided we should go over there so that neither of them would be offended.

Mrs. Walker said that it was only a short distance and that we could walk or take my car. I suggested that we take my car, since we were already late.

As we drove, Mrs. Walker pointed out different people's houses and suggested different families with whom I should talk. When we got to Mrs. Jones' house, Mrs. Walker walked to the door and knocked. Mrs. Jones, calling from inside her house, asked us to come in. After we entered the house, Mrs. Jones offered us a seat. Before we sat down, Mrs. Walker introduced me to Mrs. Jones. She looked up at me and then she said, "Just what is it you do?"

"I am trying to get my Ph.D. I am going to write my dissertation about black family life."

I felt that I could talk with her in this way because she was an educated woman. She had graduated from a college up North. Mrs. Walker had told me that she was a school teacher. Mrs. Jones responded: "You came to the right place to study the black family. You're gonna pick up more gossip than you can deal with. People 'round here sure like to talk, especially about other people. You gotta make sure you talk to the right people, otherwise all you gonna get are lies."

"Who are the right people?"

"You stay here long enough and you'll know. I can tell you and Mrs. Walker can tell you, but it's best you find out for yourself. Now, don't get me wrong, all the people 'round here ain't that bad, it's just some of them—those I call 'low-down' because they are always trying to bring in the low-down about other people who may be getting somewhere and they can't."

"Well, if I do my work right, I'll have to listen to the 'low-down' as well as the 'high-up.' It would be wrong for me to pick out certain things some people say because they live another kind of life. I am interested in every aspect of black lifestyle here in Vera Ridge."

"Black lifestyle! What about people like us? People who aren't black. I'm not black and Mrs. Walker's not black. All colored people aren't black."

"Oh! Mrs. Jones, he don't mean it that way. I know I'm not black in color. It ain't your color they're talking about. It's the spirit. Now you know what he meant."

"I know, and I don't like it. They're trying to lump all of us into one big smut-pot. Now you can call me Colored or you can call me Negro, but don't call me black.

As I tried to explain to Mrs. Jones why it was necessary to include the terms 'Colored' and 'Negro' in presenting a total picture of black family life, she laughed. But I think that for the most part she understood what I was trying to explain to her about my work. She interrupted my explanation by saying, "Well, would you like to see the room I have prepared for you?"

She took me to the room. After seeing it, I was sure that I didn't want to rent it. The whole house smelled of age. She kept it closed with drapes drawn. There was also the odor of medicine. The room looked recently cleaned; however, the rest of the house needed dusting. She began to tell me what she would expect from me as a boarder. She said, "I don't allow people coming into my house unless I know them. I have diabetes and the slightest thing upsets me and that isn't good for me. I usually go to bed 'round nine o'clock, so there can't be any noise after that. You can't take any young ladies into your room. I don't mind you bringing them here, but they have to sit on the porch."

Both Mrs. Walker and I looked at her; then we looked at each other. Mrs. Jones asked me to go outside and take a look at the backyard while she and Mrs. Walker talked. I walked outside the house. She had a big backyard that had been well-kept at one time. There was a large fishpond with a few very old goldfish that had lost their color and looked almost white. The yard was fenced in, with a wooden picket fence that had rotted and fallen down. Wrought-iron yard furniture was arranged neatly, but the white paint that had coated it was chipping and peeling, and the iron was rusting. The grass had gotten tall and brown; it badly needed cutting and watering. Two kids walked by and stopped. They stood there, staring at me, so I called them over.

They hesitated. I asked them if they wanted to see the fish. They said "Yes!" I asked them to come closer, but the little boy said "No! We can't do that. That old lady will get mad at us."

"Oh, come on. She won't care."

"You sure?"

"Sure!"

They slowly crossed to where I was and stooped to look at the fish. There were water lilies that were so thick that the fish easily hid. I was moving some of the lilies aside when someone yelled. "Get outta my yard. You kids know better than to come in my yard."

"He told us to come. It's his fault; he told us!"

"But you know better. Now go on home where you belong."

The kids ran as fast as they could. I stood and looked in amazement. While I was standing there, Mrs. Jones asked me to return. She said that I should not have asked the kids in her yard without her permission. Then she said that she would have to notify her nephew before she made a final decision about renting the room to me. She said, "My nephew handles all of my business and he would have to approve whatever I do first— before I do it."

I told her that would be fine by me. She asked me, "How many meals would you like? I don't mind cooking, but you'll have to cook your own breakfast because I don't get up 'til afternoon. I can cook your dinner. What sort of food do you like to eat?"

She asked me so many questions that I was overwhelmed, and simply responded to the last one. I told her that I liked soul food and she said, "What's soul food?"

Mrs. Walker laughed. She tried not to, but every time she attempted to speak, she began laughing again. I could see that Mrs. Jones was becoming annoyed. Finally, Mrs. Walker said, "Now Mrs. Jones! You know what soul food is."

"Well, I don't cook no collard greens. I can't stand the smell of them in my house. However, I don't mind if you cook them yourself. I'm not used to eating that kind of food myself. Can you cook?"

"Yes, I can cook. I've been cooking since I was thirteen years old."

I told Mrs. Jones that I would think over her offer and let her know as soon as possible. Mrs. Walker said that she was in a hurry, and that we had to leave. We bade Mrs. Jones good evening and Mrs. Walker was still laughing when we left Mrs. Jones' house. I told her that maybe she did not know the name "soul food," even though she might know what some of the foods are. Mrs. Walker said, "Oh! She knows the name soul food. I just can't understand Mrs. Jones—why do she keep pretending she don't know about something she knows?"

We got into my car, and I started for Mrs. Walker's house. She told me that she had to go by a dry cleaner's shop where she wanted to introduce me to a Mr. Smith, the owner of the shop. She said that he could help me find a place if I did not like the room at Mrs. Jones'. I told her that I did not feel that I would be comfortable living with Mrs. Jones. She said, "I understand; I don't blame you. That woman even gets on my nerves. Mrs. Jones, pretending that she didn't know what soul food was. She knows what it is."

She started laughing again. I said to her, "I wonder then, why did she pretend that she didn't know?"

Mrs. Walker said, "You see, she used to be a 'society lady,' while her husband was the principal of the high school. She used to travel to Europe and other places out of the country. Her husband built the first and only black clinic we had here in Vera Ridge. She worked there and she also taught at the high school. I hate to say this, but it pays to be nice to people all the time, 'cause you never know when you might need them. Mrs. Jones was a society lady. She only had certain people at her home. Now look at her and look at her house. She don't have a penny. Don't say nothing about this, but I understand that she had to mortgage her house to the bank. The bank is threatening to take over her house because she is not making payments. Mrs. Jones used to turn up her nose at people. Now when she needs them, no one will have anything to do with her. Once in a while some of her relatives come over and help her 'round the house. But more and more even they stop coming. You see, that house used to be the best kept house in this community. Now look at it. It just don't pay to try to be something you can't stick by. It will sure come back to haunt you later on down the road. Now it look like most of the other shacks 'round here. The poor old soul, she's really suffering. I feel sorry for her, honestly I do."

Before Mrs. Walker finished talking to me about Mrs. Jones, we arrived in front of Mr. Smith's shop. She made me sit in the car until she had finished telling me about Mrs. Jones. In spite of her feeling sorry for Mrs. Jones, she laughed about her present situation. We then got out of the car and walked into Mr. Smith's shop. He was sitting at a table in the corner, talking with two other men. Mr. Smith stood up and said, "I'm happy to meet you, Reggie, I understand that you are looking for a place to stay. I'll keep my eyes and ears open, and if there's a place to rent here in Vera Ridge I'll know about it. I'm proud to see our young men going to college and getting their Ph.D. Anything I can do to help you, anything you want to know about Vera Ridge, just let me know. Come to me, I can tell you everything. I have lived here, right here in this same spot for over twenty-five years. I've seen them come and I've seen them go. I've seen them born and I've seen them buried. I know the 'low-down' and everything there is to know about almost everyone living in Vera Ridge. I know who you should be with and who you should stay away from. I know you're in a hurry, but remember, anything you need to know just come back and talk with me, I'll always be right here. The only time I'm not at home, I'm at the barber shop and that's twice a week."

I did not know exactly how to feel about Mr. Smith. It struck me as being odd that he would come on so gracious, especially after just meeting me for the first time. Even though I had just arrived in Vera Ridge and was tired from the trip, I wanted to sit down and just let Mr. Smith talk with me until he got tired. I believed him to be a potentially invaluable source of information about Vera Ridge. Quickly, I said to myself, find yourself a place and get on with it. Mrs. Walker said that she had to return home, as Mr. Smith continued to talk. Mrs. Walker said that I could stay if I wanted to, and that she would walk home. I told her I was leaving. I wondered how Mr. Smith came to know so much about me. Later I learned from Mrs. Walker that she had told him earlier in the week about my coming and about the nature of my work.

As we were returning to her house, I asked her about Peggy's mother and where she lived. She said that Peggy's mother lived in the green house across from her. As we pulled up in front of her door, she pointed to the house. She said that she would take me by later in the evening, that Peggy's mother was a very nice lady, and that I should not be upset if she seemed not to respond to me once we had met. She said, "She is late in years and she is very sick. Sometimes she doesn't even recognize me."

We got out of the car and walked into her house. She talked about my work, and said that she had a son in Africa who was getting a degree. She told me that her husband was away at a meeting and probably would not return until the following day. I asked her what I should do with my things in the car, and she said, "I gather you are not interested in renting the room from Mrs. Jones. Well, I don't blame you. Why don't you unpack your things and put them in the living room while I clean up the back room where you can stay until you find a place of your own. Of course, this depends on what my husband will say, and I think he will agree."

As I began unloading my car, one of her sons came home from school. She introduced him to me as James. James did not seem to be interested in talking with me. She told him to help me unload my car, but he went out of the back door into the project housing nearby.

Later that evening, I met the older of the two sons living at home. His name was Larry. He was not too concerned about my presence, either. He disappeared somewhere into the house, and I did not see him again until the next day. It was much later that I found out that neither James nor Larry appreciated my being there. James said that his mother seemed to be giving me more attention than she ever gave him. Larry told me that his mother and father used me as an example when criticizing him for not liking school. Because of his resentment, Larry would eat all the food, leaving nothing for me when I returned from my interviewing for the day. All the while, Mrs. Walker assumed that I had eaten. I never told her otherwise. It was not until I found my own place that I began to get along with James and Larry.

James was in grade school, and Larry was in high school. They were not the biological sons of Mr. and Mrs. Walker. They had adopted them from Mrs. Walker's oldest daughter, of a previous marriage. Larry said that his biological mother is like a sister. He calls her "Nancy." Nancy ran away from home when she was twelve years old, to live with her mother's sister. When she was fifteen, she had Larry, and a year later she had James by another man—neither of whom she married. This last man she stayed with convinced her to leave with him for Boston. When Mrs. Walker found out about this, she decided that she wanted Larry and James with her. After being in Boston three months, Nancy and the man she stayed with separated. Nancy took James and Larry to her mother's sister. The sister contacted Mrs. Walker, who went there and brought them back. She decided to legally adopt them to prevent her daughter from reclaiming them.

Larry said that he has seen his "real" mama, but would not live with her, even if she wanted him to. He has also seen and continues to see his half-brothers and half-sisters that his mother Nancy now has. James and Larry are only a few years younger than Mr. and Mrs. Walker's youngest twin daughters. Larry said, "It's strange for me to call them aunts. I don't think of them as being my aunts. I think of them as being my sisters."

Neither Mr. or Mrs. Walker ever told me that James and

Larry are not their biological sons. All the information I received about James and Larry came from Larry, and from a few of the community's 'gossips'—especially Almira, the secretary at the funeral home. Mrs. Jones was right about the local gossips; Almira was one of them. All you had to do was get her started and she'd tell you something on everybody in Vera Ridge. After knowing her for only three weeks, she was telling me about events that happened between Mr. and Mrs. Walker. She said that he is very jealous of her, but that he "mess around with everybody he can." She said that Mrs. Walker knows he messes around, and, "One day she knew he was in a motel room with another lady. She went up there. He came out of that room and beat her and beat her. He beat her so bad she stayed in bed for days. He told her she better never come where he is again. Do you know after he beat her and sent her home, he went back into that motel room with that woman?"

Almira said she felt sorry for Mrs. Walker, that she would not live with a man who treated her that way—always beating on her. However, she and Mrs. Walker do not get along very well. Rumor has it that Mr. Walker and she were having an affair. She has a daughter, and Mr. Walker is said to be the father of her daughter. Carol, another of the local gossips, will tell you, "Don't she look just like Mr. Walker? She look just like one of the twins when she was that age. Lordy! I don't know what this world's coming to. Everybody's children belong to everybody else. It's getting so you don't know who the father is anymore; only the mama really knows—and sometimes she don't even know."

After I had unloaded my car, and crowded the room where I was to sleep with all of my equipment, clothing, and other items I had brought with me for my year's stay in Vera Ridge, I took out my ledger and began writing up all that had occurred during my first day there. I always wrote a daily account of what happened, whether I used my tape recorder or not. It was the most effective way of collecting conversational data when the tape recorder was not available. I had a knack for remembering detailed conversations. I think it had a lot to do with being an actor for ten years. I could learn my entire lines from a play in one night.

As I was writing, the pen seemed to flow with recollections. After I had put down all I thought had occurred, I re-read what I had written for the day. Since I had not had a full day in Vera Ridge, I was quickly through with my daily writing and evaluation of the data. A full day's research would take me five or more hours to write up. When I had finished, I lay across the bed to rest.

I must have dozed off, because I was awakened by James, telling me that his father wanted to see me. Mr. Walker had returned from his trip sooner than expected. I went into the living room and waited for him. He walked into the living room and spoke to me in a deep voice, saying: "How do you do, Mr. Kennedy? I am Mr. Walker. Don't get up; that's not necessary around here."

As I looked up at him, I could not help registering surprise. He must have been close to seven feet tall and weighed about two hundred pounds. He extended his hand and as I shook it, it nearly swallowed mine. His hands were huge and I thought he would break every bone in my hand. I had to literally pull it away from him. By this time, Mrs. Walker had entered the living room and said, "Albert, this is Mr. Kennedy."

"I know, I already introduced myself to Mr. Kennedy."

"I hope you don't mind, Mr. Walker, but I would feel more comfortable if you called me Reggie."

"I don't mind calling you Reggie, if you don't mind calling me Albert. Now let's go into the kitchen so that we can eat and talk."

I told him that I was not hungry, because I had already eaten. He suggested that I watch television until he finished eating. He seemed to order his wife around. He yelled, "Frances! Fix me some food."

He appeared as funny to me as Mrs. Jones did to Mrs. Walker

when she said she did not know what soul food was. Under my breath I had to laugh every time I imagined him standing before me in his bright-red dinner jacket, looking like a redwood tree. I had to grind my teeth to keep from laughing aloud. Finally, he finished his food, and yelled for me to come into the kitchen so that we could talk. As I walked into the kitchen, he was sitting there, having eaten neckbones—some scattered on the table and others still on his plate. His whole face was greasy with fat. He told me to sit down, and offered me food for the second time. Again, I refused it, and he said, "Let's get down to business then."

Our conversation centered around how much I would be charged, and what services I could expect while living in their home. It was decided that I pay them on a daily basis for my room and board, including one meal a day and my laundry once a week. Mr. Walker arrived at eight dollars a day—a rather large amount, I thought. I did not protest, however; I knew that I would not be living there very long.

After the living arrangements had been settled, Mr. Walker began making out a schedule that I was supposed to follow. He decided when I was to go, where I was to go, and whom I was to see each day. I would not have any time to do my work (the way I wanted to) if I were to follow his expectations. I told him that I could not regiment myself that way; but he insisted that I should give it a try.

As the days passed, I managed to let him know that I would have to visit the "undesirables" as well as the "desirable areas" of the community. I told him my work entailed contacting all the black people of the community who were accessible to me. I also had to explain to him that he could not monopolize my time, that I had to be free to do my research. Eventually, he realized this, and began letting me work the way I wanted. Of course, on occasion I had to go with him to meet "certain people" of the community, as well as those outside the community. Actually, he was a very good source for many of my contacts and materials. He was also to be indirectly responsible for a major problem I had during the first three months in Vera Ridge.

It was about one-thirty before I got to bed, my first night in Vera Ridge. I took a shower; and as I lay down to sleep I started wondering if I had made a mistake in coming there. A lot of memories of what it meant to live in the South filled my mind. The living conditions I had already seen angered me. I was angry with the whites for keeping the blacks down, and even angrier at the blacks for allowing themselves to be kept down. I wanted to get out of bed and begin packing my things, to get into my car and drive straight through without stopping until I had crossed the Mason-Dixon line. When I remembered I had to spend a whole year in Vera Ridge, I felt trapped; the need to escape preyed on my mind. Somewhere between plotting my escape and reconciling myself to my situation, I fell asleep.

JUDGMENT DAY
AND THE
AFTERMATH

*T*HE first two weeks in Vera Ridge were surprisingly uneventful. I approached people, and began conversations with them with little or no difficulty. I told them I was a college student at a university in the East, and that I was working on my Ph.D. I told them I had come to Vera Ridge to do a study of how black families lived in a southern town. I had no organized method of approach for the first weeks. I just wanted things to happen as they did, and to record whatever happened at the end of each day. I collected some names of people and places; but my major concern was finding a place to stay. One thing that struck me was that the people seemed to know a lot about me before I knew anything about them. For example, they knew where I lived, that I was a stranger, an outsider, and the work I "pretended" to do. My presence in Vera Ridge became known very quickly, even to the white community. The word got around that there was a "stranger" in town asking a lot of questions. The white merchants knew that there was a "nigger" who seemed to have lots of money, buying film and other supplies. The white policemen got on my trail, and often followed me back into the black community.

Mr. Walker arranged for me to visit and be interviewed at

the white-owned (but black-operated) radio station. He also took me to the town meetings and to places as distant as Lakeview (about a hundred miles away). But I became annoyed with the manner in which he presented me to people, and with his insistence on taking me around. He wanted me to meet particular people and to go places he had checked out as "safe" for me to go. Every time I met someone, he would introduce me as "Mr. Kennedy," as if I were someone of importance. He would say, "This is Mr. Kennedy. He's doing a study in Vera Ridge on black folks. He's getting his Ph.D. at a big university in the East, and he's staying with me—at my house."

I got the impression that he did not care about me as an individual, but was concerned only with my status as an "important person staying at his house." It seemed as if he was trying to build a name for himself. When I mentioned to him that I had no trouble in interviewing people, he said, "That's because you're living with me. I know most of the people 'round here, and they know me. I had a lot of pull 'round here."

He was right; he had a lot of pull. He almost pulled me down with him. He was wrong about my living with him being a blessing; it was a contributing factor that led to a nightmare I was to remember forever. He singled himself out as the most important black person in the community. He did have his wits about him; however, he did not know how to explain my work to others. He would always start out by saying, "Mr. Kennedy is doing a study on black folks," and then he added, "you tell them what you're doing."

He would leave me to explain the nature of my work, not because he wanted me to speak, but because he was unfamiliar with my work. When we went to the town meetings, he would introduce me to the chairman of the committee. The vibes I got from the chairman and other white committee members seemed to be, "So what, he's just another nigger who thinks he knows so much. He has to be watched."

Mr. Walker would let me start my explanations, but almost

immediately he would cut me short by saying, "I have another meeting, so we'll have to cut this one short; maybe we can get together later and talk about your work." Of course, that talk never materialized. Mr. Walker was right about one thing; many people in Vera Ridge knew him. But all who knew him considered him as a "trouble-maker, a power-seeker, or a stupid person who was trying to get ahead by stepping on anybody he could—black or white." This feeling about Mr. Walker was shared by members of the black as well as the white communities.

In my spare time—that is, when I was not meeting "important people" (which was rare)—I got a chance to go out on my own and talk with black people in the community. One such group was the four black men I had met the first day I came to Vera Ridge. These were the ones who said they could find me a place to live, and called me a fish as I was leaving them. The next day, they had taken me to the previously mentioned hotel and showed me a room where I could live. But the hotel was a place for transients and prostitutes. The bottom floor had two cafe-restaurants and a curbside market. I knew it would be impossible for me to stay there because of the noise from the establishments below, the arguing and fighting of people on the sidewalk, the street traffic, and the train. How could I possibly concentrate or conduct serious interviews there?

On the way to the hotel, they kept insisting that I drive them to Polksville—some ninety miles away. They said they would pay for the gas. I continued to refuse them because I had early interviews the following day. We went up to the room of one of their friends. At the room, they bought some wine, and offered me a drink. I rarely drink with people who seem as questionable as they appeared; however, I did not want to appear unsociable. They drank, and agreed to answer my queries. I had taken my tape recorder along; so I asked them if they would mind if I taped the conversations. They all agreed. But the interview was totally unsuccessful because they never attempted to answer any of the questions I asked; instead they asked me why I wanted to know the information, or else they changed the subject of any question I would ask—almost always returning to the idea of taking them to Polksville. After an hour of what I considered wasted and fruitless effort, I told them I had to leave because the Walkers went to bed early, and I did not have a key—although of course I did.

But they tried to keep me there. One of the young men grabbed the tape recorder and said he would keep it if I did not take them to Polksville. I managed to talk him into giving it back, after promising that I would take them at a later date. I gathered my things and started to leave. I became angry, and pushed my way through the doorway. Once we got down to the street, they cornered me in the alley behind the hotel. One of them took a knife out of his pocket, and threatened to kill me if I did not take them to Polksville. You feel strange when something like that happens. You don't want to believe that it is happening to you, and even with the knife at my throat, I could not think of dying—could not think of death. It was only when he gripped me tighter and pressed the blade harder to my throat that I began to imagine what could happen to me, and the pain I could go through.

I had been in areas of the country where people got killed every day. But to be in a little place like Vera Ridge, and to be told by someone that he is going to take your life, makes you afraid and unafraid at the same time. Luckily for me, a drunken man came out of the back door of one of the bars; as they heard him, the knife was put away and they ran off. I stood there, shocked in disbelief. I slowly picked up the things I was carrying and composed myself. When the realization of what had happened, and what could have happened, came to me, I made a dash for the Walker house, scared to death. I unlocked the door, and hurried to my room. Mr. Walker, who usually waited for me to return, heard me come in. He called to me to come where he was. I had to quickly think of a reason why I couldn't and told him I had to write down some information I had received

before I forgot it. He said he understood, and told me he would
see me in the morning.

I put my equipment in the corner of the room, took out my
ledger, and began to write up the day's events. It was very difficult for me to concentrate on my writing. I kept thinking of
what had happened to me only a short while ago. Several times
I stopped writing and put my head on the desk. I tried to tell
myself that the event did not happen. My fear of what had
occurred began to turn into anger. In my mind, I planned to go
and find these guys and confront them with what they had
done. However, I know that I was happy to be in the safety of
my room. Finally, when I had written down all the things I
could remember of the day—with most of what I had to write
pertaining to the event of the evening—I got ready for bed. It
was hard for me to fall asleep. When I did, I dreamed all that
night about being murdered. I wanted to tell Mr. Walker about
the incident; but I was afraid and decided not to. Many times
during the night, I woke up—I thought I had been screaming,
and wondered if anyone heard me. As I fell asleep for the last
time (before awaking in the morning), I was imagining packing up my things and preparing to leave Vera Ridge.

The next day, I was eating lunch in a cafe and talking with
the owner, who said he could possibly rent me a room. It was
hard for me to concentrate on anything. I kept remembering
the previous night, and wondering when and where those four
guys would pop up again. While we were talking, a man came
up and introduced himself as John Plummer. He said, "I've
heard about you. I was wondering when I would get a chance to
meet you. I saw you coming into this place, so I decided I would
make the first move. My sister has been waiting to talk with
you ever since you got here."

"How did you and your sister know about me, and how did
she know I was in Vera Ridge? Why is it so many people are
interested to see and talk with me?"

"Oh! We know. My sister, she know everything that happen
around Vera Ridge, especially when it involves strangers asking

a lot of questions. We want to know who you are, and what you are doing down here, asking so many people so many questions."

"Is there any reason why she wants to talk with me, other than wanting to know why I'm here?"

"Yeah! She want to make sure you are who you claim to be, and that you are not here to start any trouble for the black people who are trying to bring some respect to our people. We have had people here before—blacks claiming they were for the cause. They turned out to be spies for the white man."

"Well, I can assure you that I am not a spy, and that my purpose down here is to study black-family lifestyle in Vera Ridge. Whatever it takes to prove to you, and to anyone concerned, that my intentions are to do fieldwork for my dissertation, I will be happy to prove."

"Well, we'll find that out in time. Now don't let me stop you from eating your lunch; your food's getting cold. We can still talk while you eat."

"I'm not that hungry now; and anyway, I am more interested in meeting people than eating lunch—actually, I am even *more* concerned about finding a place to live."

"Well, you finish your lunch, and we will work on things— one thing at a time. First, we got to make sure you are who you claim to be."

"What kinds of things do you and your sister do to improve the black peoples' position down here in Vera Ridge?"

"No questions, especially about that; in time you will find out everything—maybe."

"O.K. No more questions until I have been given the go-ahead."

I finished my lunch, and told John I would go meet with his sister. He told me to drive my car back to the Walkers'. He would take me around in his car. After I had parked my car, I went to his, parked about a block away from the Walker house. I asked him why he had parked so far away; and he said, "You will know in time. Remember, no questions."

He drove me to a curbside market, and there I was introduced to a young woman he referred to as "Linda," his sister. He turned to me and said, "What did you say your name was?"

"Reggie."

"Reggie, this is my sister, Linda."

"I'm glad to meet you, Linda."

"Maybe the feeling will be the same; right now I don't know. I was waiting for you to come 'round so that I could see where you was coming from. I knew you was in town two weeks ago."

"How did you know that?"

"That's my business. It's for me to know and you to find out. I would not be too nosy at first, if I was you. We don't accept strangers too easy down here, especially if they're from up North."

"If you knew I was in town two weeks ago, and you wanted to talk with me, why didn't you come by the Walkers' house, where I live? Or why didn't you call or get in touch with me, so that I could come and see you?"

" 'Cause, you are staying at the Walkers' house, and we don't get along. I hate that pig—Walker."

"What's wrong with Mr. Walker?"

"You've been over there for two weeks and you don't know? You'll find out. There's too much misunderstanding between our people today. I don't want to start any more misunderstandings. It's for you to find out for yourself; otherwise, I would come right out and tell you."

"Well, he does seem very bossy and demands that you do what he wants you to do; but other than that, he seems like a pretty good person to me."

"You'll find out in time. He thinks he's the spokesman for all of the black people in Vera Ridge; actually he ain't shit in my book; he's just another Uncle Tom, sucking up to Mr. White Man, while they use him like a jackass."

I started to ask her questions about the situation of black people in Vera Ridge; but she would not answer. She only said, "I gotta make sure who you are . . . what's your real purpose for being here. You got two strikes against you already for living at Walker's house. Anytime a man know his house is going to be bombed and let his wife and children stay in that house while he hides out in his funeral home should be strung-up on a tree. Yes, his wife and children was asleep in that house when some white folks placed dynamite near it, and they were lucky they weren't all killed. He pretended he fell asleep in the funeral home. He should have been laying in one of them coffins he have in there—sleeping for good."

Then she started asking me questions, and outlined the conditions under which she would eventually talk with me. She fired questions at me so fast it was impossible for me to follow what she was saying. I stood there, frustrated and angry, because I could not ask her questions; also because of the fact that she knew she had me on the spot. All I could do was listen to her mouth going a mile a minute. I did not like some of the conditions she laid down. I did not like her, although her demands seemed fair in some respects. I thought she wanted me to prove that I was not working for the "pigs" (police). That seemed to be her most important demand. She told me that a month ago, two blacks and one white person came to Vera Ridge and, "A few days after they left, twenty black people were arrested on charge of possession of drugs. They had said that they were Civil Rights workers. I want you to prove to me that you aren't gathering information about the black community to take back to Whitey."

She let it be known that she was the spokeswoman for the "leading citizens" of the black community—of whom there seemed to be several. She said that she would arrange a meeting the following Sunday, where I could prove my good intentions. She gave me the option of not attending—along with a warning that my absence would make my stay in Vera Ridge very difficult. I was annoyed at myself for being intimidated by her. As I left her shop, I told her I would be back to see her again, and she said, "You do that."

Once I had returned to the Walkers' house, I kept picturing

her face in my mind: I had seen it whenever there was a disturbance on a college campus—hard, mean, suspicious, weary, tired, without a sign of positive leadership.

Mr. Walker must have noticed the concern on my face when I reached his house because he said, "What's the matter, Reggie?"

"Oh, it's nothing, really. I just met some of the people who live down the road a bit."

"Did they give you any trouble?"

"No; I just talked with them and they talked with me."

"You probably didn't like what you saw. We have a lot of poor people living here in Vera Ridge. We also have some who think that they are bigshots, those you should stay away from. They will get to you. And, the first thing you know, you'll be giving them money and they will be taking you for everything you got. You gotta watch out for folks like that here. Now I told you the people you ought to be talking to, but you won't listen."

I thought to myself, "Yeah! Just like you are doing to me." He made me feel like they would take the money he would be getting from me for staying in his house. However, I said to him, "I listen, Mr. Walker; it's just that all the people you told me to talk with only represent a small portion of the total black population in Vera Ridge. How can I say I am doing a study on the Vera Ridge blacks if I choose only a few carefully screened people that you have recommended for me to interview? I have to talk with as many of the black people as I can—from all walks of life. Can't you understand that?"

"Yeh! I understand; but I also understand what kind of trouble you can get into if you don't watch your step, if you don't stay away from certain people . . ."

"Getting into trouble is a hazard in doing fieldwork where you are not a member of that community. It's the chance you take; it's the data you record; it's black-family lifestyle. It is black lifestyle in general."

With that, I headed for the kitchen. As usual, there was not much food for me, but I did not care because I was not very hungry anyway. I was afraid he was going to follow me into the kitchen and insist on my telling him with whom I had talked. He did not; and I wondered whether or not I should tell him. If Linda was correct about him, it would only cause more trouble if I told him; so I said nothing. After eating some corn bread and collard greens, I took a shower and retired to my room, where I began writing in my ledger. Afterward, I went to bed.

Early in the next morning, I walked over to Linda's brother's house. He lived in the section of Vera Ridge I refer to as section B. I decided I would spend several weeks meeting people in section B before going on to other areas. When I got to John's house, he was in the yard, raking trash. Without giving me a chance to offer to help, he said, "Hey! Grab yourself a rake, Reggie, and give me a hand."

I did; and he began talking to me about his school work. He was working part-time for his Master's degree in Earth Science. He talked about the trouble he had had while going to school—especially because he could not devote his entire time to school work. He said, "If my wife wasn't working, there wouldn't be no money coming into the house. How do you think I feel, not having a job and not bringing in at least some money to support my family?"

"But, John, that's the reason you're going back to school—to get a higher degree so that you can get a good job and be able to take care of your family."

"I know, man, but I've been in school over two years already, working on my Master's degree, and I really don't know how close I am in getting it yet."

While we were raking, a friend of John's stopped by. John called to him, "Curtis, come over here. I want to introduce you to Reggie."

Curtis came over, extended his hand, and said, "How are you doing, Reggie? I have heard about you, and now I have a chance to meet, in person, Reggie. What brings you to Vera Ridge?"

"I bring myself," I said, hoping and trying to be humorous,

to get a laugh out of him. I was hoping to break the iron look on his face; but he kept his composure and replied, "I know you bring yourself; I mean *why* did you come to Vera Ridge?"

I realized that he was serious; and so I said, "I came to Vera Ridge to study a town where the black population is small enough for me to know everyone—almost everyone."

"What kind of study do you want to do with *us* blacks?," he said; and he laughed as he looked at John. John began laughing also.

"I'm interested in how black family members organize their everyday lives."

"Black family life? Why do you have to come all the way to Vera Ridge to study the black family?"

"Well, Vera Ridge isn't the only town I could have come to, but the main reason I am in Vera Ridge is because it is the home of Peggy, and I wanted to come to the place where she grew up."

"You talked to Peggy? I don't believe it."

"Why do you say that?"

" 'Cause everybody say that they talk to Peggy, just because she's a famous person. I bet you don't even know her."

"Well, I have a letter from her. This letter is an introduction to Mr. Walker."

"I know that's a lie. Peggy can't stand Walker. I got to see that letter before I believe you."

"When I return to Mr. Walker's house, I'll get a copy of the letter and show it to you."

"Hey!," John said, "Why don't we go to my house and sit down and have some coffee while we talk?"

"I would," Curtis said, "but I have to get to work."

I asked him when he thought he would be able to talk with me, and he said, "I don't know if I want to talk to you. You ain't showed me nothing yet. And, if you don't come over right with me, you won't talk to nobody 'round here."

"Well, I've already talked with some people, and they didn't seem to mind."

"Yeh! I know exactly who you have talked to, and what they told you. What makes you think people 'round here are going to talk to you before they get to know who you are and what you're all about?"

"It seems to me that people either act the way you do or they are very nice and friendly. I can understand people being skeptical. But overt hostility—that I can't understand."

"Well, if you live around here, you may be hostile to strangers too. We've had our problems, and things are going to get worse, not better—you got to be careful if you're going to survive."

"Linda said that she was going to set up a meeting, and I could let the people know who I was and what I was all about."

"Oh! That reminds me," said John, "my sister set the meeting time for seven o'clock in the evening at the Community Club House. She told me to tell you."

"Where is the Community Club House located?"

"It's over there; I'll show you later."

Curtis said good-bye to John; and then he added, "I'll see you on Sunday—at the meeting."

After we had finished raking, John took me to his house; in the back is the house where he was born and raised. He had built his present home mostly by himself. The house needed additional work, but John said that he did not have the money to buy the necessary materials. It was a one-story structure and you had to walk around the back to enter. John asked me if I wanted a cup of coffee. While drinking the coffee, I asked him about the meeting I was to attend on Sunday. He said, "You wanted to meet with the people of Vera Ridge; well, you will meet them—not all of them; but you are going to meet some characters."

"What do you mean by 'some characters'?"

"Oh, there will be church people there, militant people, people who are interested in strangers who come to our community to do a study on us."

"Are you going to be there?"

"No!"

"Why aren't you coming?"

"Because I know what will happen. You see, they have good intentions; but by the time the meeting is halfway over, they'll be arguing between themselves. Everyone think his own idea is more important than other people's, and that his question is better put than others; and they will bitch and argue between each other 'til people get tired and decide, 'what's the use?', as I have already said. Now, I don't attend any of them meetings; but you have to, because if you don't, you will upset many people here in Vera Ridge, and that could possibly make trouble for you."

"Well, I guess I had better go; but somehow I would feel much better if you were there. I don't know if you will be any different from them, but at least I feel comfortable being around you."

"I'm sorry, but I have to study my lessons. Sunday evening is the only time I am not busy doing other things around the house; but you can bet I'll hear about it when it's over."

I spent the rest of the week in and around John's house. I followed him wherever he went—to his sister's curbside market, to a cafe-restaurant his mother owned, to his college some ninety miles away, to other people's homes, and to playgrounds with the children. John introduced me to his mother, Ola May. She was a very pleasant woman, and invited me to come into her home. She told me that if there was anything I wanted to know about Vera Ridge or its people she would tell me. She added, "When the time is right, we'll sit down, and I will keep your ears burning."

I met John's wife and his four-year-old son, Sammy. Sammy took to me right away. John's wife, Sarah, was very pleasant and as nice as the rest of his relatives, not including Linda. During the days leading up to Sunday, I helped John do lots of chores around his and his mother's house. I even helped him put up shelves in his sister's curbside market. I went with him to different wholesale houses to purchase items his sister sold.

On occasion, Curtis would join us; but he never talked about anything other than sports, school work, or how he someday wanted to return to college. Curtis headed a social organization designed to provide welfare for the poor; he was very proud of his directorship. He had a staff of about ten women working for him. I learned from John that the organization was not going to be funded much longer, and that Curtis would soon be out of a job.

The closer it got to Sunday, the more ill-at-ease I began to feel. I cannot describe what was bothering me. I just felt that something was wrong. For example, people with whom I had already talked now refused to talk with me, and told me to wait until after the meeting. Many times I asked John about the meeting and what I could expect from it; but he told me nothing new.

Then came Sunday. I had promised Mr. Walker I would attend church services with him and his family, but I awoke too late. Church services had already begun, so I decided not to go. I had butterflies in my stomach. Anticipating the meeting that evening, I drank a cup of coffee and spent most of the day going over notes I had already written. I also packed a carrying-case so that it contained all the proof I felt necessary to show people that my goals were legitimate.

I left the house about six-thirty. It was only a five-minute walk to the Community Club House; but I wanted to arrive early. People had already begun to assemble. I looked around the hall; but I did not see John. There were many faces I didn't recognize. I walked over where Linda sat; she motioned for me to sit in a chair she had prepared, so that I would be in full view of all who attended the meeting. Linda then introduced me to Mrs. Mables. I learned that Mrs. Mables was related to a famous black politician and that worried me. Linda sat to my left; Mrs. Mables to my right, while the rest of the townspeople sat in full front view of us. I asked Linda and Mrs. Mables if I could tape the session; they immediately responded, "No!" They did not want anything they said taped.

That made me even more suspicious of their motives. However, I thought they simply wanted to protect themselves. After all, they did not know who I was or whom I represented.

The kangaroo court began. I was immediately placed on the defensive and was not allowed to respond to anything until they were ready for me to do so. I felt like getting up and walking out; but knew if I did not stay and face them they would always have reason to be suspicious of me. By the time they would turn to me for a response, I had forgotten many of the questions and their sequence; so my responses were somewhat vague and not always to the point. It would not have mattered how I responded, though, because every time I tried to explain myself I was called a liar.

It was a strange feeling sitting there, being humiliated by people you barely knew. They were tense and intent on "getting to me." My blood seemed to boil; I thought at times my head would blow up from the anger rising in me. The lies that were being said about me—even more so, the people who knew they were lies, spreading the lies—enraged me. Linda pointed out that I was staying with Mr. Walker; and Mrs. Mables saw that as a sign of my "no-good" intentions because, as she said, "It was Mr. Walker who was responsible for me being dragged from the courthouse by them white policemen."

It is so hard to think of yourself as an outsider, as a researcher, so that you sit there and take the shit and do nothing about it. Suddenly I became *me*, a person being attacked. I had feelings just like them; and I could not just sit there like some iron dummy and not respond to my feelings. They are just people, I said to myself; I've done nothing wrong, so why should I just sit here? I looked out over the room; and the people seemed to be enjoying seeing me sit there, squirming in my seat. The more they seemed to make me squirm, the more pleasure appeared on their faces. I realized that most of them could care less who I was, as long as they got satisfaction from the state of uneasiness in which they placed me. This seemed like a play or a movie or something. It couldn't be real, I thought. Nobody had the right to make another feel the way I was feeling. But I sat there still as I could, even though my mind and the thoughts that came to it raced with rage.

During the meeting, the four men who had wanted me to take them to Polksville accused me of having taped their conversation without their knowledge. This was just too much; however, fortunately for me, I could remember the exact sequence of events, and tried to persuade them to recall that I did indeed ask their permission. I reminded them that they had asked to listen to the tape at one point during the interview. I also pointed out the fact that they had stopped talking while a train passed so that they would be heard clearly. Even so, they held to their original story, and insisted that I had taped them without their knowledge.

I wanted to point out how they had tried to take my tape recorder; but decided that if they admitted to it, it would probably be used against me. They would say that they had discovered me taping them and tried to get the tape recorder. This particular accusation caused many of the others to suspect me. I noticed that neither Linda nor Mrs. Mables seemed surprised when the charges were made against me. It was as though they had planned exactly how the meeting would proceed, and when particular pieces of information should be brought up.

I wanted to describe how they had put a knife to my throat, how they had manhandled me and demanded that I take them to Polksville or die. But then I turned and looked at the four men. They did not say anything; but I knew that I would be in serious trouble with them if I brought it up. They were bent on destroying me. And the men could deny it; they had me, no matter what I would say. After all, they were members of this community and I was but a stranger, an outsider. The verdict would have gone against me merely because of the fact that I was on trial, not the four men. So I did not mention the Polksville incident.

Mrs. Mables turned to me and said, "Did you use the tape recorder, or didn't you?"

"Yes, I used it."

"You used it without them knowing it, didn't you?"

"That's not true. I told you it wasn't true. They knew the tape recorder was there, and they knew it was on. One of them even fooled around with it, to see how it worked."

"Well, they said they didn't; now who do you think we're going to believe, them or you? We know them; we don't know you. Why should they lie about something like that?"

"I don't know. Why don't you ask them?"

Linda, who had been looking at me during Mrs. Mables' interrogation, turned to the four men and asked, "Did you guys know he had a tape recorder or didn't you?"

"No! We didn't know he had it, we already told you that; he's lying," one of the young men stood and said.

"Well, that's good enough for me," Linda said. "You used the tape without their permission. Now, let's get on with the meeting."

And so they did. As the meeting progressed, I became more and more angry. At first, I tried to answer their questions, thinking they were really after the truth and that all I needed to do was to prove to them who I was and what I was all about. Later, I felt more and more sure that they were not interested in the truth, but wanted to show how much power they could exert over me, and how small they could make me feel.

At this point, I stood up and said, "Damn it! I'm sick and tired of being accused of something I didn't do. You people are worse than any white person I've ever known. Here I am, trying to make something out of myself. Trying to show the white man that we are just as smart as he, that all we need is a chance. But who's trying to throw up blocks? My own people. Well, you're not throwing up a block against me. You are throwing it up against all black people who fight the shit they have to in order to get somewhere. And most of all, you're throwing a block against yourselves. Who needs this? I don't need it and you don't need it."

This response seemed to surprise everyone—even Linda and

Mrs. Mables—and you could hear a pin drop in the quietness. But I wasn't through with them; I continued, "Listen to me for a change. I know that none of you have to talk to me. I know that you can make my stay here in Vera Ridge miserable. I thought you called this meeting in good faith. I thought you were interested in finding out the truth about me. This stranger wanted to become friends. But what you are doing, or trying to do to me, shouldn't be done to a dog. I don't have to take this from you or anybody."

Linda, on one side of me, and Mrs. Mables on the other, took hold of me and asked me to please sit down. They told me not to become so excited. I lowered myself to my seat; but I wasn't through yet. Sitting back in my chair, I said, "You said that you wanted to prove that I wasn't 'the man' or working for 'the man,' but every time I offer you proof, you ignore it by calling me a liar, or going on to another point. What is it that you want from me? Now, these four guys said that I taped them without their knowledge. I can prove to you that they knew they were being taped, and that I had asked permission before taking the tape recorder from its holder. They saw the tape recorder; it was right in front of their faces. They even asked me, as I was setting it up, how it worked. Now, if you really want to know whether I am lying or telling the truth, why don't you let me go and get the tape and play it back for you?"

With that, one of the four guys stood up and said, "He asked our permission to use the tape recorder. We were all aware of it being there."

The other three angrily turned to him; and one of them said, "What did you go and say that for? We had the cat going." "I know what 'um doing," he said "We didn't come here for that. Ain't no use to lying about something just to put the dude on the spot. Yeh! Hey! We knew he was using the tape recorder because we gave him permission to use it."

For a moment, I began to breathe easier, because the people had begun to argue among themselves. Then one of the women in the audience stood up and shouted in a loud voice: "Hey! We ain't getting nowhere like this—arguing between ourselves. We ain't on no trial; he is, and I must say, he's been better about this than any of us. Now let's get back down to business—what we came here for in the first place."

People quieted down; and then came new charges. One charge after another was leveled against me. They ranged from "spying on them" to "causing trouble for the community." As soon as I tried to answer one charge, another was made. I was beginning to lose my patience again; my anger got the better of me. I no longer felt that they were interested in testing my honesty—they were demonstrating their control over me and the pressures I would have to face if I did not "see things their way." I grabbed my briefcase and took every document I had brought to prove where I was in Vera Ridge. I spread them on the table for all to see. The documents included the grants that were financing my research. Having them see the documents was a big mistake. Now the four men were sure I had lots of money. When I showed the grants, the meeting began to get out of control again. Attention momentarily shifted from me; and the people began to argue, once again, among themselves. Mrs. Mables finally pounded her hand on the table and shouted, "That's just like us Colored people. We can't settle nothing among ourselves without getting into arguments. Already we're at each others' throats. Why? Why do we do this to ourselves? Now let us get back to what we came here for in the first place! Let us cut out this damned nonsense and get back down to the real reason why we're here."

My relief because the attention had shifted from me was short-lived. Mrs. Mables seemed to be blaming me for their arguments. I was asked to provide further proof of my purpose. I had a letter of recommendation from Peggy. She was very highly respected by the community, not only because she was a successful entertainer in New York City, but also because her mother was warmly regarded. This letter should have been sufficient, had it not revealed what they considered a contradiction. A man in the audience said, "No way! Peggy wouldn't suggest that you stay at Walker's house. We know Peggy and we know Walker, and nobody here cares for that man and neither do Peggy care for him."

I tried to tell them that Peggy did not arrange for me to stay at Mr. Walker's house. She had asked him to help me find a place to stay.

"Then why are you staying there?"

"Because I can't find any place else to stay."

"We'll find you a place to stay."

"You can stay at my house," one of the women said.

This appeared to alleviate most of their suspicions. Their final question raised the issue of what I could do for the black community of Vera Ridge. Linda said, in an annoying manner, "You've come to get something out of our community. People are always coming down here to get something—to study us. Are we some kind of freaks or something? What do we get? Nothing. What are you going to give to us?"

I told her that the best I hoped to offer was an honest report on the structure of the black family and black lifestyle in Vera Ridge. I told her that I hoped that my study would help to clear up what I felt to be a gross misunderstanding of our people and our ways of living.

One of the four men stood up and shouted, "We don't need nobody to tell us about black family life; we already know about our families. Tell us what you gonna do about people who don't have jobs, people who can't feed they families, people who are poor and hungry—tell us about that."

"These problems many communities such as Vera Ridge have," I said. "I don't represent the government, although I can voice my own opinions; and I had hoped that one of you would volunteer to help with my research." A lady stood up and asked, "Is there any money in it?"

"Yes, there is some."

"How much?"

"That depends on how many hours you give each day."

Suddenly, everyone wanted to become my assistant. I told

them that I would need some time to consider each person, and asked everyone interested to leave his or her name with me. Thus, the official meeting was over. People began to drift to the place where Linda, Mrs. Mables, and I sat. The confrontation seemed never to have happened. I couldn't believe it had taken place; and yet I was still uncertain that it was really over—even when people appeared friendly. Some of them seemed unhappy at the outcome of the meeting. They had wanted to see something "done to me." On the other hand, some offered congratulations. One person said, "You sure seem all right to most of us —at least you do to me."

With the exception of the four men, the people seemed pleased with me by the time we were ready to leave the Community Club House. I asked some people if they would give me their names, so that I could keep them informed of my progress. I wanted them to feel that I was making sure they would be a part of anything and everything I did in the community. Most gave me their names and phone numbers, with the exception of the four men, who appeared very antagonistic.

As I was leaving, some of the people commented to me, "I hope you didn't think we were too hard on you."

"You can't take chances with nobody these days."

"Good night, Reggie, it was a pleasure talking with you."

Was I glad that this night had come to an end! I had a kind of numb feeling as I left the meeting place. I did not know whether I was still angry or unhappy, or merely at a loss to describe my feelings. I hurried toward Mr. Walker's house. Several people had offered me a lift there, but I'd refused. I wanted to walk back alone.

On my way, a woman from the meeting called to me, "Reggie, I heard you say that you needed an assistant; I'll be your assistant."

I turned to her; but, still annoyed at what had just happened to me, said, "No! Why should you? What makes you think you are any better qualified for the position than any of the other people at the 'trial?' Since all of you decided to put me on trial, bring your court back! Let it decide who my assistant should be."

I realized immediately that I should not have answered her in anger and so I apologized. I told her I would think about it and let her know when I had reached a decision.

As I returned to Mr. Walker's house, I considered whether to tell him about the meeting. If I told him, should I tell him all that had happened? I decided to tell him, for it would let me test his reactions and in this way I could begin looking into the allegations made against him. I walked into the house. As usual, he wanted to discuss my daily activities. I told him about the meeting. He wanted to know who was there. He said that he knew all the "respectable people" in Vera Ridge, and that none of them would ever attend such a meeting. How badly I wanted to see how he would react if I told him what others said of him! However, as usual, I refrained. He asked the names of the people who had been there. I decided not to give him any names, because I wanted to forget about the meeting. But, of course, I could not forget; and the reverberations of that meeting continued to affect me for some time, while the four men began to terrify me.

YOU GOTTA
DEAL WITH IT

A few days after the meeting, I was approached by the same four men who had caused so much trouble during my trial. They demanded, once again, that I take them to Polksville, about ninety miles away. But again I refused. It was good I did, because later I was to learn from them that they were planning to kill me and take the money I supposedly had with me. I was beginning to feel I could not go anywhere without one of them —sometimes all of them—following me. As I started to talk to different community members, they began to open up to me and sometimes warned me against the four men. They told me the men used drugs, and that I had to be careful of them at all times. But these four men continued to hound me every time I stepped outside Mr. Walker's house. They got so bold as to begin stopping at his door. Mr. Walker sensed that something was wrong; he sometimes asked me if I had invited them over. I said I had, to keep him from investigating the situation. He also warned me about them. I finally decided I must confront the situation. But it seemed there was little I could do.

One day, I was on my way to check out the possibility of renting an apartment in a housing project when I saw the four men approaching. They had a big German Shepherd with them on a leash. I wanted to head back toward Mr. Walker's house, but because I did not want them to think I could be intimidated by them, I slowly continued toward the housing project. I made a plan. I decided to cut through the back of the project to reach the office, rather than continuing along the sidewalk. I was hoping they would not follow me back there, because I did not want to be caught where no one could see what they were up to. As I emerged from behind the first set of buildings, there they were. Instead of walking fast, I began to run. Then they unleashed the dog and let it chase me. I sensed I could not get back to Mr. Walker's house in time, so I ran around the building, back onto the sidewalk, and headed for the housing project office. I could see the dog coming, and I could hear them telling the dog to get me. I ran as fast as I could. Just as I got to the steps of the office, the dog caught up with me and grabbed my leg. It sank its teeth deep and if it were not for Jim, the project manager, who came out of his office with a board and chased the dog away, I cannot imagine how badly it might have mauled me. The dog ran off, and Jim told me to go into the office quickly. He said that if he had had his gun, he would have shot the dog.

My pants were torn, and blood was running down my leg. Jim lifted my pants leg to assess the dog bite. He said the bite was deep—it had ripped my muscle—and he advised me to go to a doctor. I told him I had better wait in his office for a while, to make sure the dog had gone. I said the four men had set the dog on me, and that I was afraid that they were still out there waiting for me. He asked if I wanted him to go home with me. He said he'd get his gun, and if anyone tried to bother me, he would take care of them. I thought I would rather wait in his office to see what would happen.

Jim said that he would have an apartment available soon, but I would have to go downtown to put my name on a waiting-list. He indicated I would not have much trouble getting the apartment, but that I could not tell the authorities who I was, because the housing was only for poor people. While I was sitting in his office, talking about the apartment and the men who had been causing me trouble, a young woman came in. Jim knew her "very well." She looked down at my leg and said, "What happened to you?"

"Oh, a dog bit me."

"Well, you better take care of that, 'cause it looks pretty bad from where I stand. Let me take a look at it."

She walked over to me, lifted my pants leg, and said, "Wow! You better go to the doctor. What if that was a crazy dog! You can go crazy and die—'um telling you the truth."

She walked over to where Jim stood, and they began talking about the possibility of her renting an apartment. He said he did not want her that close to him, because she was a married woman. Then he said, "I understand you had some trouble down your way the other night."

"It's that sister of mine. I caught her at it again. She and my old man. Here I'm out working, trying to keep a roof over all of our heads and some food. There she is, laying up in the bed with my old man. I put her ass out."

"What about your old man?," Jim said. "She couldn't do it if he didn't let her."

"I put his ass out, too. But can you dig it? Your own sister . . . after you try to do something to help her out. If you can't trust your own sister you might as well forget about it."

She turned and looked at me and said, "Honey! You better take care of that leg, and soon. Did you say a dog bit you?"

Jim responded, "Some damned fools sicked the dog on him."

The woman said, "I wished somebody sicked a dog on me. I'd kill the dog, then turn 'round and kill whoever sicked the dog on me. If I didn't kill 'em they'd wish they was dead."

I asked them where a doctor was, and Jim said, "There's Doctor Benson, but I don't know about him. I wouldn't go to him, but he's the only black doctor we have now."

"All he will do is give him a shot," the woman said. "He can do that. 'Course you may die from the needle he use."

"Where is he located?"

"Right down the street here. Just make a right at the corner and ask anybody. They'll tell you where he live."

"You mean his office is in his house?"

"Yeh!," the woman said. "He's been there for over twenty years. Come on, I'll take you by there."

"Just a minute, Reggie," Jim said. "You better let me take you. Going with Gladis, you may never get there for one reason or another."

"What are you saying to that young man? Do you think I would do something bad to him?"

"Come on, Reggie; just give me a minute to lock up the office. Let me get my gun out of the back room. If we meet up with that dog again, I'll take care of it."

I stood on the porch with Gladis, and waited for Jim to lock up. I looked down the street to see if I could see the dog or the four men, but they were not in sight. Jim came out of his office, putting his gun in his back pocket. We started down the street, and Gladis went home. When we got to the corner, I saw the men standing at the next corner with the dog. When they saw us, they ducked out of sight behind the housing project. The doctor's house was only three blocks away. Jim pointed out the house, and told me he would see me later. I walked to the front door and knocked. A lady came to the door. I told her that I wanted to see the doctor and she said, "What do you want to see the doctor for? He's not holding office hours now."

"Well, I got bitten by a dog, and I thought maybe he would take a look at it."

"Well, go 'round to the side door and I'll see if the doctor will see you."

I walked around to the side door and waited. It was nearly five minutes before the doctor came to the door. He invited me in and took a look at my wound. He cleaned the wound, and then told me to roll up my sleeve. I saw him take a needle from the table. The needle was not covered, and it looked a bit rusty. But I didn't want to say anything to him about it. He took a piece of cotton and doused it in alcohol, rubbed it against my arm, and injected the needle. It was very painful, but I pretended not to feel it. It was painful because the needle was dull. I thanked him, and asked how much I owed him. I was surprised when he told me there was no charge. I thanked him again, and left.

As I walked out of his office, I looked around; but I didn't see either the men or the dog. I hurried to Mr. Walker's house. It was only four blocks away. Just as I reached the house, I saw the four men with the dog. I quickly looked away from them, and continued toward the door. Every step I took, I could feel that dog chewing on me; but I was not going to run this time. If they released the dog, it would catch me. This time, I was fortunate, for they kept the dog in check. I got to the door of the house and turned around to look but they were gone.

Shortly after this incident, I was able to rent a trailer-house, and for the first time in almost a month I could live by myself. What a relief! Although it was good to be alone, I was afraid that now that I was no longer under Mr. Walker's roof, I would be bothered by the men. And, just as I had feared, my problems with them became worse. They would come over at all hours of the night, and would not go away until they had eaten all the food and drink I had on hand. They would deliberately come by late at night, because they knew most of the people who lived around me were in bed by then. There was no way I could refuse them entry, since they would keep banging on the door, on the walls, or throwing things on the roof, shining their lights into my windows, and calling my name. It was a good thing I never kept cash around the house. They would come in and put their feet on the sofa or the chairs, rummage through whatever caught their fancy, and, after a long stay, usually three or four hours, they would leave.

While all of this was going on, I still continued to do my field-work. Whenever I had interviews, I was able to push all my worries behind me. I am not saying that the quality of my interviews did not suffer, but somehow I was able to carry on my work. Sometimes I would frequent a bar close to my trailer-house. Here I met and talked with some interesting people. I met a man named Harry; and we talked on many occasions about his family, his problems, and how he had straightened up. Eventually, I told him about my troubles with the four men. He said he knew them and did not think much of them. He told me if I paid him a certain amount of money each month, he would see that they did not bother me again. He said that he was a boxer at one time, "a damned good one," and that I could ask John if I didn't believe him. I did ask John, and he did agree that Harry was a good boxer. John added, "He just couldn't stay away from that bottle and them women. Those two things are dangerous when you are training to become a boxer."

One night, I invited Harry to come by my house. I wanted him to stay as late as he could, just in case the four men came over. He was telling me about his problems with his brother. I knew his brother because I had met him in the bar many times. Each time I saw him, he was very drunk, and he was always "hitting on" someone for a drink. On several occasions, he asked me to buy him a drink and I did. One night, when I was sitting in the bar, Harry's brother got into a fight. The man he fought beat him very badly, and I was surprised that he didn't try to defend himself. I told Harry about this incident; and he said, "I know, I've always had to take up for him, but if he don't do better, I'm going to be through with him. I'm the only one left that will have anything to do with him in our family. He don't do nothing for himself. He's always begging other people. You saw him that night, well, that's the way he always is—drunk and fighting."

While Harry and I were sitting there talking, there was a knock on the door. I knew it was those men; and this time I gladly opened the door. I told them to come in. They started to enter, but when they saw Harry they stopped and said, "Oh, man, you have company; we'll come by later."

But Harry said, "Come on in; I may be here for a long time."

"No! That's all right, man, we'll come back another time."

"There's no time like now; come in and have yourself a drink. Reggie don't mind, do you Reggie?," Harry said.

"Oh, no! Help yourself; you know where everthing is."

They reluctantly came in, got themselves a beer, and sat down. None of them said a word. Harry had to do all the talking. After staying only for about five minutes or so, they decided they had to leave. This time, Harry did not stop them. They told me they would see me later, and left. Harry turned to me and said, "See! They know me, and they won't fuck around with me and with you neither, so long as I'm around. All you have to do is say the word."

"Harry, there must be another way. I can't afford to pay you anything. What I mean is, I don't want to have to pay anybody to take care of my problems. What is the difference between paying you or them? No, that's not the way. There must be a better way."

"The difference may be your life. But all right, suit yourself; but if they hurt you, don't blame me. They play rough. They are for real. They play for keeps. Those guys use drugs, and they'll do anything to get them. I'm not just trying to scare you, 'um telling you this for your own good. Have you ever seen anyone who is on dope, and needs it, and don't have the money to pay for it? They'll steal from they own mother if they are hurting bad enough. Do you think for once they care about you? Those guys use the hard stuff; they use the needle."

"Tell me, Harry, why do you want to do this for me?"

"I told you, man, I'm in it for the money—that's all."

"But I thought we were pretty good friends by now."

"What do friendship have to do with business? As far as friends go, we are. But friends is one thing and making some money is another. That's just the way it is."

With that, Harry said he had to get home to his wife and kid. He said good-night; and he stopped coming around to see me. Two days later, I was again visited by the four men. They came into my house and one of them took a knife from his pocket and put it at my throat. Then he told me that if I didn't give them money, he would use the knife. He said, "This is the second time you had a taste of my knife. If there is a next time, you're dead. I will cut your mother-fucking-head off, and you better believe it."

I told them I didn't have any money in the house, that I never kept any money around, and that I only received money once a month from my university. They told me that they would give me another chance, but if I didn't give them the money when it arrived, they would kill me without thinking twice about it. They threatened to burn me out and set fire to my car. Every day they began loitering around my mailbox. I decided to rent a box at the post office. But they told me I would never leave Vera Ridge alive.

I finally took my problems to John. Even though he seemed to disbelieve some of the things I told him, John would listen with what seemed like great interest. Yet, he offered me no advice. I then took this problem to Linda, his sister, the one responsible for the meeting. I discussed each event with Linda as it had happened. When she fully realized the complexity of my situation, all she would say was, "*You gotta deal with it*."

When I asked her what she meant by "*deal*," she said, "Do what is necessary."

I told her that I would call the police if things got any worse, and she said, "No! don't call the pigs. You have to deal with it yourself. Keep the pigs out of it."

My situation began to worsen. One night, when I returned to my house, I found them inside. I knew I had locked the door when I had left earlier that day. They had no lights on, and as I unlocked the door and turned on the lights, I saw them sitting on the sofa. Now I experienced a double fright; I had not expected anyone to be there, and here were these people who had been intimidating me. The stronger of the men grabbed me and put my right hand behind my back in a hammer lock. The one who seemed to be the leader took a knife from his pocket again. He let me hear the blade open; and this time he pressed it tightly against my throat. I was sure I had had it this time. I was really scared and I shook; and they knew I was afraid. The man holding the knife said, "This is the last warning we are going to give you. I mean the last one. If you don't come up with some money, the next time we won't do no talking. If it was up to me, I'd just as soon get it over with right now. Hear me? *Do you dig?*"

I got a knee in the testicles and I slumped to the floor in pain. He said, "That is just a taste of what you will get next time. And just to 'sure you we really mean business, we're going to rearrange your house."

They went through every room, and completely tore things from the places where I had them; and everything ended on the floor. Even my equipment was thrown to the floor. My clothes were taken from the closet, thrown to the floor, and stepped on. They ground the soles of their shoes into the clothing.

I lay on the floor, slumped and doubled over, still in pain. One of the guys rolled me over on my back, and put the knife to my throat again. I tried to say something; but with the knife pressing against my throat, I produced only a guttural sound. The man who was holding the knife on me lifted me up and threw me against the wall. After they had put my house in a shambles, they decided to leave. As they were going, the guy with the knife said, "I hope you know now that we mean business. I should cut your balls off. You just keep holding out, they'll be taking you away from here in a coffin." They walked out and slammed the door behind them.

I wanted to go and tell John. I wanted to go and see Harry; but decided the guys might be outside, listening or waiting for me. I could not sleep that night, nor was I able to write much in my ledger. I kept all my lights on and stayed between the two doors, so that if they came in one, I could leave by the other. I felt if they wanted whatever I had so badly that it would make them continue to threaten me, they could have it—all of it. Sometime during the night, I must have fallen asleep sitting between the two doors. When I woke up, it was morning.

It took me hours to straighten up my house from the previous
night's incident. After I had finished, I decided to visit with
John. I spent the rest of the day at John's house. I kept telling
him what they were doing to me, and how difficult it made my
work. I told him that I had had about as much as I could take
from them; and I wanted to know what could be done about
them. I told him about Harry's offer; but he said, "You can't
have other people solving your problems for you. It's no good.
You'll find yourself in the same predicament, only a different
situation."

"What do you mean by that?"

"Well, it's like this; you're jumping out of the fire into the
frying-pan. In other words, the heat is still there; it's just being
supplied by somebody else. I say you solve your own problems
the best way you know how."

"Well, tell me, John, just tell me, how in the hell do I do
that?"

"You gotta deal with it."

"I know I gotta 'deal with it.' You've said that a hundred
times already. But how in the hell can I 'deal with it?' What do
you mean, deal with it?"

When I proposed calling the police, John, like his sister,
Linda, had said that I shouldn't; that I should keep the police
out of the situation, and that I had to deal with it myself. Now I
turned to John and yelled, "What the hell am I supposed to do?"

"Calm down, Reggie. Just calm down. Don't get upset."

"Calm down! How can you expect me not to be upset?
Wouldn't you be upset? What the hell would you do about it?"

"Well, I'll tell you this: if someone comes to my door and I
don't want him to bother me, and I had already told him so,
then I'll take whatever step is necessary to keep him off of me—
except calling the pigs. I'd know what to do; and you can bet
he wouldn't bother me no more. The thing is, *you gotta deal
with it yourself, nobody else.*"

"That's fine for you to say; you're a member of this community. Your family is well known here in this town. You

know if you have to do something, you have people to back you up. Look, one of the men is your neighbor. Yeh! You can say that you'd know what to do. But you're not in my situation. It's because of your sister that I'm in this hell of a mess in the first place. If she hadn't stirred the people against me and forced me to reveal my financial situation, I wouldn't have these guys on my back."

"Well, dealing with it means knowing what you have to do in each situation and doing it. Then you'd see how things will work out. You're not all that much of a stranger to this community now. You're not that much outside of it. You take care of this business, and you'll see how much of a stranger you are to a lot of people. Everyone knows you, Reggie; they know more about your situation than you think. So just calm down."

I realized that John was trying to tell me something; but I couldn't get the message. Why couldn't he just be straightforward and tell me? Why was he beating around the bush? I was growing more confused; and I decided that maybe if I walked around, I could think this situation out more clearly. I dashed out of John's house and as I headed down his steps, I saw the four men with the dog. I returned to John's house and pointed them out to him. I told John that I was going to buy a gun, and if they bothered me again, I was going to use it. I said I wouldn't shoot to hit anybody—just shoot it, and maybe if they knew I had a gun, they'd leave me alone. John stood there, looking outside, and said that he would know how to handle the situation, if it were he. Then he turned to me and said, "You can get a gun if you want to, but already you have the wrong idea. I don't say hurt anybody, but you got to make them believe you will do it, or they will keep picking on you. I'd know what to do, yes indeed; no one would come in my house or bother me if I didn't want them to."

I reminded him again that in a way he was responsible for my situation, along with his sister, because he was the person who had "set me up," because the men learned about me at that meeting. I asked him why he hadn't attended the meeting, and he responded, "I knew what was going to happen, and I didn't want no part of it. But don't blame your problems on the meeting, and don't blame me and don't blame my sister. You was 'the mark' for those four guys the minute they spotted you as a stranger. All I got to say is prove to them that you are just as much a part of this community as they are."

Then I asked him why he hadn't warned me before, and he answered, "It's good experience for you. You said you wanted to know something about the people of Vera Ridge. I figured the sooner you meet these people, the better you will understand what goes on around here."

"Thanks! Thanks a hell of a lot."

"Reggie, don't be too hard on us; don't be too hard."

This phrase, "Don't be too hard on us, Reggie," I was to hear repeatedly during my stay in Vera Ridge; it later took on an even greater meaning as I began to know what he really meant by it. John had sensed that things were going badly for me, and I was thinking of abandoning my work in Vera Ridge. Almost daily, he would come by where I lived, or I would go to his house. No matter how much I would speak against certain people, John would eventually end up by saying, "Don't be too hard on us, Reggie."

I decided that on my next visit to "the city," I would buy a gun. I had met many people in the city, and knew that I would have no difficulty purchasing a weapon. I knew this guy named Robert. He dealt in everything the streets had to offer. I gave him a call and he asked me what kind of gun I wanted. I told him something that was big and looked frightening. He said he knew where he could get something like that, but it would cost me one hundred dollars. I told him I would have the money waiting for him. He said he'd see me shortly.

About six-thirty that evening, he came to the hotel where I stayed in the city. He called from a phone outside the hotel. It seemed that a black man had used the top of this very hotel some time ago to fire on and kill several people. That is why he didn't want to bring the gun into the hotel. I met him in the parking lot and we went to my car, where I asked him to show the gun to me before I paid him. He suggested we get into my car and drive around. As we drove, he showed me the gun, which had been broken down. He assembled it and demonstrated how it worked. It looked like something I had used in the military. I asked if it was automatic: "only semi." I told him to break it down again, and I would stop the car so we could put it into the trunk. The gun was a carbine, but not the kind used in the military. Once the gun was in the trunk, we drove back to the hotel. I paid him, parked the car in the hotel's parking lot, and returned to my room.

Several days later, when I returned to Vera Ridge, chilling thoughts ran through my mind. What if I was stopped by the police and they found the gun on me? In the South I knew the problems I would face if caught with a gun. So I stopped the car—something I never did along this stretch of road I traveled —and when no cars were passing by I opened the trunk, took the handle part of the gun, and placed it under the front seat. I figured in this way, if I was stopped and the police didn't find a complete gun, I would not be in as much trouble. I hurried as fast as I could. Soon I was on my way again.

Still, I could not shut out the thought of all the probable consequences to me if I was stopped by the police. So I drove carefully and cautiously—always looking in my rearview mirror. Any place I thought a police car might be waiting for a speeding motorist, I would slow down. My fears of being stopped by the police lessened as I thought about the reason I had bought the gun in the first place. I felt that once I had the gun back at my house, my problems with the four guys would be over. I was never so happy as when I pulled into my carport, took the gun from the car, and safely put it in my house.

The fact that I had a gun didn't seem to change my situation with the four men. I had new locks put on my doors, thus making the trailer more secure. The only way they could now get in would be to break down the door or break in a window, which they might do. I had one factor in my favor: my neighbors. They would stop anyone from fooling around with my house when I was not there. So, if someone tried to break in, the neighbors might prevent it—provided they saw or heard him.

One night when it was getting dark, and I was sitting at my table writing in my ledger, I heard a knock at the door. I asked, "Who is it?," but there was no answer. I asked again, and this time I heard someone say, "It's Ralph."

"Ralph! Ralph who?"

"Open up the door, man. You know who I am. I want to talk to you."

"Hey, man! You just better go away. I have had all I'm going to take from you guys."

"Man! I'm trying to help you. It's just me out here. Come on, hurry up and open the door."

"I have a gun in here, and I know how to use it. Now, if you try to get in here, somebody will have to carry you out. I mean what I say."

"Listen man, I'm by myself. Ain't nobody else with me. I want to help you, make it easy on you. Now, if you don't listen to me, you're going to be in a whole lot of trouble. I'm warning you."

"Well, say whatever you have to say out there, 'cause you ain't getting in here."

"Reggie, listen to me man, I can't stand out here. If they knew I was here, I'd get into trouble with them myself."

I took my gun and held it in one hand, then I peeked out of the curtain. I didn't see anyone but Ralph, so I decided to open the door. Before I got the door completely opened, he pushed through and I brought the gun up as if I was going to use it. He yelled, "Hey! Wait a minute, man! Don't point that thing at me. Can't you see 'um by myself? I just come here to tell you how you can get out of this thing. Can I sit down, man?"

"No! Because you won't be staying long."

"Give me something to drink, 'um thirsty."

"I don't keep anything to drink in this house anymore. And even if I did, I wouldn't give any to you. Now, what do you want to say to me?"

"All we're looking for is a little change. If you give us a little change—a few bucks—we'd leave you alone."

"I bet! Sure, all I have to do is give you a little change this time and a little change the next time, and then there will be the next time, and on and on and on. Anyway, I don't have any money to give to you."

"Man! We know you have money. We saw all them papers on the table at the meeting. We know what they mean. You think we are stupid or something? Man, you gotta have some kind of bucks. I tell you, if you give me some money, I'll keep them other guys away from you."

"I know, just as soon as I give you some money, what's to stop the other guys from coming? What's to stop you from coming back, yourself?"

"Hey man! You have to take my word for it—believe me."

"You know what? I could have paid Harry, and he would probably ask for less money than you guys. But I'm not going to give any of you money. I would rather trust Harry than any of you; and he has the force to back up his word. I've seen the way he's handled men before. You guys are punks; and if I was a member of this community, Mr. Walker's funeral home would be jumping with business, believe me."

"Well, if you think Harry's so bad, why don't you pay him to take care of us—you'll see who's the punk. I don't appreciate you calling me a punk anyway. Now I came over 'cause I felt sorry for you and I wanted to help you, but I don't have to take no shit off of you. You just may be digging your own grave with them kind of words."

"Let's assume that I was going to consider your offer—and I don't say that I do—but just let's assume. Why should I believe you any more than any of the rest of them. Anyone who uses tactics as you have is hardly a person one should believe."

"Um tellin' you, man—just take my word."

"If that's the case, why did you have to sneak here, and why were you so afraid the others would see you?"

"I have my reasons, man, believe me. You best listen to what

I told you. These other guys, they mean real business. They'll take care of you, man—that's for sure."

"What's all that 'believe me'; it seems to me that you are trying to convince yourself more than you are trying to convince me. Are you hurting for something, man?"

"We're all hurting for something, ain't we? But if you mean do I need some dope, I wouldn't be so quick to say that if I was you."

I told him again I didn't have any money in the house, that I never kept money on me. I told him I would get twenty-five dollars and give it to him tomorrow. Even as I was saying this, I was not sure in my mind that it was the right thing to do, and if I would really do it. He agreed, and told me that my problems were over, but that I shouldn't mention this to anyone. Then he left. I had mixed feelings about what I had agreed to—that I had given in. On the one hand, I was opening myself up to everything they could throw at me. Yet, on the other hand, I thought, maybe I had solved my problems. It sounded so good to me to hear him say, "Your problems are over." I convinced myself that this was true; and that was the night—the first night— I had a good sleep since I had moved into the trailer-house, because for the first time I felt safe. I finished writing in my ledger and made a bite to eat; and this time I even cleaned the dishes and swept the place. After a long, hot shower, I went to bed. I slept well, very well.

The next morning, I called John over for coffee. I told him what I had agreed to do and he said it would turn out to be the same kind of mistake as I was going to make with Harry. He said, "Now you've done it. You'll never get them guys off your back. I could have told you better than that."

"But you didn't. I asked you, didn't I?"

"Well, do it your way; but if it was me I wouldn't give them nothing."

"What do you think I ought to do?"

"It's up to you, man. 'Um telling you what I would do. I wouldn't give them a damned cent—never."

He hurried his cup of coffee, and said that he had to leave. As he was going, he looked at me and shook his head. I decided that I would take his advice and wouldn't give Ralph the money I had promised. I went about my daily activities. I met Harry on my way back to my trailer later that evening; he said he wanted to stop by. I told him that I had some work to do, and that I would not be at my house very long. He said that he had something very important to tell me, so I invited him to come along. On the way he said, "I hear you're going to give someone some money."

"You did? Who told you that? Where did you hear that?"

"Never mind who told me or where I got it from; I tell you, there's not much that goes on around here that I don't know about. Now I made you a proposition and you turned me down, but you think you can trust Ralph. 'Um telling you, you're making a serious mistake. You're getting into trouble ain't nobody going to be able to help you out of. You should have listened to me in the first place."

The only person I could think of who could have told Harry was John. I wondered why John would tell Harry. I know Ralph didn't tell him. Maybe one or the other of the guys found out and told him. Anyway, I asked him, "Did Ralph tell you that I was going to give him some money?"

"I told you I ain't going to tell you who. Just believe me, I know."

"Well, this has just made up my mind. I'm not going to give anybody nothing, and if I have to use this gun I have, I'll use it. Now I don't want to talk about it anymore to anybody."

"All right, man, if that's the way you feel about it. I said all I got to say about it. The case is closed as far as I'm concerned— it's over, finished, the end."

"Well, you don't have to get mad about it."

" 'Um not mad, man. Just forget it. How's your work coming along?"

"It's going along all right, considering the shit I've had to go through. As a matter of fact, I have an interview in a few minutes. I'm going to talk with John's mother."

"You never let me finish talking about *myself*. I got lots of interesting things I could tell you about myself and my family. Now take myself, I've been in trouble before. I used to do all kinds of things. I was a pimp, a dope user, and I've been in the joint many times, but I'm straight now."

"Why are you telling me all of this?"

" 'Cause I thought you wanted to hear it. Also, I want you to know what kind of a person I really am. People here respect me now. They used to not like me because of what I was. You see, all my troubles happened a long time ago. Most of the trouble I got into didn't happen here. Here I have my wife and a little baby boy, and I work every day. I do my thing on the weekend, but I'm respected."

"Harry, what you have to say sounds very interesting, but I told you I have to go and interview John's mother. Maybe I can talk with you later."

"You better listen to me now, while I feel like talking. You may not find me in this kind of a mood again."

"Well, let me call John's mother and tell her I will be late."

I got on the phone and called Ola May. She was happy that the interview would be later because she had "things to do." I told Harry I would like to put what he had to say to me on tape, but he said that he did not want to be taped, so I had to take notes on everything. He asked for something to drink. I told him I did not keep any more alcohol in the house. So, we went out and got a six-pack. As soon as we returned, he began to discuss his brother. He said, "My brother, he can't even take up for himself. You saw how that dude was just beating the shit out of him. Now the only reason why I jumped on the dude was because my brother was drunk and he couldn't help himself. The dude knew that."

Most of the time, Harry talked about his brother. He said little about his other relatives—not even his wife and his baby boy. It was as if he wanted me to talk to his brother for him. Sometimes he would pause and lower his head. I asked him if he loved his brother, and at first he said, "No!" Then, almost immediately, he responded, "Every time I'm ready to give up on him, he comes by the house and throws me a few bucks and says, 'Here, here's something for you, the wife and the baby.' Now it ain't the money, that ain't enough to buy the baby's milk. It's the idea of him trying to do something for someone else, trying to be thankful of what I do for him. Then I change my mind and say, I'll give him another chance. But I'm getting tired of his shit. Man, I don't know how much longer I can take it. None of the other folks will have anything to do with him. I'm the only family he's got."

After listening to him talk about his brother for an hour, I reminded Harry that I had an interview with John's mother.

I liked talking with John's mother. I could sit and listen to her for hours. She has filled many of my days with the history of her family. She told me often that she could write several books on her family. Between her and Mr. Smith, the man who owns the dry-cleaning shop, there is not one rock unturned in Vera Ridge. It was late in the evening when I finished my interview with Ola May. I had just enough time to eat dinner before my next interview.

When I didn't prepare food at home, I always ate at one of the many cafe-restaurants in Vera Ridge. In this way, I got a chance to meet and talk with a number of different people in the community. After eating, I hurried over to section A for the interview. It was late before I finished it. I really didn't want to go home, because I didn't want to face Ralph. But I had to get it over with.

As soon as I walked in my trailer-house there was a knock at the door. It was as if he had been waiting in hiding for me. I paused, then asked, "Who's there?" He said, "Ralph." I let him in, and immediately informed him of my decision. Then I told him to leave. As he was leaving, he said that I would be sorry. I took my gun, placed it by the table, then told him if he bothered me again, *he* would be the sorry one. I said I had talked with

John and Harry, and they were aware of what was happening; therefore, if I shot any one, John and Harry would back me up. He said, "We'll see," as he slammed the door behind him.

I waited between my doors with the gun. One, then two, and then three hours passed; and nothing happened. I started writing in my journal. After I had finished, I decided it was safe for me to go to bed. I had been in bed almost an hour when there was a knock on my door. I sprang up and grabbed my gun before answering the door. This time, it was all of them; but they said they only wanted to talk to me. I finally decided to let them in because I didn't want them to break down the door; I had my gun ready. They looked at it, and then at me. They didn't say anything—they just looked. Finally, one of them said, "Gee! What a nice piece you have. Can I use it sometimes? I like to go hunting."

Then he added, "By the way, you have until tomorrow to pay up."

Without saying another word, they left. Just like that they were gone. I didn't have to use the gun. I don't know if I would have used the gun if it had become necessary. In a way, I wished something had happened. I wanted to end this once and for all—either for them or me. I felt that I could sleep the rest of the night since they would at least wait until tomorrow before bothering me again. I wondered why I had been given so many warnings. Did they really mean to harm me or were they simply trying to frighten me into giving them money? No matter what, I was not going to let them drive me away from Vera Ridge until I had finished my research—no way. I was set on staying, no matter what the cost. But, what was going to happen next? I didn't want to think about it.

GOING TO
THE LAND
OF COTTON

DURING all this time, I had been scared stiff. In the back of my mind, I felt that maybe I had won a small victory over them, but that they were not going to give up so easily. I now had had three months of harassment, and I was beginning to get desperate. In spite of the trouble they were causing me, I still managed to do a fair amount of research. I had interviewed many people, and they had little good to say about the four men. For the most part, they told me to watch out and be careful, but only a few of them offered any suggestions as to how I could end my trouble. Mr. Smith told me to call the police or "shoot them." He was angry, and said if I didn't do anything about it, he would. I pleaded with him to let me handle the situation. He threw up his hands, and agreed to stay out of it.

I had made many tapes and written much information about individuals and their families. I had also taken lots of pictures and movies of the residential areas and the outskirts of Vera Ridge. I attended football games and community basketball games; sometimes I participated in them. I had built up good relations with some of the people in Vera Ridge. I took some of the children to movies, games, and different recreational areas.

John and several other members of the community trusted me with their children. I even took the nephew of one of the four men who were harassing me. Like John's son, he called me "Uncle Reggie." He was one of the few members of the four men's families whom I could approach without too much of a problem.

Before I decided which families I would concentrate on in my study, I wanted to make one more trip outside of Vera Ridge. All I had to do was to tell John I was leaving, along with the neighbors who lived behind and to the side of me; and, you bet, no one could even go into my yard without their knowing and chasing them away. Mrs. Andrews, who lived in front of me, would be on the watch with her children. None of the neighbors concerned themselves about my home so long as I was there, but when I was gone they made it a point to be very watchful.

I got up early the next morning, packed some equipment, and headed for John's house. I always left my keys with him, and let him know when and how long I expected to be away. I had interviewed Peggy's family, at least all of its known members living in Vera Ridge, so I thought I would use this trip to go looking for some of the members who lived elsewhere. I felt that if I was absent for a few days, maybe the four men would stop bothering me. Although I had been away before—and it seemed as if they knew when I was leaving as well as when I was going to return—perhaps a longer time away would have different results. I had wanted to put an end to this irksome conflict with them once and for all by going to Mr. Walker. However, I knew that would only make the problem worse, so I headed straight for the land of cotton.

I didn't know which was worse, staying in Vera Ridge and facing those men, or driving on the back roads in the deep South with my heart always pumping in my throat, never knowing what would happen next. I just could not shake off this feeling of being in the South. My previous experiences continued to return to my mind. I thought of these back roads as "white man's land."

The first stop I planned to make was in the town of Ludlo. It would also be my longest stretch between stopping points. Vera Ridge was considered a nice-size town, with its thirty thousand or so people; between Vera Ridge and Ludlo all you had was Hickville, USA. I always got lost, no matter how well I planned a trip. Sure enough, on the way to Ludlo, I got lost. No matter how badly lost I was, I would never stop to ask a white person for directions, for fear of what might be said or done to me. I remembered the experiences I had had in the South before; I knew the problems I could encounter with white people if they decided they didn't like me. Therefore, I was determined not to take anything from any of them; and I knew that my reactions could endanger my life.

A young black male, standing beside the road as if he needed a ride, indicated for me to stop; so I did. He asked me if I was going to Red Clay. I told him I didn't know where Red Clay was located, and that I was trying to find the right road to Ludlo. He told me that Red Clay was in the same direction as Ludlo, and that if I gave him a ride, he would show me the way.

He had been riding with me for no more than five minutes when he said he wanted to get out, because we were in Red Clay. He pointed out a gas station where I could ask for the directions to Ludlo. The station was white-owned, but there were several black people working there. Across from the gas station was a structure where some black men were "hanging-out," and another that looked like a house, with some people sitting on the porch. The rest was field after field of cotton. I decided to have my gas tank filled, since the place seemed less hostile than others I had passed. I got out of the car and walked over to where the black men stood. There was a tall, heavyset black man who seemed to be the center of attraction. I heard him say, "That's the trouble with you niggers, you don't stick together; all you do is talk, and the minute you see white folks, you close your lips so tight a crowbar couldn't open them."

A man standing next to him said, "Willie, one of these days that mouth of yours is going to get you into a whole lot of trouble."

Willie said, "I was trouble when I was born. My mama told me I liked to kill her in birth, and I'll be trouble 'til I die. So what?"

The man responded, "Well, it ain't gonna take long fur that to happen if you keep on acting the way you do."

I walked over to where Willie was standing, and said, "Mr. Willie, can you tell me how to get to Ludlo?"

"Who is you, and how did you know who I was?"

"My name is Reggie, and I heard that man over there call you 'Willie'."

"Well, how come you be here?"

"I'm on my way to Ludlo, but I'm not sure I'm on the right road."

"Well, if you buy me a drink, I'll tell you how to get to Ludlo or anywhere else 'round these parts you want to go."

So I said I would buy him a drink; and we walked inside the structure that looked like a makeshift bar. Willie asked for two beers. I told him I was driving and did not really want a drink. He said that both of the beers were for him anyway. He drank one beer, then turned to me and said, "Now where is it that you said you wanted to go?"

"To Ludlo."

"Well, I tell you what you oughta do. It ain't too difficult. You just git right back on that there road, the one you came off of, and it will lead you straight into Ludlo. Go in the same direction as you was going. Now tell me, what are you really doing here?"

"I'm down here doing some research on the black families in Vera Ridge; and once in a while I track some of the people's kinfolks wherever they are located, no matter how far it is from Vera Ridge. But no matter where I have to go, if I see some black people, I always like to stop and talk with them."

"You better be careful down here who you talk to. These white folks don't like no niggers from up North coming down here talking to us Southern niggers about nothin'. They don't want you to put no smarts in us. You see, in that way, we'll always be they dumb niggers. They may think you're up to somethin' like that, and 'fore you know it they done gone and got you, and it ain't gonna do nobody no good to come down here lookin' fur you. You be done gone man—dead gone."

"Tell me, then, how come you can talk the way you do down here and get away with it?"

"That's 'cause I'm not afraid of them whitefolks. I ain't never been 'fraid of nobody . . . anyway, I'm from this here area, and all the white folks 'round here knows me and knows my folks. See, that there house over yonder way, well, I was born in that there house; now just look 'round you, tell me what you see."

"Mostly cotton fields."

"That's exactly what you see; but if you look closer you'll see a old broken-down shack somewhere in the middle of them cotton fields. You see, out here, ain't no nigger got no land, and they don't live close to each other. They all scattered miles apart; that way they can't get together and start no trouble for the white man. The only reason why so many of us is here is because we came to go to work—pickin' cotton; but it is too wet, the fields are covered with water, so when you can't work you might as well stand 'round drinking to pass away the time."

"Is this the only place where blacks can go for fun?"

"The only place 'round here; but if I was in your shoes, I wouldn't be asking so many questions. Tell me, where did you say you come from?"

"I was born in Florida, grew up in California, and go to school in New Jersey."

"Boy, you've been 'round. Tell me somethin', how's California? Is it really as good as people say it is—for black folks, I mean? I heard so much about California when I was in the Army."

"Mr. Willie, I'll tell you like this; it's good and it's bad. There are some blacks who are doing fine; and there are some blacks who are poorer than some blacks down here."

"No! No way. Nobody can be poorer than us blacks down here. You're puttin' me on."

"No! Not really. What it all boils down to is that you have those that have and you have those that have not; and they are in California as well as here."

"Say, are you comin' back this way soon? If you do, I will take a ride up to Ludlo with you."

"Mister," the man who told Willie he would get into trouble some day said, "you better stick to your plans and travel by yourself. You'd be a fool to take Willie 'long with you. He's bad company; and sooner than not, he'd get you into a heap of trouble."

"Whatchu talkin' 'bout, old Uncle Tom! You just stay outta this if you know what's good for you. If the man wants me to come 'long, let him say so, don't you go puttin' ideas into his head."

I gave it a few seconds' thought, then decided perhaps Willie would get both of us into trouble with his mouth; so I told him, "I'd like to have you come along, but I won't be back this way for a couple of weeks or so, at the earliest."

"Well, then, I guess there ain't no useta me goin' then."

I thanked Willie for giving me directions, and paid for my gas, got into my car, and jotted down as much of the conversation I had had, so that it would be easier to remember that night when I wrote up my daily activities. I headed up the road to Ludlo. About forty miles from Ludlo, I spotted another black male seeking a ride. I pulled over, and offered him a ride. I asked him where he wanted to go, and he said, "I'm going home to help out Mama and Granddaddy. My daddy died, so they need me back home to help out.

"Where are you coming from?"

"I was living with Grandmama, and going to school there. I sure hate that I have to come back, 'cause they ain't got no school near where I live. I was beginning to like school too."

"You mean you don't want to help your mama and grand-daddy?"

"No, man, I didn't say that. I love my mama, it's just that I was going to school so I could be somebody, but coming back here, all I can do is work in the fields, picking cotton."

He didn't talk much then, except to answer my questions. He sat back in the seat, with his hands folded. He looked sad and unhappy. I wanted to think of something I might say to cheer him up; but what could I say? So we drove in silence. About ten miles up the road, he said, "Where are you coming from? I mean, I couldn't tell from looking at your license plates where you are from."

I told him that the license plates were German, because I had bought the car overseas, and had not changed the plates where I lived in New Jersey. He asked me to remind him to take a good look at them when I let him out. We drove past endless stretches of cotton fields and an occasional shack where a black family lived, in the middle or at the edge of a cotton field. I saw a small church sitting at the edge of a cotton field. I told him I wanted to stop and take some pictures. He said he went to that church, and that his daddy was buried here. While I was taking pictures of the church, he walked back to the graveyard. When I came to the graveyard and started taking pictures, he asked me if I would take a picture of his daddy's grave. So I returned to the car, got my Polaroid, took a couple of pictures, and gave them to him. He was very grateful. It was a small graveyard, just to the side of the church, in a small clearing in the cotton field. The graves were covered with plastic flowers. He told me he lived only a mile or so up the road. Then he said, "I want to thank you for these pictures, but I don't know your name."

"It's Reggie; what's your name?

"Jimmy, Jimmy Robinson. Thanks a lot, Reggie. Do you have time to stop at my house for a little while?"

"Sure, I've been driving a long time; and the rest will do me good."

He directed me to turn off the main road about a half mile out of town, and down a dirt road between two cotton fields. After a mile or so, he pointed to a place to park. The road was too sandy to drive further. We walked about an eighth of a mile to where he lived. He told me that I didn't have to worry about leaving my car, because the road was traveled only by people who lived in his house. We walked up the road until we came to where he lived. His house looked as if it would tumble down or topple over if you pushed against it. Boards were nailed in all directions; and there were cracks between the boards. The roof was constructed of galvanized iron, some of it old and rusty, and some of it new. An old man was sitting on the front porch as we walked up. Jimmy yelled, "Granddaddy!"

"Is that you, Jimmy Lee?," the old man asked.

"Yeh, Granddaddy, it's me."

"I was gettin' worried 'bout you, Jimmy Lee; your mama said you'd be here yesterday. What happened to you?"

"I didn't have no money, Granddaddy, to come on the bus. I had to hitchhike all the way here."

"Jimmy Lee, I done told you 'bout travelin' on these here roads all by yourself. Some white folks come 'long and ain't no tellin' what they'd do to you."

"Oh, Granddaddy, I know how to take care of myself. It wasn't too bad. I got a ride half way and Reggie brought me the rest of the way. Granddaddy, this here is Reggie."

I extended my hand and said, "How do you do, sir?"

It was only when he thrust his hand away from where mine was that I realized he was blind. As we shook hands, he said, "I want to thank you for bringin' my boy home. Jimmy Lee, you must be hungry; there's some food in there on the stove. Fix some for you and Reggie."

I really did not want to take the food; but I had learned that an offer of food was a way of welcoming a stranger. Jimmy invited me to come in. He began to apologize for the condition of his house, but he relaxed when I told him that my family grew up in a house much smaller and worse off than his. Inside the house, the rooms were divided with cardboard. There were containers on the floor to catch the rain that leaked through holes in the roof. The house was heated by a wood stove, which also served to cook the food. Once inside, I told Jimmy not to fix me too much food, because I had a long way to go, and if I ate too much, I would become sleepy. He fixed both of us a sandwich; and we went back and sat on the porch with his Granddaddy. His Granddaddy said to me, "Reggie, where's your folks?"

"Some of them in California and some in Michigan, while others live in Washington and Florida."

"California! I heard so many things about California. Tell me somethin', do they really treat colored people like they treat white people there?"

"Well, Mr. . . . ah . . . I don't remember your name."

"That's because I didn't give it to you. Just call me Robinson."

"Mr. Robinson, to tell you the truth, I don't think there is anywhere in the world that black people are treated the same way as white people. I don't care what people tell you. And, it will be a long time before that happens, if it ever does. California is different from here. Blacks have some opportunities. California doesn't have all the problems between the races that you may have here, but it has other problems. All in all, I guess it's safe to say that California is better in some respects for black people than here."

"Reggie, that sound like a sensible thing to say; 'least you didn't try to make it seem like black people's heaven. I'd sure like to visit California; but I guess I'll never see it. I'm too old now."

We talked about my folks, and where I was going, and what I was doing in Ludlo. I stayed with them for a couple of hours. These people were really kind and friendly. I wished that all the people I had met were like them. Just thinking about those four men in Vera Ridge made me angry at the way they acted toward me. I told Jimmy and his Granddaddy that I had better be on my way, because I wanted to reach Ludlo before dark. The Granddaddy said, "I don't blame you for wanting to be in Ludlo before dark; that place done more against our people than any other place in the state. You be careful, you hear, and I hope you do well in your work. Do you know somebody there?"

"Yes, I met them in Vera Ridge, and I'm going to visit with them. So, if I can't find a place to sleep tonight, I can always sleep with them."

I said good-day to them, and walked back to my car. Then I backed up until I found a good place to turn around. I returned to the main road and sped on my way to Ludlo. The sun was just beginning to go down when I arrived. I had no idea where the family I was going to visit lived. I decided to call them for directions, instead of trying to find the place by myself, or asking someone else. Luckily for me, I was only six blocks from their house. When I drove up in front of their house, Mr. and Mrs. Grey were waiting for me on their doorsteps. I locked the car, took my shoulderbag that contained all my equipment, and followed them into the house.

Mrs. Grey offered me something to drink; and Mr. Grey and I immediately started talking about his family. We had already talked to each other when they were in Vera Ridge, visiting other family members. Mr. Grey started by saying, "A white man by the name of Doctor Grey bought my grandfather . . . my grandfather was sold to him . . . for three dollars."

Mrs. Grey said, "You mean three hundred dollars."

Mr. Grey said, "No! Three dollars. . . ."

Mrs. Grey added, "Now you know nobody don't buy nobody for no three dollars; it musta been three hundred dollars."

"All right," Mr. Grey said, "three hundred dollars. My Granddaddy was a carriage driver for Dr. Grey. Now, this was in Texas. Later, he left Dr. Grey and moved to Oklahoma; and that's where he died. And that's all I know about him."

I asked him how many children his Granddaddy had; and he said, "Only one, that's my daddy—J. L. Grey."

"How many children did J. L. Grey have?"

"Oh, I don't remember—fifteen or sixteen of them."

"Do you remember their names?"

"Yes, the oldest boy was named Bobby; the next child was named Sally; the next child was named Willie. . . ."

And he continued until he had named all of them. They were sixteen. He told me that some had died in infancy. I asked if he had any children of his own and he said, "No," but his wife interrupted. "Yeh! He has a daughter; her name is Gracey Lee. You see, he's been married twice, and he had a daughter by his first wife."

After he had given me his genealogy as far as he knew it, we started talking about the connections of some of his kin and their relation to Indians. I thought he had said his mama was part Indian, but I wasn't sure. So I asked him again and he said, "Full-Indian, no part nothing. My Grandmama was full-Indian; my Granddaddy was full-African."

I asked him if he knew whom his father married; but he said, "I know, but I can't tell you."

When I asked him why he couldn't, he said, "I can't tell you that, either—you understand?"

"No, I don't understand. Why?"

"I can't tell you that."

"I think I know why you can't tell me. If I tell you, you tell me if I'm right. You see, you told me when you were in Vera Ridge."

"Oh! No! I didn't!"

"Well, didn't you tell me that he married the wife of Dr. Grey?"

"No! I didn't tell you that. He didn't marry his wife; he married the doctor's youngest daughter. Now I told you I couldn't tell you that. You see why?"

I finally understood. His Granddaddy had married a full-blooded Indian; and his father ran off with white Doctor Grey's daughter. I asked him about his father, and he said, "My daddy was a hustler; he did everything. He was a hunter too—a good one at that."

"Do you remember your daddy?"

"Remember him! I was crazy about my daddy. My daddy ran bloodhounds. He used to train them. He trained the bloodhounds to catch the slaves when they ran away. Daddy would be over a hundred years old if he was still alive."

We talked about five hours before he decided that he was tired and had to go to bed. They prepared a place for me to sleep in their extra bedroom. After I had said goodnight and retired to my room I became hungry, but I didn't want to ask them for food, so I started to write up my daily activity in my ledger. I remembered Willie in Red Clay, and how he would be called a troublemaker if he was in Vera Ridge. I wondered if he could have survived, had he lived in Vera Ridge. It is so frustrating to see blacks who are still afraid of the wrath of the white man that it is refreshing to meet people like Willie. I thought of Jimmy Lee, having to return to the cotton fields, just when he was beginning to enjoy a new kind of life for himself. There was no future for him there. I had told him that I would stop by on my way back to Vera Ridge to see him. Maybe I could work something out so that he could continue his schooling. After writing for a couple of hours, I became very sleepy. After I had gotten into bed, it was not long before I had fallen asleep.

The next morning, I was treated to a typical Southern breakfast: eggs, grits, bacon, and hot biscuits. After breakfast, Mr. Grey took me around the community and introduced me to friends and other relatives. I had only planned to spend one day in Ludlo before continuing on through the land of cotton; but so much interested me about this family that I stayed in Ludlo for three days. The people were friendly and cooperative. They were as different from the people in Vera Ridge as night and day. I thought to myself: these people here knew me less than the ones in Vera Ridge did, yet they did not make things difficult for me. Maybe, I thought to myself, if I were to stay in this town for a year, things might be different. At any rate, it was such a relief to find people so warm and friendly that it was difficult to think of myself as being a stranger. The day I left

Ludlo, the people I had met came by Mr. Grey's house to wish me well, and to offer me their hospitality should I return.

Since I had new information on Mr. Grey's family, my next stop would be where some of the people he mentioned lived. That meant that I was on my way to Lina, a few hours from Ludlo. I got there in the early evening, but had trouble locating the family members. Fortunately, there was a black section of the town, so I didn't feel uncomfortable about asking for directions. I stopped at what looked like a cafe-bar. It was a very small place that could only house about twenty people at any one time. So most of the people were outside. I asked a man if he knew where the Greys lived and he said, "Which Greys? There are two or three families of Greys here."

I gave him their first name, and he didn't seem to know them. However, he said that he would ask a man named Richard, and that if anyone knew them, Richard would because he knew everyone in Lina. He took me inside the bar. He told me that people were not allowed to drink inside, because they could not have whiskey in the place. I had noticed men standing about, passing pints of whiskey around. We made our way through the crowd of people until he saw the person he called Richard. He said, "Hey Richard! Here's a man asking about a Wilbert Grey. Do you know any Wilbert Grey?"

"Who is this person who want to know about Wilbert?"

"Me. I would like to know where he lives."

"Who are you, and what do you want to know that for?"

"Well, I'm studying the Grey family in Vera Ridge; and I was trying to locate all the members of the family, so that I could talk with them. I just came from Ludlo; and I was told that members of the Grey family by the name of Wilbert Grey lived here."

"What do you mean, *studying* them?"

"I'm talking with many families, to compare their lifestyles."

"Whatever that means, Wilbert lives here. I've known Wilbert all my life. He lives over near the Reddicks. You can ask anybody over there; and they'll tell you where Wilbert live."

A man named Larry walked over to us and said, "I'll take him over there. I'm just about to go home myself, and it's right on the way, soon as I go to the toilet."

I told Larry that I needed to go to the toilet myself, and asked if he would show me where it was. We walked out of the building and down a dirt path that still had puddles in it from the rain two days ago. It was an outdoor toilet and you could smell it before you reached it. I was accustomed to outdoor toilets by now, so it didn't bother me. However, when we got there, it was being used. Larry went in and I stayed outside, holding my nose. He came out and said, "If you want to do something, you better go on in. Old Charley's in there and no telling what time he'll be through."

Charley yelled from inside the toilet, "Come on in boy, ain't no use in being bashful."

I walked in. The smell was bad enough and the flies were worse—but Old Charley, squatting on top of one of the holes —that was just too much for me to take, so I walked out. Larry asked if I was ready to go and I said, "Yes." I followed him about a half mile down a dirt road that wound through some cotton fields, across a railroad track, down a clay road, and then we stopped in front of a house. Larry got out of his truck, came over to my car, and said, "Here's where Wilbert live; but it don't look like anybody's home."

We walked up to the door and knocked. There was no answer. We knocked and waited, still there was no answer. An old lady next door came out of her house on to her porch, and said, "They ain't there. No tellin' when they'll be back."

We thanked her; Larry said I could wait at his house if I wanted to, and mentioned that his wife was related to Wilbert. I didn't have anywhere else to go, so I thought this would be a good idea. I followed him down the road until we got to his house. There were some children playing in the yard and he told them to "get in the house before I take a stick to you."

The smallest child was about four or five. He came to where we were and said, "Daddy, Billy hit me with a stick."

Larry replied, "He did? Well, did you hit him back?"

"Noop, I didn't."

"Why didn't you?"

Larry picked him up, held him in his arms, and said, "Why didn't you hit him back?"

" 'Cause he's too big."

"Well, you're my big man, ain't you?"

"Yep! But if I hit him back he'll hit me back, and he hit harder than me."

"Billy!," Larry yelled, "I don't want to hear telling you hitting on your baby brother no more—you hear me?"

"But Daddy, he hit me."

"I don't care what he did—did you hear what I said?"

"Yessum."

Then Larry put the child down, and invited me into his house. Once inside the house, he introduced me to his wife. She had finished high school and had started college, but had to drop out when she began having children. She said she had always been interested in sociology, and asked me if that's what I was doing. I explained my work to her, and both she and Larry wanted me to demonstrate how I went about doing my research. I told them I would if they would be truthful about the information they gave to me; they agreed.

I began with his wife, Clara. I asked her to talk to me about her family. I was especially interested in them when Larry said that she was related to Wilbert. The first person she talked about was her Granddaddy. She said, "My Granddaddy was named John Grey."

"Oh, are you related to the Greys I came to see?"

"Yes, we are cousins somewhere down the line. My Granddaddy was a slave. He was sold as a slave. I remember him a little bit, 'cause I remember he ran a blacksmith shop."

"If your Granddaddy was a slave, how can you remember back that far? You aren't that old, are you?"

"No, I ain't that old, but 'um old enough. You see, the man I call Granddaddy was really my great-granddaddy. But we all called him Granddaddy. He was so old that the hair 'round his eyes almost covered his eyes from seeing. He musta been way over a hundred. I would have to ask my cousin; she keeps the record of all of us. She could tell you better than me. My Granddaddy he had, let me see, it was, it was five boys and three girls. My uncle, one of his sons, went to college. Now all of his children are dead. I can name 'um all. There was Van Grey, William Grey—that's my father—Floyd Grey, Webster Grey, L. T. Grey, and ah, Lula, Georgia, and Mary Grey. All of them are dead, but they have children."

She went on to name all of the children who were still alive and those who had died. She mentioned where they lived, and how often she saw them. I was hoping she would give me the names of some Greys who would tie into the Greys I had met already. Perhaps after I talked to Wilbert, things would become clearer. I asked her to talk about her mother, and she said, "I can't tell you too much about my mama. You see, my mama was raised by her auntie. Her name was Molley. You see, my mama's mama died when she was very young. There was three of them: my mama, my mama's sister, and my mama's brother. Well, my mama's daddy left when she was young, and her brother did too. She never heard of her daddy after he left, so she was raised by her auntie. You see, she was a King—I mean, her last name was King before she married a Grey; but I didn't know nothing about her side of the family, the Kings."

I was amazed at the way she could remember how many children each person had, their names, where they lived, if they had moved away, when they moved, who had married whom, who had left whom, and so on and so forth. She said that her mother's auntie had some children, and that one of them was named Fred Grey. I had talked with a Fred Grey in Ludlo, and wondered if they could be related. Clara told me that most of her people had grown up in the same state she had, and some of them had moved to Ludlo, where Fred Grey lived. She was not sure, however, whether Fred Grey was living or dead. I continued to listen to her, to see if there would be any further cor-

responding information with what Fred had told me. She said
that Fred was the son of a Sam Grey, but the Fred I knew had
told me that his father's name was J. L. Grey. She said, "Fred
was cousin Sam's daddy. I can't get this right, but I think that's
the way it goes. No, cousin Sam's daddy was named Charley,
wasn't it, Larry? Or, he had a brother named Charley. I don't
know, I can't get it right, but I know they're related somehow."

She could remember that there was a John L. Grey in the
family. It was difficult for me to connect these members of the
Grey family with those in Ludlo and Vera Ridge; but I knew
that if they were connected, I would find out before my study
was over. After two hours of talking, Clara said that she had to
fix supper and Larry asked me if I wanted to eat with them. I
quickly accepted the invitation and had one of the best soul-food
meals I had eaten since returning to the South.

After supper we went by Wilbert's house again, but he was
not there. The lady next door again came out, and said she
thought they had gone up to Oakley and that she didn't know
when they were going to return. Larry asked if I needed a place
to stay and I told him I would try to find a motel. He said there
was one in Lina but it would be better if I went into Stanford, or
I could spend the night at his house. Since Clara had told me
about a C. Q. Grey, who lived up the highway, I thought I would
go by and talk with him the next day. So, I spent the night at
Larry's house. I asked Larry if he didn't mind taking me back to
the bar where we had met; he said that he would.

First we went by the state store to buy some whiskey, because
they do not sell whiskey in the bar—the state does not allow it.
I thought I would buy a fifth instead of a pint, like most of the
people. Larry told me not to buy a fifth. He said you could not
hide a bottle that size under your coat, and if they caught you
with it, you could go to jail. He also said, "You don't want just
anybody drinking out of your bottle; and the more you have,
the more people gonna come up and ask you."

So I bought a pint of whiskey and gave it to him. After we
got back into the car, he opened it and took a swallow. Then he

passed it over to me. Well, since I don't drink, especially not straight liquor, I merely put the bottle to my lips and pretended to take a big swallow. But the little I gulped burned so badly I could hardly stand it, though I tried not to make too much of a face.

There were about twenty-five people in and around the bar. Larry introduced me to one of his friends, Seaborn. Seaborn was about my age. I asked him why there were no women present, and he said they were not allowed. I asked if that was a state law and he said he didn't know. Then he turned to me and said, "But don't worry, let's just hang around here for a little while."

I wasn't sure what he meant by that. Rather than ask, I thought I would just wait and see what happened. Every once in awhile, Larry would come by to see how things were going with me. It didn't seem to him that I was having a good time, but I told him I was really enjoying myself. I told him I liked talking to and meeting new people. I don't think he believed me, because I saw him walk over to Seaborn and pull him aside. They talked about five minutes, and then Seaborn came over to me and motioned for me to come outside. Once outside, he offered me a drink from his bottle. I faked drinking from it, and passed it back to him. Then he said, "Let's go."

"Go where?"

"Just follow me."

"Where are we going?"

"You'll see."

We walked behind the bar, toward the outdoor toilet. Then we started up a hill toward a house. I asked him if we were going to that house and he said, "Don't ask so many questions."

"Well, I would like to know where I'm going."

"You'll know when we get there. Don't worry, 'um gonna take care of you."

When we reached the house, he knocked on the door. A middle-aged woman came to the door, and told us to come in. She was in her nightclothes, or what seemed like nightclothes. She asked us to sit down, but Seaborn told her that he had to go and, pointing to me, said that he just wanted her to meet a friend of his. He introduced her to me, and she offered me a drink. I knew or felt I knew what was going on, but pretended not to. While she was fixing me a drink, Seaborn started to leave. I walked out behind him. Once outside, he asked me where I was going, and I said, "with you." Then he said, "Oh! Man! What's wrong with you? I set you up and you're acting like this. What's it with you?"

"Well, I don't know what's going on. You didn't tell me nothing."

"Do I have to tell you? Can't you see? All you have to do is give her five bucks—that's all."

"Give her five bucks for what—one drink? I can buy a whole bottle for half that."

"Hey Man! I tell you what, let's go. You just wait right here. I gotta go and talk to her. I'll be right back."

He went into the house. I stood there, knowing what it was all about, but I didn't want to tell him that I didn't want sex with such an old woman. Seaborn came out and headed back toward the bar. He didn't say one word to me all the way to the bar. When we got there, he headed straight for Larry. They talked for a few minutes; then Larry came over to me and said, "Didn't you like that, man?"

"Like what?"

"The woman. She may not look young and beautiful, but she sure know what to do."

"You mean she is a prostitute?"

"She's a married lady; but her old man don't care, 'long as she gets something for it."

"Well, why didn't Seaborn tell me that before? I could have told him I don't do that with a married woman."

"Oh, it would have been all right. I guess we better be getting on home. I got to go to work in the morning."

All the way home, Larry didn't say a word. I thought he might be embarrassed, so I didn't say anything else. When we got to his house, he showed me where to sleep, and said good-night. After I had finished my writing, I went straight to bed.

I got up early the next day, and thanked them for allowing me to stay overnight. I was undecided about where I should go next. It would be nice to visit with C. Q. Grey, and get additional information about the Grey family. My luck had been very good with all the people I had met since I left Vera Ridge. Perhaps, though, this time I wouldn't fare as well, so maybe I should go on to Stanford. Finally I decided against it and headed for where C. Q. Grey lived.

I remembered how to get there from the directions Clara and Larry had given me. It was just as they had said, right in the middle of the cotton fields. Of all the houses I had seen in this area, this one was the most in need of repair. The whole house was tilted, and looked as if it would topple over at the slightest push. It began to rain and by the time I reached C. Q.'s house, there was a pool of water in his front yard. I got there just as some children were climbing off a school bus. On the porch there was a tall, thin man in overalls, who appeared to be in his late sixties. I hurried out of the car and onto the porch to get out of the rain, but noticed that almost as much rain was falling onto the porch as was falling in the yard. I told the man who I was, and where I had been, and why I had come to see him. Without any further conversation, he invited me into his house.

Inside, the house was just one big room, without any dividers. There was a young woman, who looked to be in her middle twenties, cooking on a wooden stove, and several children. One of them was a little baby, sleeping on the only bed in the house. C. Q. told me that he had gotten a call from Clara. As we began to talk, it struck me as strange that everyone I had talked to about their family began with a mention of their Granddaddy. C. Q. Grey also started with his. He said, "Um gonna begin with my Granddaddy, and come on down. My Granddaddy was named John Grey, and his oldest son was named Sonny Grey. . . ."

The children were making a lot of noise and C. Q. told them to go to a corner of the room and be quiet. He asked me to excuse him while he directed them where to sit. While he was directing the children, I looked around the house. You could see light between the cracks. I wondered how they kept warm during the winter. I thought it odd that they should have a telephone; I wondered how they could afford it. However, if they didn't have a phone, stuck way out in the middle of a cotton field and no one around for miles, they would be in trouble in case of an emergency.

By this time C. Q. had returned. He began to name every child his Granddaddy had, including C. Q.'s own mother. I began to tie this family to all the Greys when he talked to me about his father's sister. It turned out that his father's sister was the mother of Peggy, the entertainer from Vera Ridge. He first named his Granddaddy's children, and then named and talked about his own mother's children. She had had one set of children by one man, and another set, including himself, by another man. He said, "My dear mama's children was all raised up in Grey's name, but they lived in her daddy's house."

In trying to explain this to me, he pointed out that these children, the ones his mother had by another man, were "illegitimate." "So they call it, but they were raised up in Grey's name," he said. It turned out that his "blood daddy" was a Young; but he, C. Q., was raised in the name of Grey. As my talk with C. Q. continued, many questions I had had about the Grey family were answered. He even repeated some of the stories the Greys I had already talked with told me. We talked about an hour and a half. His wife was cooking, and he asked if I would like some supper. I told him I would, even though I was not too hungry. I was glad I did, because they were having one of my favorite meals. His wife cooked some good old biscuits on a wooden stove, and fried some "titty bacon." We would sop the biscuits in some hot syrup and tug at the titty bacon. It was good!

After eating, I talked with C. Q. again. His wife never said a word; he did all the talking. He would not even allow his children to interrupt him while he and I talked. For a few minutes,

I thought I was a kid again, growing up in Florida with all of my brothers and sisters, cousins, and other relatives, sitting around a wooden stove on a rainy day, sopping biscuits in syrup and tugging on titty bacon. We would top off our meal with roasted peanuts. I thanked C. Q. and his wife for allowing me to come into their home and eat and talk with them. Afterward I headed on down the road for Stanford.

I felt good. In these past few days I wouldn't have traded my position with anyone. Not only had I accomplished a lot in terms of my work, but I had also had a chance to meet and talk with such "real nice" people who had taken me in and given me some of whatever they had.

It was still raining when I reached the city. There were several people I had to look up in the city of Stanford. There were two sets of Greys with whom I wanted to talk. Stanford was a big city; and I got there during rush hour. It seemed as if it took forever to get to the black section. Since it was late, I thought I ought to find a motel and stay there for the night. From there, I hoped to call the people I wanted to see.

I saw a black cafe, and decided to stop and ask if they knew of a motel where it would be all right for me to stay. I sat in the cafe and talked with some of the people, but they all seemed to be suspicious of me. Finally, I got back into my car and headed for the motel. After settling down, I got on the phone and began calling the people I wanted to talk with. I got no answer to the first phone call. In response to the second, I was told that the people I was looking for didn't live there anymore. The last call reached the remaining people I was looking for; they said it would be all right if I came over to talk with them. I arranged to talk with them the following day.

Settling down on my bed, I turned on the television. I could hear the rain as it fell. I was pretty tired, and this would be the first time in days I would have a chance to get some sleep without feeling I was imposing on someone. I took out my ledger and began to write up the day's events. I found myself getting sleepy, so I turned off the television and soon fell asleep across the bed.

In the morning when I awakened, I was sweating. I must have had a terrible dream, because I was soaking wet, as if I had been running. In the back of my mind were the four guys of Vera Ridge. I began to feel upset about them. I started to think about the people I had talked with in the last few days and how wonderful they had all been; and when I remembered how some of the people in Vera Ridge treated me, I became angry. Suddenly I found myself loading up my car and telling myself I was going back to Vera Ridge and that I was not going to take any more from those four guys. If they wanted a fight, I would give it to them. The more I thought about it, the angrier I became, and the more I wanted to get back there as soon as possible. I was going to *deal with* those four guys, once and for all. I got into my car and drove straight to Vera Ridge, stopping only for gas.

It was about seven o'clock in the morning when I left. I knew I had to return to Stanford again, and figured that I could get in touch with the Greys at some other time. It rained all the way back to Vera Ridge. I was very tired and just as angry. Over ten hours' driving didn't abate my anger. On returning to Vera Ridge, the first place I went was John's house. I knocked on the door and when he said, "Come in," once inside I told him I had had it with the four guys and a few other people in Vera Ridge. I told him that the people in Vera Ridge complained about "not having this, and not having that, and that they were cutting each other's throats telling on this one, and telling on that one, trying to win favors from me." I suggested he go to the cotton fields and see how hard black people really have it there, and how little they have, but how wonderful they are. I said, "I have taken all the shit I'm going to take from some of these people who have bothered me, and if I have any more trouble with them they will regret it. If I have to use my gun, I'll use it."

I grabbed my keys from him, and strode out of his house and

over to his sister's curbside market. I told her the same things. After I had finished, I went to the house where one of the four guys lived; I told him the same, only with more force. I knew I only had to tell him and the rest of them would hear about it. I was raving mad! Then I drove back to my trailer and flopped on the sofa. I was angry, tired, and, at the same time, a little frightened. I took a hot shower and went straight to bed.

That night they came to my trailer. I got my gun. I didn't say a word. I let them knock and pound on the door. I carefully walked to the other door. I opened it quietly, so that they would not hear me. I took my gun, pointed it to the sky, and fired it several times. They ran, stumbling over themselves, trying to get away. The story got around town very fast. I never was troubled by them again. As a matter of fact, during the last few months of my stay in Vera Ridge, we became friendly enough to play cards together. I had *dealt* with it.

I can truthfully say that I wouldn't have traded the experience of meeting and learning to love the people of Vera Ridge. John's family was one of the four families I studied intensively. John also became my best friend in Vera Ridge; and his son affectionately addressed me as "Uncle Reggie." I asked John if he had told his son to do this, but he swore he had not. John was the one person I felt I could really trust. He had made it possible for me to gain access to people at several colleges, as well as well-known figures in professional sports who originally came from Vera Ridge. In addition, I spent many hours talking with his mother, Ola May. Linda, John's sister, was the only member of the family who didn't have much to say to me.

There were times, God knows, when I wanted to leave Vera Ridge because I felt that my situation was hopeless. But John dropped by frequently to check up on me. When I expressed my feelings about Vera Ridge, and the trouble I had been having with some people, he would say, "Reggie, you gonna leave us?"

Sometimes he would ask, "Reggie, you're still with us?" But always he would say, "Reggie, don't be too hard on us."

He would have a cup of coffee and we would talk about the

progress in my fieldwork. He kept checking on me, to make sure that I didn't stop doing my research, because there were times when I threw up my hands and said, "I'm through! Finished! It's not worth all of the hell I keep getting from those guys."

This general ethnographic background, and the accounts of the conditions under which I did my study, will present the reader with a picture of the area and its people. It also portrays my state of mind as a fieldworker. How I felt from day to day is bound to have influenced the way I viewed situations. Whatever their effect on me emotionally, some of the incidents gave me considerable insight into the character of the community under study. For example, my conflict with the four men revealed to me the importance of self-preservation in a black context: as I was told repeatedly, I, and only I, had to "deal with it." Even though some members of the community did feel a certain sense of responsibility for me, both their general discussions and their specific attitudes toward me seemed to have been marked by individual autonomy—a recurrent theme that may be seen to pervade the entire lifestyle of black society.

*A*T last I had established a position for myself in the community. I was not a member, yet I had obtained certain rights that afforded me some measure of trust and respect, even though still an outsider. For example, I had a temporary territory within the community that was referred to as "Reggie's place." This referred not only to a geographical location, but also to a social level within the community's system of social stratification. I had a voice in community decisions. I was called on for advice to mediate family disputes, to argue with landlords over rent, to coordinate activities, and to host community functions that were usually hosted by community members only. There was a poor woman with two children who were somewhat retarded and I went to see them almost daily. She was not able to take care of her two children, so I offered to adopt them. I wanted to put them in school. The woman began to think I was interested in her sexually, and started to visit my home. She said she would let me adopt her children if I would marry her. I was not interested in the woman sexually, but I was touched by her concern for me.

I now felt very comfortable in the community, and at this point chose the four families to concentrate on and began to map out methods and techniques for obtaining the information necessary for my research.

I had observed the community of Vera Ridge, and had interviewed a wide range of its black population. So I knew I should select at least one family from each of its three clearly defined sections. I decided to choose two families from the most populous section because half the black community's population (section B) lived there, and also because this was the original black settlement of Vera Ridge. Together, these four families represented a cross section of all the people of Vera Ridge. Members of these families filled diverse occupational roles and had different educational backgrounds. Some had no formal education, while others had become teachers. The living facilities of the families ranged from a single family dwelling to several family dwellings. In this way, I included in my sample all the family types representative of black lifestyle. These would form the basis for delineating black family structure.

The family from section A represented people living under separate roofs, but relying on each other for necessary services. The day-to-day activities of these members presented a means for me to explore family networks. One of the two families from section B owned a small business. I was thus able to get to know an educated family whose members provided its own support. One of the family members had become a scholar; another was attending college; while a third operated the business. This family had the fewest members present in Vera Ridge at any one time. The second family in section B was chosen because it had the largest kin network. I felt it would amply illustrate the structure of a family whose members were still concentrated, for the most part, in the general Vera Ridge area. The family in section C was selected because it represented a typical family in the black community of Vera Ridge.

I used three methods for obtaining my data: participant observation, open-ended interviews, and surveying, including some spot-checking. None of these methods was used totally independent of the others. That is, when I was observing behavior,

I also did some interviewing and vice versa. There were times when I had intended to restrict my research to observation only, but I almost always ended up interviewing the people I observed, in order to understand better what was taking place. I didn't begin my survey until I had collected enough data to generate broadly relevant questions. For example, the idea of "relative" became an important concept in investigating and understanding the black family; therefore I questioned every informant (whether or not he or she was a member of the four families involved in this study) about relatives. I did spot-checking of people who weren't part of the four families to verify data already collected.

I was not always able to have my tape recorder with me when I collected data; however, I did carry a pencil and pad with me wherever I went. In this way I could, if it was convenient, jot down enough information to actually use the conversation. Where it was not convenient to take notes, I did so at the first opportunity. The dialogue I have recorded may not always be verbatim, but it accurately represents the content of the conversations that took place. It was my intention to record the exact language the informants used in describing their accounts of events, whether they were responding to questions I had asked formally or conversations I had overheard. Therefore, when the conversations couldn't be recorded on the spot, I jotted down pertinent information; where possible I arranged for a formal interview with the person or persons involved.

My participant observation occurred in many places: colleges, bars, universities, schools, churches, barber shops, pool halls, and other spots where people congregated for social activities or for work. Of course, most participant observation occurred in households, especially in those of the four families. Interviews weren't always possible in the places where participant observation occurred, for example, at work, in churches, in classrooms—especially when I was using a tape recorder. Nevertheless, most interviews occurred in the same places where I had made my observations. When on-the-spot interviews weren't possible, I sometimes could arrange to hold them elsewhere. In addition to concentrating on the representative families, I also randomly interviewed people. I followed up incidents when onlookers expressed approval or disapproval of the people involved. The collected data suggested new questions. For example, each family study revealed members who were considered "family" but weren't related by blood or marriage; therefore, in the course of my surveys, I began asking questions about relationships to obtain further information. I also talked to people who weren't related to the families. Some of these people lived in the community, and others were located in other states.

Thus, beyond the family context, participant observation consisted of discussing family members' behavior outside the family context. For example, I discovered that sex roles and gender distinctions, especially with regard to division of labor, did not play as important a part in the household as they did outside. To understand what appeared to be an absence of sex role-playing between male and female labor within and without the household, it became necessary to observe and talk with people whose behavior was challenged by others. So, I began to visit places where people gathered and I observed what they were doing, how they were doing it, and what would explain why they behaved that way. I asked the people involved, as well as those viewing and commenting on the behavior, to explain to me what was taking place. In this manner, participant observation allowed me to begin to understand this apparent dichotomy in male and female roles within and without the household contexts.

As the interviews produced more and more data (which will be presented shortly), important questions arose that necessitated the collection of data from sources other than the home environment. Now I began to conduct interviews in public places already mentioned. Sometimes I would stop people walking on the street and begin a conversation. Some of the responses were unhelpful: "I don't know," or "I don't have the time."

Others led to a wealth of information and to associations with new people who became informants during my stay in Vera Ridge. During this phase of my study, interviewing became my main source of data gathering. I relied less on observational experiences that didn't include interviewing. The tape recorder proved a useful device; few people objected to its use.

Shortly after I began to use interviews instead of participant observation, I increased my traveling outside the community. Although my purpose was to follow up the interviews with the four families, travel also afforded me the opportunity to do some spot-checking. I thus had an opportunity to compare the data acquired from the members of the four families as well as to obtain new data from which to generate additional questions and hypotheses that could be tested on the four families.

Traveling outside the community also enabled me to conduct surveys pertaining to important questions arising from interview data. I questioned people on such topics as: (1) Who is a relative? (2) Who is considered a family member? (3) How do you view pre or extramarital sexual behavior? (4) What does "illegitimate" mean? (5) How do you view foster parents?, and so on. My interviews can be grouped into two broad categories: (1) Intensive interviewing with the four families selected in the research, and (2) cross-checking and spot-checking interviews with people besides the family members.

The following material is representative of the data I received from the four families studied. The accounts of each family are purely descriptive, and (other than comparing and contrasting the families to each other) no attempt is made to use the technique of anthropological analysis during the discussions of these families in this section. However, each family is presented from a different perspective. In discussing the first family, I concentrate on kinship and the role of kin terminology, such as "biological" connections, in defining family membership. For the second family, I focus on "pivotal members," and discuss how membership is secured to retain a member once he or she has entered the family. Family number three exemplifies the process whereby family members related by blood are excluded from the family when they refuse to fulfill certain role expectations. The discussion of the fourth family brings out certain features common to all black families, regardless of whether the family is self-supporting or not.

FAMILY
NUMBER ONE

I first met a member of this family shortly after I arrived in Vera Ridge. I had asked Mrs. Walker, the lady with whom I first stayed, if she would take me to see Peggy's mother, Ruth. I had corresponded only with Peggy up to now, but felt that I wanted to begin talking to her mother, as well as other members of her family. Another reason I thought I should see the mother soon after my arrival was because she was said to be very ill and there was a question as to how much longer she would live.

On the evening of the first day I spent in Vera Ridge, Mrs. Walker and I visited Peggy's mother. The door was answered by a nurse who was taking care of her. As I learned later, the nurse was called "Sister Child" by Peggy. They were close friends, like sisters. She admitted us into a big and imposing house, and then returned to her duties with the invalid mother. A woman named Alice came immediately from the kitchen to greet us. Mrs. Walker introduced her to me, and then went into the bedroom where the mother lay, so that Alice and I could talk briefly about my work. She said she was Peggy's cousin and wanted to know how I knew Peggy. I explained that I had only corresponded with Peggy but had never formally met her.

Alice remarked, "That's just like Peggy. She's a friend to every-body. She takes after Aunt Ruth, her mother."

As I sat in the living room, I glanced at the other parts of the house. The living room made you feel quiet and peaceful; it was big, and had a high ceiling. There was a fireplace on the east wall. Over it was a picture of Peggy, her mother, father, and brother. On the mantel there were many other pictures—one of Alice. We sat on a long, soft, and modest sofa. The sofa, along with the chairs and other furniture, blended well with the room. There was a record-player, with a few albums beside it. The simplicity of the furniture, drapes, and other decorative items in the living room made you feel as if you had been there before— that you were at home, and not sitting in a strange place for the first time. The people I met there also made you feel the same way.

I wanted to go through the whole house, but knew that would not be possible at this time. However, I was able to see it on a later visit. It is a big, two-story house, with five bedrooms, a large living and dining room, a large kitchen, two bathrooms, and a front and back porch. Perhaps its most remarkable feature was how spotless it was kept. Everything was in place; there was no dust on the furniture, and the floors were always vac-uumed or polished. In the dining room, a large dining table occupied the center of the floor and a chandelier hung low over the table. There was a buffet and two smaller tables against the north and east walls. This furniture was old, but very well kept. It was similar to that in the living room. In the kitchen, the stove and refrigerator looked new; however, the rest of the appliances were older. Nevertheless, they all were spotless. The tiled floor looked as if it was just waxed.

There were two twin beds in every bedroom. All the bed rooms had wood floors, with throw-rugs between the beds and the beds and the dressers. There was nothing fancy about the furniture in the bedrooms. However, everything was neatly in place; the beds looked as if no one slept in them. Both porches were enclosed with wire screens. On the front porch there was a large swing hanging from the ceiling. Other chairs were arranged around the porch. On the back porch there was a washer and a dryer. Some of the space was used for storage. I was happy that I had had a chance to see this house.

While sitting there talking with Alice, I looked into the bedroom where Mrs. Walker was visiting with Peggy's mother. The mother occasionally shifted her eyes back and forth, and from side to side. She wasn't responding verbally to Mrs. Walker. Alice and I continued to talk. She showed me albums that Peggy had recorded. Then she said, "This is all that we have. Dumpling—that's what I call my aunt—she keep giving them away to anyone who asked for them."

I noticed that the only recordings that remained were spirituals. Mrs. Walker motioned for me to come into the bedroom where the mother lay. I stood there for what seemed a long time. The mother stared at me. She moved her eyes as if she were examining me. Mrs. Walker was continually talking to her during this time. After awhile, the mother slowly raised her hand and extended it toward me. I reached to shake it. I was very careful not to grip it too tightly. I feared that I would disturb her. She gripped my hand, ever so slightly. I stood there until she finally released it. She looked up at me, then shifted her eyes to Mrs. Walker.

I returned to the living room. I felt good all over. It was as if I had experienced all the great things I had heard about this woman. I thought to myself, here she is, on what could be her deathbed, still trying to encourage others to succeed in life. I felt a strength from her that rippled through my whole body. It was the same feeling you get from someone on whom you've modeled your life. He or she tells you personally that you've arrived—that's the way I felt. I wanted to go back and hug her, pour the life that I had into her, so that she could live forever. I thought about how often you try to establish a line of communication with people you like, but it takes so long and is so difficult; yet I had obtained this communication with her in a short time and with someone I had just met. I only wished that I had known her many years before. But I knew the feeling I got from her would be with me the rest of my life.

A few minutes later, Mrs. Walker said that she had to return home, but that she would come back tomorrow. Alice saw us to the door; and on the porch she talked with Mrs. Walker. She said, "I don't think she's going to make it this time. She's too weak. She has lost all of her spirit. I think she's ready to give up."

Mrs. Walker commented on how strong the invalid mother had been in the past, and how she had fallen sick and people thought she would die, but that she had then pulled through. Alice shook her head and said, "I don't think so this time." We said good-night to her and left.

The next day, I saw Alice. She was on her way to Peggy's mother's house. She invited me to come with her, and we sat on the front porch after she had gone into the house and checked on her aunt. She told me that she spent her days attending to her aunt; at night she would go home to an apartment in the project housing in section B. She said that Peggy was to return on the 17th of the month, unless her mother became worse. I asked her how often Peggy got in touch with them, and she said, "She called every day after Dumpling got sick. Otherwise she calls every Sunday, no matter whether she is in California or Europe. She not only calls, but she writes me and Dumpling. That's one thing you can count on, whenever she says she's going to do something, she'll do it. I haven't seen it fail yet. Just like her mama—just like her for the world."

Alice was called by the nurse. She asked to be excused, and I waited on the porch for her to return. When she came back, she said, "Maybe I shouldn't say this, but I don't care, I'm gonna say it anyway. There's one thing wrong with Peggy, she don't know how to say *no!* Sometimes I think she let people run over her. Now Dumpling, you can't do that to her—no Lord. When she says 'Yes!' she means 'Yes!,' but when she says 'No!,' she means 'No!.' Ain't no way you gonna change her mind once it's made up. She's the sweetest person in the world. You can't ask for a better person."

All the people with whom I talked and who knew Peggy's mother—and almost everyone did—said the same things about her decisiveness. Many said that she was the person who delivered them or their children when she had been midwife in in the black community.

For the next two weeks, I was unable to hold long conversations with Alice. Her aunt had become worse, and so our meetings were brief. At this time, she was describing her life, and telling me about other members of this family, when she could recall them. Alice was fascinating in that she could remember back to her great-grandfather's life as if it was yesterday. She knew where every living member was now. She knew how many children each had. She told me who was married to whom, and who had become separated from whom. She recalled who had died and when they had died, who came to the funeral, who cried, and how the death affected other members of the family. Alice also told me a great deal about the next-door neighbors, Phillis and Jim. She said, "They are the nicest people you ever want to meet. They helped raise Peggy and her brother Terry. Many times they would come home from school, and Dumpling would be out somewhere delivering a baby or looking after other people's problems. Peggy and Terry would go over to Phillis and Jim's house and eat just like they were at home."

I asked Alice if Peggy and Terry were still as close to Phillis and Jim as they were when they were growing up, and she said, "Right today, if they come home, before they could sit down, Phillis would be here asking them if they wanted a potato pie or a chocolate cake. They are just like another mama and daddy to them. When Peggy comes home, she always brings something for her mama and me; she has something for Phillis and Jim too. Most of the time Dumpling would give it away because she says she don't want or need it. When she brings her mama and me something, she brings Phillis, Jim, and Carol, the woman she call 'Sister Child,' something too. And, when her daddy was alive, he used to love to see his children come home because they always had something for him too. If Phillis or Jim got sick, they'd be right down here the same way they'd be for their own mama. They're crazy about Phillis and Jim."

I asked Alice how long she had known Phillis and Jim, and she replied, "Ever since I've been in Vera Ridge. I grew up in this house next door to them. Of course, I'm not as close to them as Dumpling, Peggy, and Terry. You see, I moved away from Vera Ridge and went to live with some white folks up next to Whitefield—I worked for them. When I came back, I was grown up. I had a child of my own by then. I didn't stay here when I came back. I stayed right over there in that same apartment I have now. So, I never really got too close to Phillis and Jim. Still, they are very nice people and I respect them very much."

I didn't see Alice for two days after the last interview. One morning, I got up early. Some man from the local newspaper was supposed to come by and take a picture of me, to go with a story they were going to print in the *Vera Ridge News*. After I took a shower and went into the living room, I was told by Mrs. Walker that Peggy had arrived in Vera Ridge at six o'clock and that her mother had passed away at seven. This came as a shock to me, because I thought I would get another chance to visit with the mother. I also didn't want to have to introduce myself to Peggy under the circumstances of her mother's recent death.

After I finished a cup of coffee, I asked Mrs. Walker if I should go over and see Peggy. She said, "I don't think it would be a good idea yet, but both of us could go over there tomorrow."

I walked outside and looked in the direction of Peggy's house. I saw a woman beating a rug on the back-porch steps. Although I had never seen Peggy up close, I felt that it must be she. I guess my staring caused her to glance in my direction. She paused briefly, then resumed her beating. Finally I waved to her, and she returned the wave, then disappeared into the house.

I left the Walkers' home for an interview at eleven o'clock and didn't return until one in the afternoon. Mrs. Walker said that she had paid a morning visit to Peggy and had mentioned me. She said Peggy had told her it would be all right if I came that day. I decided to go over right away. If I delayed, I felt our meeting would probably be very awkward. You see, I have never been able to face death under any circumstances. I know that it can happen, and eventually does happen to everyone. But I never know what to do or say in its presence, especially at a funeral. So I couldn't think of what to say to Peggy, who had just lost her mother; moreover, this was to be our first meeting, which made it even more difficult. To think about this would simply make me more diffident. Therefore, I decided that if I went right over, I might take everything in stride. So, I walked over to Peggy's house and knocked on the door. She came out. While I stood there, not knowing what to do or say, she said, "You're Reggie."

I nodded and she invited me in. Once inside, I conveyed my sympathy to her, and she acknowledged it kindly. Then she said, "I wish you great success in the work you are doing, especially because you are doing a fine thing."

For lack of anything more appropriate to say under the circumstances, I talked about the work she was doing, and how much I enjoyed her music. She accepted my compliments graciously. I said, "I'm sorry that I have to see you under these circumstances. Perhaps I should come back later."

She replied, "Oh! I'm sorry that I didn't have time to change my dress for you, but this is all I have right now."

Even though I realized that she didn't want me to feel uncomfortable, I thought I should leave; but she said, "It's all right. I don't mind talking with you."

I kept complimenting her on her career and she responded by praising the work I was doing, and so I ended up thanking her.

Apparently she had heard of my problems in Vera Ridge and was concerned about them more than her own. To relieve her mind, I told her that I devoted most of my time to my work and didn't let things bother me. She replied, "But a person has to have some kind of social life."

I thanked her for the help she had given me in getting to Vera Ridge; and she said, "That's quite all right. Anything I am able to do, let me know. I would be only too happy to do more."

She offered me a drink, and I asked for scotch. Then we sat and talked about fifteen minutes, mostly about her work and mine. Finally I thought I should go, even though I really wanted to continue talking. So I told her I had an interview and excused myself. She saw me to the door, and said, "Reggie, now you come by anytime. Give me a week and I'll be ready for your interviews; but you're welcome to come by anytime!"

The next day when I saw Peggy, she said, "Kinfolks and relatives are coming from everywhere. Some in cars, some in buses, some in trains, and some in planes. I didn't know I had so many folks. Some of them I've never seen—didn't know I had."

I told her that I had a car, and would be happy to pick up any of her kinfolks from the airport or stations as they came in. She said, "Reggie, that's very sweet of you, and I certainly will call on you if it becomes necessary."

Later I had the chance to meet and talk with most of these people. Perhaps the most exciting part was that everybody talked about the things they knew about each other. They recalled good times, bad times, and hard times. They remembered so far back that some members said, "Wait a minute, I wasn't even born then." They spoke of being young, of growing up, where they used to live, how they used to live, and with whom they lived. Relatives wanted to know about other relatives and kin; and kin wanted to know about other kin and relatives. In this family, as in other families that are a part of my study, there was a distinction made between "kin" and "relative." Kin were the "immediate family" or the "family"; whereas people who were considered "relatives" were usually outside the "immediate family" or "family." They were usually referred to as "distant relatives" or "relatives." Immediate family for Peggy was members with whom she had close ties, close relationships, frequent interactions and communication. Those people she felt a responsibility toward or an obligation to. On the other hand, the people she included in the general category of relatives were people related by blood or marriage; however, she didn't communicate with them except on special occasions. Since they were all talking with one another so readily, I didn't have to ask questions at this time.

The people grouped themselves into old people, young people, and men and women. There were two women who moved from group to group, saying things like, "Jack, you go talk to Mary. Terry, you go talk to Uncle Robert over there in the corner. Resa, you've been talking to these young men too long; go over there and keep Aunt Susie company."

When too many people gathered in one place, these women would disperse them into less crowded parts of the house. All this time, people were busy in the kitchen. Food was being prepared and served. Drinks were being poured and consumed. Both men and women helped in these services. I kept darting in and out, because I would run across the street to where I lived and write down information I had received, then run back to Peggy's house to gather more information, until the evening was over. I was busy in this way—collecting data on this family—for two days. Then came the funeral; and the day afterwards, the same intense data collection continued for two more days.

Each night ended for me when most of the people had gone to the places where they were to sleep. Some slept in the house itself, while others were with friends and relatives throughout Vera Ridge. I was always one of the last to leave for the night. The final night ended with Peggy saying, as she lifted up the tablecloth where she sat eating in the dining room, "I've got to sing in a few days. I've got to find me a voice from somewhere."

I knew then that she would be all right. Somehow I had begun to feel responsible for removing the sadness in her heart—at least, I wanted to. Now I was assured that she would continue her career, even though she had just lost "the dearest person in my life—my sweet mother."

After I returned home for the final time each night, I would go over my notes, to see if I could add any information left out. I was exhausted by the time the funeral was over and people returned to their homes in Alabama, Pennsylvania, New York, New Orleans, California, and various points throughout the state itself.

It was another week before I began my interviews with Peggy and Terry, her brother, who had remained behind. I had noticed that there were no children at this gathering. Most of the people were thirty-five years old or older. At first I thought that the children had been left behind because of the funeral. Further investigation proved me wrong: there were only three children in this family. They were the children of Terry and his wife.

I had also noticed that at no time did the situation get out of hand. There was a remarkable amount of cohesion among all members. Perhaps it was because of the circumstances under which they had assembled. However, I didn't know what might have taken place when I wasn't there. But the speed and efficiency with which those present went about their tasks reflected a great deal of understanding among them. One person did say to another, "You need a rest; you have been working all day. Let me do it for awhile."

I also observed that people always showed a great amount of respect for age. For example, when there was a conflict of opinions among some, three of the older people who commanded everyone's respect were called on to settle the differences. When their decision went against a particular person, he or she didn't challenge it, or if he or she did, the challenge was mild and short.

Friends and other associates who wanted to show their respect to the family members came in at all hours. If someone did come by at night, he or she would be met at the door. The visitor delivered condolence and/or gifts—food in most cases—and then left.

In this family, the mother had been addressed by Peggy and her brother Terry as "Mama." This was also the term by which they referred to her. Alice, the mother's niece, addressed the mother as "Dumpling." She also referred to and called her "Aunt Ruth." Jim and Phillis, the next-door neighbors, addressed and referred to the mother as "Ruth." Sister Child, the nurse, called her "Mrs. Smith." All these people are considered by each other as members of the family. Other kin terms used among members of the family include: Peggy to Jim—"Cousin Jim"; Peggy to the nurse—"Sister Child." Sometimes Peggy addressed Terry as "Baby Brother." He called her "Peg." Otherwise, members of the family were addressed or referred to by first names or by nicknames.

In the family, "mama," "aunt," and "brother" were used for biological family members. "Cousin" and "sister" were used to refer to those who were affiliated only by mutual consent. I found that if I used a kinship term while interviewing a family member, he or she would use the same term in his or her reply. For example, if my question was, "Who is your mother?," the reply would usually be, "My mother is. . . ."

In this family, the term "family" refers to two sets of people. One set included Peggy, Terry, Ruth, Alice, Jim, Phillis, and Sister Child. Peggy sometimes referred to them as "immediate family." The other set of people contained all the other kin and relatives. Peggy sometimes referred to them as "distant family." We can see here that a single kin term, for example, "cousin," may appear in both categories of family; however, it depends on the closeness of the relationship between the members. For example, Alice was Peggy's and Terry's cousin; but she was grouped in what Peggy referred to as immediate family. All the other cousins present were categorized as distant family. Therefore, it isn't the term that determines which family a person may belong to; rather it is the relationship between the members.

The mother lived alone when she was in good health. Although she was in a house by herself, people always looked in on her daily. After she became ill, Peggy and Alice, along with Sister Child, became an integral part of her household. Peggy was with her whenever she wasn't away working. Alice spent days with her, and nights at her own apartment. Sister Child spent days and nights with the mother. When the mother became critically ill, Alice was with her all the time. Alice had grown up in the mother's house. She stayed there until she had finished high school. Peggy was away only when she had to perform. She would have given up performing and remained with her mother, had it not been for her mother insisting "Do your work, no matter what."

I remember when I first intreviewed Peggy, I referred to her as "Miss Smith," and she corrected me by saying, "Well, first thing is to make the situation easier for you and me. My name is Peggy, so . . . ah . . . we'll get that out of the way."

"Oh, I didn't know, I. . . ." She laughed and said that I could even call her "Peg," that the only time she insisted on being called "Miss Smith" was when there was a contract to be signed. I asked her about members of her family—whom did she refer to as "family"? She replied, "Mama, Daddy, Terry, Alice, Phillis and Cousin Jim, and Sister Child . . . Gee! There are so many that are gone now. For me, I guess, that's it."

She lowered her head and continued, "Mama used to keep track of all the family. If ever I wanted to know something about a cousin or an uncle or an aunt, all I had to do was call Mama. Now I don't know who's going to take care of keeping the family together."

Of the members Peggy named, Phillis and Jim weren't related either by blood or marriage to others she mentioned. Nevertheless, Peggy, Terry, and other biologically related members consider them a part of the family. Peggy said, "From what I just told you about relatives, the people next door, Phillis and Jim, are more than relatives to me. To be a relative doesn't necessarily mean that you love him. But the people next door, I do love. And, I think they love me. What I mean is that they are closer to me than some relatives."

Jim, Phillis, and Sister Child were family members because of their continuing relationship, which had been marked by mutual consent. Peggy said, "Phillis is like a second mother; I consider her to be a member of my family. I consider Cousin Jim, Phillis' husband, also to be a member of my family by virtue of the fact that I have no hesitation in going to their house and feeling the same warmth and relaxation as I do with my own mother and father. That includes food [she laughed], words of inspiration, faith, opinions, just the same as I would find in my own family; and we aren't related by blood."

Terry, Peggy's brother, was always academic during our interviews. He was a government official, and was very much concerned with the "youth generation." Terry and Peggy had different ideas about what a man and a woman should do as members of a family. Whereas Peggy thought in terms of a clear distinction between chores for men and chores for women, Terry felt that sometimes a man may have to perform chores that would be considered appropriate for a woman. For example, Peggy said, "I'd prefer a man not to do any chores that a woman should be doing. I don't want my man in the kitchen. Of course, if I couldn't get anyone else, then, if he cares about me, he would cook or clean the kitchen if he had to."

On the other hand, Terry said that he often does kitchen chores. He said, "I often get up in the morning and cook my breakfast; and when my wife was sick, I took care of my daughter. Not so much from having to do it, but rather from being able to do it. Now I may spend all damned day in the kitchen, but we were brought up that somebody would come by to make sure that the kids are fed. I used to bathe my daughter, but I would call a friend to come by and comb her hair—it's just that simple. There's a point when a woman's touch is needed."

Terry told me that his father played the male's role for many relatives, in addition to himself and Peggy. He said, "A man's role is not restricted to his children. For example, my uncle was father to my two cousins. In fact, my own mother and father were closer to them than their real parents. My cousins would come to my mother and father with problems before they went to their own."

When I talked with Peggy earlier, she was trying to determine how a cousin of hers became a "double" cousin; but she was unable to figure it out, and so was I. She asked Terry; but he too was at a loss. They both said they would ask their cousin, Alice. I finally figured it out. Their mother's brother's daughter married their father's brother's son. "No! No! No!," Alice was to tell me. "It goes deeper than that. Now listen to me carefully, because sometimes even I get mixed up when I'm trying to tell it. It goes this way. Peggy's mother's, brother's, daughter—now let me see if I got that straight—Yes! She married Peggy's father's brother's son—now let me see if I got that straight—Yes! Yes, that's the way it goes, and that's what makes them double cousins."

Alice would take over from where the mother had left off in her knowledge of the relatives and their relationships to each other. She would also keep the lines of communication open between the relatives, and let each know from time to time how different relatives were doing.

During this set of interviews, Terry did most of the talking, and Peggy mostly listened and agreed with him. Being in the government, Terry had had to deal with many family problems characteristic of people from lower-class families. Therefore, his perspective was wider than purely personal concerns. In our interviews, he often asked me questions about the possible solution to "today's problems," and sometimes he would use his own upbringing as a model for how young people of today should be reared. He said, "If I was out on the streets, doing something, and it was wrong, a man didn't have to be your father to come up and correct you."

Peggy interjected, "We were talking about that last night." Terry continued, "For example, if Jay didn't see me in church two Sundays in a row, but he knew I was home, he didn't have to ask my parents' permission to find out why I wasn't in church."

"How old were you then?"

"I was in college. He would take it upon himself—follow me? So, you had that masculine concern outside your family. As kids, we always patterned ourselves after people we held in high esteem. So, when you talk about the male role, you don't have to be talking about family matters; you can be talking about friendship."

Terry, Peggy, and I spent several days talking about their family, and what they expected from family members and vice versa. I was able to talk in depth with Peggy and Terry, because they were concerned about the same things as I. They really became excited during the interviews when we were discussing male and female role behavior. As usual, Terry did most of the talking—Peggy, even when she disagreed with him, often remained verbally silent—and even when she voiced her disagreement, she did it with a certain amount of reverence; as if to show respect for the man, but even more so, respect for her brother. Terry said, "People who were friends could provide you with guidance and things like that, things that your father or brother would provide."

Terry was particularly interested in showing that the male was a strong figure in the black family; and in spite of his role participation it didn't weaken his position of authority. He said, "The fact that my mother worked as hard as my father didn't reduce his position as head of the household. He was the *man!* My father was the *King,* and this was his *castle.* The fact that she made more money than he did didn't make her feel superior to him."

"Is it important to think of the father as 'head of the household,' being 'a man,' or as 'King of his castle?' Aren't we, by acknowledging what the black male does or doesn't do in relationship to that of the female, devaluing the roles played by the male and strengthening those played by the female, while at the same time elevating the male, but not the female?"

"I don't think people should talk about somebody doing something because he's a man and she's a woman, although there are chores that I did because I was a man and Peggy did because she was a woman. What I'm trying to say is that if the chores had to be done, and Peggy wasn't about or my mother wasn't about, and I could do them, I would and did. It's pride, it's protection, it's learning how to take care of yourself."

Terry returned to his government job the next day, and Peggy returned to her work in New York a few days later. Although I didn't see Terry again, I visited Peggy back East.

In Vera Ridge, I continued my interviews with Alice. After she recovered from the funeral, and from hard days and sleepless nights over the death of her aunt, she invited me to her apartment to talk. Alice said she would remain in Vera Ridge, although she now lives alone. I asked why she didn't go up North to live with her daughter, and she replied, "My daughter wants me to live with her, but I'm not ready yet. I feel that she should have her young life with the things that she enjoys. I feel that I want to have my own place. Until maybe I don't want to stay here or something like that. I am as close to her as the telephone. I call her once a week and sometimes twice. And, if I'm one minute late in calling her, that phone goes to ringing. When I'm ready, I'll go to live with her, or she'll come and live with me."

Thus, the black family pivots around the mother—in this case. She provided information about all other members and all family situations. Through her, many relationships were formed and maintained. In the case of Clara, who lived in Lina, the mother kept alive relationships between Clara and Peggy. Whereas Peggy had little communication with Clara, Peggy's mother kept both Peggy and Clara informed of each other's activities. Now that Peggy's mother is dead, the communication between Peggy and Clara will probably change, although it need not.

C. Q. Grey, of Lina, turned out to be Peggy's mother's father's brother's child; but when I talked with Peggy, she said that the only thing she knew about C. Q. was what her mother had told her. She said, "When we used to send out Christmas cards, I would help Mama back the envelopes, and I always remembered the name C. Q. Mama used to talk about him a lot. Now I know some of his people. You see, wherever I'm performing throughout the states, Mama would always let me know what kinfolks live there, and tell me I should get in touch with them. But that's all I know about them."

C. Q.'s account of his family illustrated how a family's household can change when the pivotal person in the household dies, or is removed. C. Q. said, "I had eleven brothers and sisters. Most of us lived in one apartment building. Our Mama lived in one of the apartments; my sister and three brothers lived in the others. I lived next door to the apartment building. Another brother lived five blocks away, and another lived about a mile away. My Mama's youngest sister lived with her children only eight blocks down the street. I had a brother living in Chicago. My youngest brother was living with my uncle in Cleveland. Things went along well. We could always call on each other any time. My Mama would call us or we would call her every day. None of us missed a day seeing or talking with each other. When Mama died, I thought it was the end of the world for us.

"All we knew was Mama. Now we didn't have no Mama. Some of us looked to Mama's youngest sister to be our mama. I remember my Granddaddy's wife calling us and telling us she would be our mama now; but we didn't want anything to do with her. On Christmas we always got together when Mama was living. I don't have no more Christmases, except what I have with my kids. But it ain't the same somehow. None of my brothers and sisters want to go home. Most of us moved away after Mama died; and it took some time before we knew where everybody was. Mama held us together. Now just look at me. I have my own family now; but the rest of my family is scattered over the country."

The death of Peggy's mother created a lot of changes, not only between relatives and kin, but also among kin and other members of the community. Peggy said, "My Mama and Daddy was mama and daddy to two of my cousins, one on my Mama's side, the other on my Daddy's side. When they wanted to go to school, or to work, or had disagreements with their husbands, Mama's house is where they came to stay. Alice stayed here also with her daughter for awhile. So, this has always been an open house and a place where Mama and Daddy took people in and took care of them."

I asked Peggy if her career had affected her relationship with other family members. That is, had her relationships changed because of her fame. She said, "I feel like I'm a failure in life. It still is a psychological problem with me, not making a family for myself. You see, if you are raised in a religious, warm family, and then don't marry by the time you are twenty, people look at you as if you are crazy. What is more important than creating another family, having children, taking care of them, and raising them in the way you were raised? But this hasn't happened in my case. My aunts said, after I had finished school, 'Why do you want to go on . . . haven't you had enough? When are you going to get married?' "

Peggy and Terry had reached a high social level. She is a famous entertainer, and he holds a high-level job with the government. Peggy's statement sums up the attitudes held by most members of this family when she said, "I am not going to change my lifestyle as far as how I was brought up. I will continue to live the way I have always lived, as far as my relationships to the people who raised me, who brought me up; I mean, my friends and my family. The basic values are untouchable— even while I'm wearing this thousand-dollar dress to some party I have to go to because 'it's the thing to do.' When the party's over, the dress comes off, and I begin to live again. That's just being flexible. It's temporary. The dress will cover me, smother me, and I don't like this part of my career. You know how it is: you play the game so long as you know it's a game, not to you, but to them. Some of our people forget that it's a game; and that's where they go off. Mama, collard greens, and corn bread is what I grew up on and what I will carry to my grave."

ONE day, when I was sitting in a cafe eating lunch, a man came over and sat down next to me. He said that his name was John Plummer and that he had heard about me and wanted to meet me.* While we sat there talking, he told me that he was going to college to get his Master's. Since he drove over a hundred miles each way, several times a week, he asked me if I would like to go with him to Marysville the following day. Having just met the man, I didn't want to appear too anxious, so I told him that I would let him know later.

John invited me to his home. He said that his sister also wanted to meet me. We dropped some packages at his house, then walked over to a barber shop around the corner. To one side were several rooms, two of which were used for the curbside market his sister operated. She, Linda, was placing food on the shelves when we walked in. John introduced me to her, then walked into the next room and began repairing some shelves. Linda said, "I heard about you, and was wondering when you would come around. What are you doing in Vera Ridge? Things

---

* This is the John Plummer of which I earlier spoke as becoming my best friend during my stay in Vera Ridge.

are really bad here. We are really hurting down here. I knew you were in town the first time you got here. I also knew it would only be a matter of time before we met."

At the end of a very unfriendly conversation, in which she did most of the talking, John, his son Sammy, who had come home from school, and I went to John's house. John lived there with his wife Sarah and his son. The house was located on the front of a lot. At the back was an older house where his mother, Ola May, lived with his sister Linda and a male boarder. John had built his own house, and said he was going to fix up his mother's soon.

John's house was constructed with old and new materials. Some he bought; others he acquired from houses being built in the area, as well as odds and ends he picked up from different friends who were building their own homes. The unique aspect about the furniture in John's house was the tremendous stereo set he had in his living room. Every component imaginable made that up, and the rest of the furniture was moderate and very inexpensive. He and Sarah purchased their furniture from one of the department stores where you can buy four rooms of furniture for six hundred and ninety-five dollars. The furniture was worn, especially the sofa and chairs, which were slip-covered. There were end tables and a coffee-table, all of which had broken or unstable legs. John said that in time he was going to replace all the furniture in his house, but because he was going to school and only his wife worked, "It takes all the money she can make to keep me in school."

All the rooms in John's house were not completed, and were extremely small. In the living room, the panel for the walls had not been finished. Part of the ceiling required additional tiles. Only some of the light fixtures operated. In the kitchen, the cabinets weren't completed; they didn't have any doors. The counter had a loose board with a cut-out for the sink. The tiles on the floor were mismatched. There was a stove with an oven that didn't work. The bedrooms had doors that were only temporarily hung. But, as John said, "This is good enough for now.

When I finish school and get a job, I'll fix it up just the way Sarah and I want it to be."

I told him that he had done a good job, having been the only person building it or doing the major work on it. He said he was going to enlarge the rooms, as well as put on additional ones. Compared to many of the houses in Vera Ridge, John's was considered exceptional—it was the only new house in its immediate area. It was built mostly of brick, whereas the rest of the houses in the area were dilapidated wooden ones. John was very proud of his; he said, "It isn't much, but it's mine. That's the most important thing. I don't owe anything on it."

John showed me his entire house, and explained exactly how he built it, from its beginning. Then we went into the living room, and he put a record on his stereo. The sound was fantastic. Sammy asked his father if he could go out to play and John told him, "But don't play in the mud holes, and don't let me catch you going across the street."

Sammy ran happily from the room, and stepped on my foot as he ran. John caught him, and said, "What are you going to say?"

" 'Cuse me, Reggie."

"Is that all you are going to say to Reggie?"

"Noop!"

"Then say it, and take your finger out of your mouth."

"I'm sorry. I didn't mean to step on your foot."

"That's all right, Sammy."

"O.K., you can go now," John said, as he put on some water for coffee. Then he said, "I forgot to ask you, Reggie, do you drink coffee?"

"Yes, I do; but I would like something other than coffee, maybe tea."

"Well, I don't have any tea."

"That's all right; coffee will do."

"Reggie, how are the schools up North? Do black people really learn more in predominantly white schools?"

"Not having gone to any predominantly black schools, I

really can't say from first hand experience. I can only go by what has been reported. They are supposed to be better. I don't think that's the important question to ask about schools that are predominantly white, whether they are in the North or South. I think the important concern is how well do blacks learn from such schools. Frankly, I don't think blacks are taking advantage of the opportunity they have. It's not completely their fault; but still they could do better."

"Well, I went to a small college in the Midwest. The only blacks there were athletes. I don't think I learned very much. Maybe it was me, I don't know; but I just couldn't get used to going to school with whites—that's why I decided to come back home and go where I'm going."

"I don't have time right now, but I'd like to talk with you about the educational system in black schools. I have to leave, but I'll be back tomorrow if you're not busy."

"I go to school tomorrow; but I'll be here until twelve."

The next day I went by to see Linda. She began telling me about problems in Vera Ridge with "them white folks." While we were talking, a woman, very heavyset and short, came into the store. She began complaining to Linda about her not being allowed to visit her "family" in jail. She said, "Only the immediate family could visit prisoners. I'm 'family', and he's my family. I don't see what they mean by 'immediate family.' What's that, Linda?"

"That means your wife, your husband, your brothers, your sisters, your Mama and Daddy, and people like that."

"Well, I'm goin' to see him, no matter what they say. I raised him, brought him up, and cared for him. Now why can't I see him? I mean to see him and see what they're doing to him, if I have to go up there and break them white folks' jail down. And, I can do it—I'm big enough, ain't I, honey?"

Linda and I laughed. She tried to smile also; but then pounded her hand on the countertop and said, "And, you know what else? They got them signs up there saying 'white-men toilet' and 'black-men toilet.' "

Linda seemed to be surprised and said, "They don't have those anymore."

The woman put her hands on her hips and said, "Yes, they sure 'nough do, honey! Them signs are there just as big as you please. I'm tellin' you, these here white folks is a mess."

Linda turned to me and said, "See what I mean? This is the kind of shit we have to go through down here. That's the kind of thing we have to fight for. They were supposed to take them signs down a long time ago. We are supposed to go in any toilet. Segregation is supposed to be over—but not here."

The women turned to me and said, "That's the way it is down here, honey! Things ain't changed; and it's gonna take a heap of change in these white folks' mind before we will see any of it. I don't remember seeing you 'round here before. Where did you come from?"

"Well, I was born in Florida, but I. . . ."

"Uh! Oh! You ain't too much better off down there than we is up here. I remember worser things happenin' down there in 'Cracker Town' than up here. I was fixin' to say you oughtta go back where you came from, but I won't. My name is Louise, what's yours?"

"Reggie."

"Reggie who?"

"Reggie Kennedy."

"Reggie Kennedy. Is that really your name?"

"Yes, It is my name. Is it so odd? But you can call me Reg."

"My! Them white folks really messed with us, didn't they? Some of the names they done give to us is somethin' else. Reggie Kennedy—I guess that ain't so bad. It could be worse."

She walked up and down in the store. Linda told her to quiet down, that there was no use in getting all upset. She said, "I'm mad! I feel like goin' up there and blowing them motherfuckers' brains out. Oh! 'Cuse me honey, but I'm so hot I'm burning up inside. And, you know what else, Linda? Black folks can't go up there 'til after them white folks done been there. White folks can visit from one o'clock to two o'clock and blacks can't come 'til after two."

She left the store, talking to herself: "Linda, you may have to come and get me outta jail 'fore tonight's over with. No telling what I might do. . . ."

Linda said to me, "You see why we have to be so careful around here. We can't take no chances who you are. I'm gonna have to go and quiet Louise down, because she don't take no shit off of nobody, and they may do anything to her. She's been in trouble with them white folks before—this won't be the first time. They got it in for her, and this may just be the time. But I really have a lot of respect for her. She's fought for us ever since I can remember. I gotta close up now. I'll talk to you later."

A few days later, I met John's mother, Ola May, and we talked while sitting on her front porch. She knew every person who passed. They all spoke to her, and some of them came over and talked with her. She told me about Vera Ridge, and how it used to be in the past. She was unhappy with the young people of today. Ola May said, "Do you know what was the causin' of young people being so bad today? When I came up, we couldn't act like that. No Lord, indeed. We would get the worst whippin' you ever did see. And, we better not say nothin' about it, or we'd get another one. You see Sammy over there; I go to whip him for something he done bad, and he go ruffin-up and puffin-up at me like he's some man. I told him, 'I bet I'd bust you up-side your head if you come lookin' at me like that.'" She started to laugh, "I love him to death, but you can't spoil a child or you'll live to regret it later, mark my word. That's why I don't care what John say, if I see Sammy doing something wrong I'll let him know one way or the other."

"You mean John lets you beat Sammy and doesn't say anything about it?"

"He better not say anything. I'll turn around and give him some of the same thing."

"What does Sarah say about it?"

"She don't say nothing. If she say anything, it's 'Grandmama caught you doing something wrong, you see what you get for being bad.' Oh! Sometime John tell me I shouldn't beat him so much and so hard. He say I should talk to him more, but I know when to talk and when to use the strap. That's the trouble with the young people these days, folks have forgot how to use the strap."

Ola May's house is so dilapidated it seems as if it is going to fall down. This seems typical of the old homes here—especially those of wood construction. It is built on cement blocks and you can see where additions were made at different times. The porch has a cover that appears to be falling. None of the boards that make up the floor of the porch are leveled. Some are warped, and nails have come out so that the boards stick up. There are many cracks, as the boards have shrunk over time. There is a rusty, torn screen-door leading into the house. As you enter, you come to a hallway. Like the porch, the wooden boards here are warped, buckled, and contain cracks. The hallway leads to the kitchen. To the left and right of the hallway are doors leading to the living room and bedrooms.

All the furniture in the house is very old. You can smell the oldness, the dampness, and the thick dust everywhere. There is only one set of boards separating the ground and the house (making up the floor); and you can see the sand below. All the rooms are kept dark, with homemade curtains. The sofas and chairs are covered with slips. Some legs on the chairs are broken; others look as if they were chewed by a dog or eaten by termites. Ola May's bedroom is the only room in the house that is completely carpeted. The living room has many throw-rugs and the rest of the rooms are covered with linoleum. There is a kerosene stove in the living room, used for heating. In Ola May's room sits a woodfed stove; the rest of the rooms have small space-heaters. The walls and ceilings of the house are smoke-covered.

In the kitchen there is a very old sink that has loosened from its structure. The faucet constantly drips. The only modern appliance in the kitchen is a stove with an oven. The floor in the kitchen is so uneven that it dips and rises in several places. There is no inside toilet—it is located just outside the back door. The tubs are still used for bathing. The only plumbing in the house is that of the kitchen sink. From the kitchen, a door leads to an uncovered back porch. However, because of its condition no one uses it. There are missing boards; two of the cement blocks that held it up are no longer there.

Ola May works a few days a week as a maid in a private home. She also receives twenty-five dollars a week from a boarder. Ola May gets a social-security check from the government monthly. And, as she puts it, "I make a few dollars a week from the cafe." John doesn't have a job because he is a student. His wife teaches at the community college. She has a yearly salary of approximately eight thousand dollars. Linda runs the small curbside market; however, she is not making enough from the business to pay the rent on the store. Ola May's sister does day-work; and her husband is a janitor for a school. However, they have a farm where they grow vegetables and raise cows, hogs, and chickens—just enough to provide food for themselves and Ola May's household. Ola May and Sarah make some of the clothing. Sometimes they pool their money and, according to Ola May, "We get by as well as the next person. What I mean is, we ain't hurting for nothing."

After several months of being around John and his family, going to Marysville, to football games and other functions in the community, and being put on trial by Linda, I became very attached to John and developed a fond attachment with his "whole family."

Members of this family live in several structures, making up eight different households. It's a large family, with most of its members living fairly close together. I have not talked about the many cousins and friends who also make up this family— Ola May provided accounts of them. Ola May told me that all family members had lived at her house at one time or another.

In some cases, a house contains only one member; in other cases as many as eight. I divide these family members into households on the basis of the degree of interaction and interdependence that each member required of another.

Several members of this family are not connected by blood or marriage; however, they are considered members because they perform and provide certain services necessary to the functioning and maintenance of the family in the same way as blood kin—in the same way that Phillis, Jim, and Sister Child did in Family Number One.

Ola May supplies information concerning everyone in this family to the rest of its members. She knows each one's situation. Her house is the central communication point for family members. She is the pivotal core in the family's communication network.

Ola May said that her husband's aunt had a child named Georgia. Georgia came to live with Ola May when she was nine years old. She continued to live with Ola May and her husband until she finished the eighth grade. Ola May said, "We raised her until she finished high school and got married. The happiest day in my life that I can remember was when she finished the eighth grade. I didn't have nothing for her to dress in. So, a lady on Main named Sue furnished everything to my niece. Sue worked in our cafe, and she was just like one of the family."

"Can you tell me what you mean by 'just like one of the family'?"

"Like one of us. We was tight like sisters. See, my sister live fifteen miles from here, and I only saw her on weekends. Sue just made me feel like I was her sister, and I guess I made her feel the same way."

Many, especially in Family Number One, had talked about people as being members of the family, even though they weren't related to them by blood or marriage. I wanted to know more about these people who were "family" or "same as family" to other members; so I asked Ola May if she could tell me what she meant by feeling like a sister to Sue, and she said, "It's how you get along. What you do together. Like when my sister come here on the weekends, she brings me things and I have things for her to take back. We go back yonder, to my bedroom, and talk about what happened to us when we were coming up— things like that. You don't be doing these things with just any-body. It's sorta the same way between Sue and me. She brings me things, and I give her things. We talk about her folks and my folks. She know my folks as good as I do. Everytime my children come home, the first thing they say is, 'Where's Auntie Sue?' She ain't really they auntie, but they call her that because they respect her the same as they do me."

Although Ola May's children referred to Sue as Auntie, they didn't see her as being their mother's sister, but, in the words of Ola May, "They respect her the same as they do me." When I talked with John and asked him who was the lady his mother said worked in the cafe with her, he said, "You mean Auntie Sue?"

"Is she your mother's sister?"

"No, but I've been calling her that ever since I knew her."

"Is she any relation to you?"

"None that I know of. But that don't mean nothing to me."

"Can you tell me what you mean by that, 'meaning nothing to you'?"

"You see, she's a real nice lady. Sometimes when I came home from school, she'd say, 'Your mama ain't here, but I got a nice supper waitin' for you.' Sometimes she was harder on me than my own mama."

"I'm not sure I understand what you mean by harder on you."

"Well, it's like this: whereas Mama would say, 'John, make sure you clean up your mess behind yourself,' then she'd just go and leave me to do it. Auntie Sue, she won't be standing right over me, but I knew she'd be somewhere watching me. Some-times I'd try to sneak away, but she'd catch me and say, 'Oh, no, you don't do that. Get back there and clean up your mess 'fore I get this dishrag to you.' I used to get so mad at her, but

I'm glad she was that strict with me. She taught me a lot of things that have stuck with me and made me the person I am today."

He laughed and said, "You may not think it's much, but I think it's a lot. I could be out there doing what so many people my age are doing; but I got my own mind and I think that's a lot. I'm going to school so that I can make something out of myself. I could be gambling away my money—if I was working—and my wife's money. I could be going out with all kinds of women, mistreating my family, my people—I don't want to do these things. The only way we are ever going to get ahead in life is not to succumb to those temptations and make a place in this world for ourselves—no matter how hard and how long it may take us."

Linda also said that Sue was a part of the family. I talked with the neighbors next door and those across the street from Ola May; they too agreed that Sue had done almost as much for John and Linda and the other members of their family as Ola May did. The next time I talked with Ola May, she brought up the topic of Sue again, and how she had provided her niece with a dress for graduation. Ola May said, "Sue gave Georgia everything she needed for graduation. At the particular time I didn't have it, and didn't know where I was going to get it. Sue didn't know I didn't have it—least I don't think so. I didn't tell her. I was going to get it somehow. I didn't know how I was going to get it. Sue just walked up and told me one day, 'I'm gonna get the dress for Georgia and the shoes.' She did lots of things for Georgia, and the rest of my children too."

Sue isn't only considered to be a member of the family by other members, but I have also heard neighbors refer to her as John's auntie. She talked about herself as a member of the family also. She told me that she helped raise "them chillun" until they were grown—"all of them." She said, "I didn't have none of my own, but they're just like mine too. I tell Ola May this sometimes and she say, 'You must have somethin' there, 'cause they minded you better than they did me.' "

Ola May talked about another woman, Resa, who did things for her and vice versa; but she didn't think of Resa as part of "the family." She said, "I still see Resa today. She married a first cousin of mine; she's living. She lives over there in her mama's house. She lived with us at the time I'm talking about. When her husband died, she lived with us. She was like a mama to all of us, and we loved her very much. So, she's over there, and that's the person I go to see every day. She's the person I took the collard greens to."

"Is she a member of your family?"

"Well, I wouldn't say 'family.' She's just a dear and close friend. She was so good to us when we was coming up. I'll never forget her for what she did for us. That's the reason you see me going over there every day. She is sick and stays in bed. She's there all alone, with nobody to take care of her. She have some children, but God knows where they are. They don't come to see her. I couldn't do my mama that way, no Lord, indeed. I musta raised my children right, because if they even think something's wrong with me they would be right here. Sometimes they fuss over me so much I tell them to get outta here and leave me alone—just like I'm mad or something. Actually, I love them for that. It make me feel so good—so proud of them. But I don't let them always know it—otherwise they'd be hugging me to death. Poor Resa, she don't deserve to be treated that way—not a'tall."

Sue's and Resa's relationships to Ola May seemed very much alike. Resa's affiliation, however, was limited to Ola May and her siblings, and didn't extend to the rest of Ola May's family. Ola May often talked about someone being "like a mama" or "a sister," and sometimes spoke of them as being the "same as mama" or the "same as sister." She didn't consider those who were "like" a relative as a member of the family. On the other hand, those people who were seen as "the same as" a relative were considered part of the family. The distinction is between "the same as" versus "similar to."

Ola May gave me many examples of people who passed

through her life and through her household; however, she would merely mention them if they weren't considered family. Mayola, the daughter of Ola May's husband's aunt, is not connected to Ola May by blood, yet she is considered a family member. Ola May said, "Mayola is the same as a sister to me. I just visited Mayola last summer. Let me tell you why she is the same as a sister to me. It is because she's the same as my real sister. When we were living on the other side of the freeway, a Mr. Clarence was her mother's boyfriend. My Daddy would stay gone all the time. Mr. Clarence would bring her mama plenty of food; and Roxanne, that's Mayola's mama, was getting the stamps from the welfare too. Because my mama was a preacher's wife, we couldn't get them. So Roxanne would always divide with us."

"Is Mayola the same as Sue to you?"

"I think of both of them as part of the family. They're both the same as sisters to me, only you could say that Sue is like an older sister. There isn't a thing I wouldn't do for both of them— not a thing in the world—if I had it."

"If Sue asked you for something and Mayola asked you for the same thing, at the same time, which one would you give it to?"

"You mean if they asked me for it right then and there?"

"Yes, so that you had to make a choice between the two."

"No! That wouldn't happen. I wouldn't make a choice between the two of them. That would never happen anyway. And just in case it did, if I couldn't give it to both of them—then I wouldn't give it to neither one of them. I would rather tell them I don't have it, and then wait until I could get another one so that I could give it to both of them. How could I choose between Sue and Resa? I told you all the things Sue did for me and my family; Mayola and her mama did the same for us. Some of the furniture my brother is sleeping on today is furniture that she gave us. Roxanne didn't have no sister, and my mama was the same as a sister to her. Her daughter Mayola and I became so close that we went for sisters. We really loved each other, and nobody could tell the difference. We were together, we were just like two peas in a shell. Wherever I was, she was and the same for me. Her mama brought something for her, she brought something for me. My mama bought something for me, what little it was, she did the same for Mayola."

Just as people who are not connected by blood or marriage can be members of the family, so people who are connected by blood and marriage may be considered not a part of the family. Ola May has had many people living with her who are thought of as family, but some blood kin who lived with her weren't considered family. She spoke of another person, a cousin by blood, as being just a "dear friend." Ola May said, "My cousin that's dead, we were very close friends. She had a sister living here. Her baby sister too. Now the reason why we were very close friends, closer than her own sister to her, was because there were a lot of things that she couldn't talk to her sister about, but she would talk to me. We were good friends until we fell out. I just had to tell her, no man can beat me like she'd let her man do it to her. So, I just jumped up and told her so. I know a lot of women who like to be beat by they man, but I just think it's a sickness or somethin'."

"Did your husband ever hit you?"

"No! Ain't gonna let no man go beating on me. My husband, he never laid a hand on me. Oh! Yes he did—once; but he never did it again after that first time. I was standing in the kitchen, cooking, and he came in late. He was tired and hungry, and he started to fuss at me for not having the supper ready. I told him if he couldn't wait until I had it cooked, he could eat it raw. He slapped me hard—right across my face. I didn't say nothing to him. I just walked in my bedroom, packed up my things, and went to my mama."

"He didn't try to stop you? He just let you go without saying anything?"

"He didn't say nothing. He just stayed in the kitchen. For over a week I didn't see him, and I didn't hear from him. My mama told me I was a fool for staying away from my husband.

But I stayed away, and I didn't try to see him or get in touch with him. Then one day, in the evening, he came over to Mama's house. He knocked on the door, and my mama answered it. I heard him say, 'Is Ola here?' (That's what he called me—Ola.) My mama came in the kitchen where I was, and told me that he was here. I walked in the living room where he was. He stood there and looked at me, and then he said, 'Ola, why don't you come home?' I asked him if he was going to hit me again, and he said, 'No!' That was all to it. I got my things and came back to our house. He never hit me again. Well, I told my cousin she was a fool for letting her husband keep hitting on her. Since I jumped up and told her that, she never spoke to me again—God rest her soul."

One of the special ways members of different families indicate who is or is not a family member (whether the relationship is by blood, marriage, or mutual consent) is by the distinct use of personal pronouns. Although this isn't a rule, it is an indicator. For example, Ola May referred to the cousin's sister (by right also a cousin of Ola May) as "*her* baby sister." Why didn't she refer to her as "my cousin?" She also referred to the same person's disagreement as "fighting each other from the same family." Why not, "fighting each other from our family?" The example is the same as: mine and his/hers, us and them, ours and yours, and so on—all illustrating a separation rather than a union of the two.

Ola May goes on to say, "Her mama [the cousin] forsaked Gracy Lee [the cousin's daughter] here, and I took her in. When she left to go where her mama was, she had to hustle up on the street to get enough money to go where her mama was. She wasn't but fifteen years old—to go where her mama was."

Throughout my fieldwork with this and other families, I noticed that the use of the possessive was an indication that a person was considered or not considered a family member. It may be an indicator, but it isn't necessarily one that produces a hard and fast rule as to who is and is not a member.

Many times, members of this family included nonbiological

or nonmarital members as part of "the family." One day I was talking with John, and he spoke of a person whom he referred to as brother. According to the genealogy I had constructed of this family John didn't have a brother. In the process of talking with John, I had noticed certain references to a person named Billy. They called each other "Bro." Because this family has a number of complex relationships with community members, I never assumed anything until it was brought to my attention. John said Billy was the same as a brother. He said, "You see, I didn't have a brother. I hated my sisters always fussing over me all the time. Billy went to school with me. We were in the same grade. I used to bring him home with me all the time. One day I asked my mama if he could stay with us. She told me that she would have to find out from his mama, and then ask my daddy. His mama and my daddy said it would be all right for him to stay. From the third grade until the eighth grade, Billy lived with us. He still calls me 'Bro' and he calls my mama, 'Mama'."

Like Ola May, John made clear distinctions between people who were considered "family" or "just like family" or "part of family," and people who weren't. As Ola May said, it is not simply an exchange of goods and services, or living in the same house that determines a person's family relationship. It is a type of closeness that, according to Ola May, encompasses a "whole lot more than that."

Ola May spoke of a schoolteacher who devoted much of her time to Ola May's oldest daughter. She said, "Me and her was just like sisters, even when me and her was at my daughter's house in Houston. Oh, we were just like two peas in a shell. And her and my mama was good friend too. You see what I mean? She was just a friend of the family."

This teacher never gained the status of a family member, in spite of the services she provided for the daughter of Ola May. Ola May said, "Miss Williams, the schoolteacher, she taught school out at Grover High. She's the reasoning of my oldest daughter finished school. When my daughter graduated, Miss Williams bought her graduating clothes. She bought her grad-

uation things for her to graduate in. She was just a friend of
the family—a good friend. She helped my daughter through
high school. The things that she needed, she got."

Ola May is always busy trying to keep every one of her relatives connected with her households. She looks ahead as she
says, "When I married my husband, I got in good with his folks
'cause he loved them. I loved him. I knew if I was going to make
it with him, I had to make it with his folks. After we married
and come to Vera Ridge, his mother would come to Vera Ridge
to see us. She would come for two or three months. Most of the
time she spent with us. She had three sisters here, but she would
stay with us. Let me tell you what I would try to do. I'd try to
get in good with all my children's wives and husband's people.
Get in good with them. If something happened to your children's wives or husbands, you can always see your grandchildren if you stay in good with them."

She spoke of a Mrs. Richards across the street from where she
lived. Mrs. Richards had four sons. They all got married and
had children, and she used to have many grandchildren at her
house. Ola May said that you could always look across the street
and see a yard full of children. Then things began to happen
with her children's marriages. One by one the marriages broke
up, till all her sons had divorced or separated from their wives.
Ola May said, "Now, that poor woman is very lonely. 'Cause
when her sons got their divorce or separated, their wives took
the children with them. Now you take Sarah, John's wife. I may
lose her; but if there's any other daughter-in-law coming in, I'll
treat her the same as I treated Sarah, whether she accepts it or
not. If something happened between John and Sarah, I know
I'll be able to see my grandchild. Now I'm not saying that's the
only reason you should stay in good with people. You should
stay in good with people all the time."

Ola May is constantly busy trying to "keep the family together." When one method fails, she uses another approach. Her
oldest daughter had two children before she died. Ola May

didn't have a good relationship with Barry, the daughter's husband. Therefore, she doesn't see her two grandchildren very much. She said, "Now, just like Barry, he won't give me his telephone number. After I see him one more time, I'm going to talk with him. I'm going to sit down and have a nice long talk with him. I'm going to stay in with Barry. I love Barry. You know why I love Barry—my daughter loved him. If she loved him, I love him too. Because the ways he's got, ain't got nothing to do with that. She stayed with him and suffered with him and died with him. I'll stay with him too. I'm still with him. You see, in this way I can see my grandchildren. He used to bring them to see me at least twice a year. Then only in the summer. Now, I haven't seen them in two years. I don't know what's going wrong. I'm going to have a talk with him. I'll get that telephone number if it's the last thing I do—you just wait and see."

Although Barry has broken off communication with Ola May, it does not stop her from trying to "get in good with him" so that she can see her grandchildren. Barry's mother lives in Vera Ridge, and Ola May takes the trouble to look after her because she wishes to reach Barry through her kindness to his mother. Ola May said, "See, this lady's been dying. My daughter and her husband sent her to Dallas to get her radium treatments. My daughter had cancer, and died from it. She left her still sitting here. Look like ain't a thing wrong with her. Last year she lost her eyesight, can't see a thing, poor soul; but look like she's just the picture of health. Last night, I mean Saturday evening, when I went by there, I stayed until her daughter went to get the groceries. She was grunting; and that's the first time I've ever heard her grunt. You know what happened? She would tell me things to make me laugh while I was sitting there. You know what I did? I got up and put hot cloths on her and when I left she was dead 'sleep. See what I mean? She wasn't hurting after I did that. You see, these young people don't know about these things. Some older person have to go by and tell them what to do. See, young people don't know about things like this. And she was 'sleep when I left. Now Barry appreciate things like that. He may not like some of the things I do, but he respects me for how I treat his mama."

Ola May is always looking ahead. She said it is "because you never know what may happen between these young people nowadays."

She told me that John had a baby by another woman before he married Sarah, and that she had expected John to marry this woman, Tessie. She said that John and Tessie had courted from childhood. When John didn't marry Tessie, Ola May went to work to keep on the "good side" of Tessie. She said, "In this way, I could always see my grandchild."

Sarah, the woman whom John did marry, is now the objective of Ola May. She said, "I have visited Sarah's mother many times, and she have been to my house. I'm going to get in good with her, and stay in good. You never know what may happen between John and Sarah."

While we were talking, Sarah came in and told Ola May (whom she refers to as "Ma") that she would have supper ready in awhile, that she had to come and bake some bread in Ola May's oven. Ola May said, "All right, honey; can I help you with anything?"

Sarah told her that she had everything under control. Sammy, John's and Sarah's son, came in while Ola May and I were talking. He wanted me to walk him across the street, so that he could buy a soda. He knew that he couldn't go across the street by himself. Ola May said, "Sammy! Can't you see I'm talking with Reggie? Now you run along and play in the back."

Sammy sat there with his lips stuck out. Ola May said, "Now you know better than that. I'll put a strap to you in a minute. Now you do like I told you."

Sammy stood up and pretended that he was going; then he took me by the hand and said, "Come on, Uncle Reggie."

Ola May stood up and pretended she was going to get a belt and Sammy ran out of the house. She laughed and said, "He knows I mean business, the little mannish rascal."

She continued to talk about her relationship with Sarah. "Now you see, I'm going to stay in good with Sarah so I can always see my grandchildren. See, there! That's what mamas don't think about. I'd try to be friends with them. You can see your children when you get ready to see them. Be friends to everybody. Now, I may not find another daughter-in-law like Sarah, and, ah, I might lose her; but if there's any other daughter-in-law, I'm going to treat her just like I treated Sarah."

Ola May saw herself as being so much in command that she doesn't talk about John, her son, in relationship to Sarah. In Ola May's eyes, it is *she* who might lose Sarah, not John. And, should *she* lose her, *she* is ready to go to work on her replacement.

Ola May said, "Sarah, she's the best daughter-in-law you can ask for. You know what? When my daughter got sick up in Houston, she went with us. That's before she got married to John. While we were going back and forth to the hospital to see my daughter, Sarah would stay at home and cook. She kept my daughter's children clean, sent them off to school, and when money got tight, she got a job on the side. Barry should be very grateful to her. She would come home tired from her job; but she didn't sit down until the house was clean, the food was cooked, and the dishes were washed. When I'd come home from the hospital, she'd be sitting in a chair—fast sleep—staying up, waiting for us to come back."

Ola May paused to wipe her eyes. It was the first time that I had seen her act emotional. She told me that I would have to excuse her, but every time she thought about her daughter, tears came to her eyes. She said that I would have to excuse her. I told her I understood, and asked her if I should come back later. She said that she would be all right, and that she would like to go on. I asked her, "How long was your daughter sick?"

"My daughter was always sickly; but during this time she was very sick. And she knew she wasn't going to make it. That's why she asked us all to come. She had . . . I can't think for

the life of me what they call it. You know what I mean . . . so
many people die from it . . . I can't remember, but it'll come
to me. Anyway, we stayed up there for four months—'till the
end."

"Did she have cancer? That's what you told me before."

"Yes, I know, but there's a name for the kind of cancer she
had. I'll think of it. Isn't it funny, when you want to think of
something, you can't; and the harder you try the more you
can't think of it. It'll come to me. Anyway, she knew she was
going to die; so we all expected it. Because we were prepared
for it, when it happened it didn't hit too hard. She suffered for
a long time. I'd go to the hospital to see her, and she never complained—not once—and I knew she was suffering. Even near
the end, when she couldn't remember too well, she would remember me. She used to say, 'Mama, is that you? Are you
hungry? Will you eat with me?' Barry, he took it real hard. It
happened that afternoon. John and me was going to see her;
Linda, she and another one of my daughters was already there.
We was walking down the hall to the room where she was, and
Linda ran up to us, crying. 'Mama,' she said, 'Lilly's gone now.'
I told John for us to turn 'round and go back home. I told Linda
to have strength, to straighten up and act right. We expected
this. She had suffered a long time. So, we went on back home.
We were all sitting 'round, trying to plan what we should do,
when Barry came home from work. I called him into the
kitchen. He said he had to get ready to go to the hospital to see
Lilly. I told him that she had passed away. He just went to
bawling. Then he busted out crying and carrying on like a little
baby. There was nothing we could do to make him stop. He
flung himself in a corner on the kitchen floor. Finally, when I
thought he had had enough, I went to him and told him to get
up and stop crying. When I told him that, he went to cussin'
me. John and Linda came in, and told him not to cuss they
mama. I told them to go on back and sit down, that I could take
care of this. He told us to get out of his house. I told him this
was my daughter's house too. He started throwing things

around. We decided it was best to leave; but Sarah, she stayed there. She's the only one that could seem to talk to him. He should always remember what Sarah done for him.''

It is reported by Ola May and John that Tessie (the woman John had a baby with) hates Sarah; and Sarah hates Tessie. Tessie's husband hates John and vice versa. The two people who keep the relationship going are Ola May and Tessie's son by John. In this way, Ola May can always see her grandchild.

Not all the people living in Ola May's house are members of the family. A roomer also lives there. There is talk in the community that he is courting Ola May, but she denies it. He is not a member of the family but "a friend," according to Ola May. She said, "I begged him to come down here and take a room, because I was here by myself. Linda was living in New York then. I don't intend to stay by myself. A lot of people are so selfish. They can just stay by themselves. I can't do that. I can't stay by myself. I begged this man to come down here and take this room. People can say anything they want about it. I'm looking out for myself, that's the main reason. You see, if that was the case, I could have went up there whenever I wanted to, he has a big house; but I needed somebody here with me. . . .''

"You know what?" Ola May said, "he don't do nothing 'round the house lately. He used to sorta clean the kitchen up. He don't work nowhere. I told him the other night to find himself a hustle. That tickled the old man to death. He gets a check. He gets a pretty good little old check. I'm hustling a little bit myself. . . . I said to him, 'Why don't you find yourself something to do?' The old man is sick. He's sick, really sick. His blood pressure was over a hundred and something last week. He's down now. He went to the doctor yesterday. He could clean the kitchen up and sweep the floor. Now he could do that, couldn't he? Now I do that while I'm here. When I come home at nights, I do it.''

I have observed the old man doing chores around the house. He sweeps the front porch over and over. When he gets tired of sweeping the porch, he sits in the rocking-chair and rocks, and talks to people who pass by. He gives his check to Ola May for safekeeping. He has unrestricted access to the whole house, with the exception of Ola May's bedroom. However, no one referred to him as a member of the family. He does not refer to himself as a member. The lady next door refers to him as "Old Man Jones." She said that all he does is "sit on Ola May's porch and rock his life away."

Even though John has his own house, he, his wife, and son sleep, eat, and cook periodically at Ola May's. Sammy comes to Ola May's house every day after school for meals. Linda stays at Ola May's house. On weekends, Ola May's sister and the sister's husband bring meat and vegetables; and in return Ola May gives them staples from her weekend shopping. Linda, although she stays in Ola May's house, takes frequent trips to Cleveland. She cannot take living in a small town like Vera Ridge "because there is no action here." Ola May and John encourage her to settle down, but Linda told me that "it won't be long before I'm gone again."

FAMILY
NUMBER THREE

*T*HE second day I was in Vera Ridge, Mr. Walker took me to the hospital with him. He was visiting someone he referred to as "Johnny's wife." He also had to visit a man named Beaufus, and someone he called "Slim." Slim had been accidentally shot by his brother who was attempting to save his life while he was fighting with another person. While we were at the hospital, I walked around the halls. I didn't want to be present while Mr. Walker visited with Clara, Johnny's wife. Outside Clara's room, a man sat, holding his head in his hands. He looked as if he were in tears. I became curious and decided to speak to him.

He told me that his name was Johnny, and that he had been at the hospital all night. His wife Clara had had surgery. He said that ever since his wife had been operated on, he had spent his nights with her at the hospital. During the day, he worked as an automobile mechanic. He went home to check on his two children—a boy seven years old and a girl of six. Then he returned to the hospital to be with his wife. He said, "My wife has female problems."

I wasn't sure what he meant by that, but didn't want to seem too nosy. Clara's mother was present in the room. After Mr.

Walker's visit with Clara, he turned to this woman—her name
was Willie Bell—and they began to talk about Clara. I heard
her say, "I have been sitting here all night with my child."

After Mr. Walker came out of the room, Johnny went in. I
talked with Mr. Walker about Johnny's wife's problems. He
said, "It's a sad story. Clara's been in and out of the hospital. If
it ain't one thing, it's another. They are a hard-luck couple.
Johnny works hard, and every time he saves up a little money,
something like this happens. He's a good husband and a good
daddy to his children."

Mr. Walker told me that this would be a good family to study.
He said that all the members belong to his church, and that he
would introduce me to the whole family next Sunday in church.
I wondered if he was suggesting that I go to church.

The first time I went over to Johnny's house, he was lying
on a sofa-bed, looking at a baseball game. He remembered me
from the hospital, and invited me in. At first, he was more interested in watching the ballgame than in talking with me, so
I watched it with him. Then he said he was resting up, because
he had to go back to the hospital. He was looking after his children and his sisters' children also. His sisters were at the hospital, visiting his wife Clara. When they returned, he would go
to the hospital. He offered me some food that he had cooked
himself. I told him I had already eaten. He said he really cooked
well. If I didn't believe him, I could ask his sister Betty. I said I
believed him, but that I had just finished eating.

Johnny's and Clara's apartment was very small—as are most
of the apartments in the housing project. They had only one
bedroom. Their two children slept on the sofa-bed. There was
one area that served as the living room, with a counter dividing
it from the kitchen. With the exception of a couple of end-tables
and a coffee-table, only a chair and sofa completed the living-
room furniture. A dining table sat in the center of the floor. The
floors were tiled and a few throw-rugs lay in the living room
and bedroom. The entire apartment was furnished with items
Clara bought from the furniture factory where she worked. She

said that it only cost her four hundred and fifty dollars. There were no slipcovers over the furniture; and even though she said it was three years old, there didn't seem to be much wear on it.

This apartment, like all the apartments in this complex, was poorly built. The electrical system was faulty, and fires had broken out as a result. Johnny said there had already been two small fires in his apartment. The walls were so thin you could hear people who lived in the apartments next door, as well as those above. The roof leaked; water stains could be seen on the ceiling as well as on the walls. The screens were torn off the windows and doors; Johnny said he had replaced them several times, but wasn't going to again. The doors didn't lock and his front door has a hole in it. Because the apartment building is built on the ground, the sandy soil is constantly brought in on one's shoes. Johnny said that he and Clara were saving money to build their own house on a lot they already own. It was a lot that belonged to his mother and father and the father had left it in his name. There was some initial dispute between him, his mother, and sisters. However, he won out. Everyone living in these apartments agreed that they were better off than they were where they formerly lived; however, "The amount of money we have to pay, we should get better than this," Johnny said.

Both Johnny and Clara worked. Their weekly combined income was approximately two hundred and ten dollars. However, Johnny only brings home fifty to sixty dollars, as Betty, his sister, said, "He throws the rest away gambling." Johnny's rent is one hundred dollars a month, but he has to pay for all utilities except water. According to his wife, their combined income would be enough to take care of their bills, pay the rent, and buy food and clothes. However, "Most of the time I don't see none of Johnny's money. He gambles it away." Johnny's and Clara's income is supplemented by Clara's mother, who provides food, clothing, and money for the children.

Half an hour later, his sisters, Betty and Cathy, and a person who lived next door, returned from the hospital. I was introduced to them. They immediately became friendly and offered me food. Johnny said, "Aha! You can eat Betty's cooking, but you won't eat mine."

Betty responded, "I don't blame him. All that red pepper you use. I wouldn't eat it either. I never saw somebody who put red pepper in everything they cook. I bet you put it in your coffee."

"You never complained about my cooking before."

"Ain't nothing wrong with his cooking, if you like hot food," Cathy, the youngest sister, said.

They all laughed, even Johnny. Then Betty said, "His cooking is all right. I was just teasing him. Actually, he can cook better than me."

We spent about three hours in talking. They wanted to know all about me, and vice versa. I ate a little, and Betty gave me more. Children came in and went out constantly. It was difficult for me to figure out which children belonged to whom. Realizing that I was having a problem, Betty said, "Honey! Don't worry about trying to figure out all the kids' names. Half of 'um belong to me. Sometimes *I* get them mixed up. They know this; and sometimes they try to trick me."

I asked if I could visit again to talk, once in awhile, and they all agreed.

I developed a close connection with all of them, as I had with members of the other families. I took Betty places she wanted to go. I even took their children to school. I helped Betty organize a group of workers who wanted higher wages; but when I saw that they would lose their jobs, I suggested to Betty that perhaps the time wasn't right. Johnny and I played pool together. Every Friday, we played cards and listened to music. There were times when we went to bars. I even went to church with some of the family. I saw at least one member of this family daily. Often I was asked to mediate family agruments that occurred almost daily between members. Also, they wanted me to go to the landlord and pressure him into repairing faulty fixtures in their apartments.

Other family members were: an older brother, his wife and

seven children; Ludy, the mother; Willie Bell; Clara's mother, Cynthia; her husband and child who are next-door neighbors; Betty's sister- and mother-in-law; and Betty's "boyfriend." Betty has five children, and Cathy, two.

The next time I visited this family, Johnny's wife had just returned from the hospital. She was lying on a sofa-bed, in great pain. Johnny was preparing food. Clara said that she was "hurting all over." I asked if there was anything I could do, and she said no. I decided this was not a good time for an interview, so I would return later. They thanked me, and asked if I would come back as soon as Clara was "up and on her feet."

I went next door to Betty's apartment, and told her about the trial I had had with some of the leading citizens of Vera Ridge— including Linda and Mrs. Mables. She told me of the problems she faced at work in the sugar factory. Her greatest problems came from within—"my own people." She said, "It's our own people that give me so much trouble. The white folks are bad enough, but our people, well, they take the cake—they're something else."

Betty had a two-bedroom apartment. She, like Johnny and Clara, had purchased a packaged grouping for every room. Because she got it through Clara, she only had to pay five hundred and ninety-five dollars instead of six hundred and ninety-five. Betty's furniture was very different from Clara's; it was more "Hollywood-like." It was large, and occupied most of the room. There was little walking space between the furniture. She had huge lamps sitting on end-tables. They were of ceramic female figures, with the light stem coming out of their heads and a wide lampshade on top of each. The living room looked more like a temporary Hollywood set. She had plastic custom-made slipcovers that had begun to rip. There were plastic flowers everywhere.

Tall, bright-red drapes, falling off their hinges, covered the windows. Betty told me not to pay too much attention to her house, because she didn't intend to put any more money into it. She, like her brother, was saving up money to build a house on a lot she said she had already paid for. Betty made only two dollars and fifteen cents an hour; and said, "After they take everything out, I only bring home eighty dollars a week." Of course, she received money from a "boyfriend" who lived in Michigan. She also received money from her divorced husband. "When he sends it," Betty said. Her divorced husband's mother and sister helped to support Betty and her children. Betty is eligible to get food stamps; however, she said, "You have to pay seventy dollars for one hundred and twenty-five dollars' worth of stamps. Who has that kind of money at one time to shell out?"

Betty works six days a week; and she says she does all the overtime she can get. Still and all, "I barely get enough money to make ends meet." She is supposed to receive alimony from her divorced husband, but said, "The last time I got anything from him was over a year ago." Because she, her brother, sister, and a neighbor pool their resources, she says, "We can get by. I don't throw away my money. Now some people, they go by the store every day, just giving that white man their money. Me, I shop only once a week. I look for specials; and I buy my food downtown at the supermarket. In that way, I can stretch my money and get the most out of it. That's one thing my kids won't have to do—go for want of food."

Betty has to pay only ninety dollars a month for her rent because of her income and the number of children she has. She said that between food, rent, and the children's clothes, her money is accounted for—"every penny of it." She said, "I need a coat for this winter, but I won't have enough money to pay for it. My children come first. I already hinted to Louis, my boyfriend, that I need a coat; I think he'll get it for me. He's always come through for me; but if he don't, I'll go without."

As we were talking, Cynthia, the next-door neighbor, came by on her way to work. She dropped off her little girl for Betty to keep until her husband returned from his work. Cynthia smiled at me, and then said she would like to talk to me sometime. After she had gone, Betty said, "I know what she wants. Actually, she is one of the family, but she's something else."

"What do you mean, she's one of the family?"

"Well, she's not related to us by blood, but we've known each other since we were kids. She's the same as a sister to me."

"Tell me, how is she like a sister?"

"It's like this: anything I ask her for, if she's got it, I know I can get it. Anything I ask her to do, if she can do it she will. All of us are working at different times. We don't have to worry about our kids eating or getting to school on time. I do the same for her. We all pitch in and help each other out. These are the kind of things you expect your kinfolks to do."

"You said kinfolks. What about your relatives?"

"Well, I know I have a lot of relatives. They are just people who may be related to you somehow. You may or may not know them. They may be scattered all over the place. But my kinfolks, no matter where they are, I know all of them and I see them almost every week."

"Cynthia is like kinfolk to me. In my eyes, she's kin. You're close to your kinfolks, and I am very close to Cynthia—we all are."

"Is Cynthia the same as a kinfolk?"

"Well, being like or being the same, is that different? Sometimes I say that people are like, for example, a brother; but I don't mean really like a brother—in the case of Cynthia, she is kinfolk, she treat me the same and I treat her the same as I do all my kinfolks."

"So, if there are people that you find out are related to you by blood and you didn't know about them, are they kinfolk?"

"If a relative came to my door, I would be nice and all that. I would invite him or her in, whatever may be the case. I would feed him if he was hungry, but I wouldn't go outta my way for someone just because he's a relative that I didn't know. He would have to prove himself to me first. I would have to get to know him—things like that."

"But you would go out of your way for Cynthia?"

"All the way! She's closer to me than some of my own blood that I know. I have some relatives I wouldn't do anything for before Cynthia. My mama, for one, but we won't get into that."

I wanted to ask her more about the situation concerning her mother, but thought it better to wait. We talked about her job instead. I told her I had to go for another interview, and asked if I could return later. She said, "Anytime."

I spent many hours at this family's residence. I went to the pool hall with Johnny. He worked on my car, and didn't charge me for his work. Betty would call me daily. She and I became very close—closer than I ever had imagined. I only realized how close when Johnny asked me if I was going to marry her. Betty would come by my trailer many times, but I never felt that our behavior went beyond a friendly "get-together." Once she asked me if I had a girl. I told her that I was married, and she said, "But your wife isn't here. You need someone here."

I asked her what people would think if they saw me bringing a girl into my house, and she said, "Who cares what people think? They're gonna talk no matter what you do. You're a nice young man and not from here. But you can slip her in at night and nobody will see you, if that bothers you. You needn't worry —before long, people will have you doing all sorts of things, anyway—so you might as well be doing some of them."

This was the second time I had found myself in a situation where a woman had interpreted my friendship as a courtship. Questions came to my mind: What was I doing that I was unaware of to create in others a sense that I was courting them? Had I placed myself in a mental condition of not being able to uncode communication that elsewhere would have been natural for me? Why didn't I see a courtship relationship developing? These are just some questions about my own behavior that I was concerned with in the attempt to understand other people's behavior.

One day, I was sitting at my desk when I heard fire engines. They seemed to be heading in the direction of Betty's apartment. I got in my car and drove over to her place. When I got there, I found that Johnny's apartment was on fire. Almost everything he owned had been or was being destroyed. An old woman was running around, trying to be helpful. She kept getting in the way of the people who were moving furniture from the apartment building. Finally, Betty said, "Mama! Will you please go somewhere and sit down!"

"But, I'm only trying to be of some help."

"I know you are trying to be of some help; that's why you should sit down before somebody knocks you down."

Johnny came over to me and said, "Man! I seem to have the worst luck in the world. Just seems like everything's happening to me."

I tried to comfort him. I remembered that I had cooked some red beans and rice, so I invited the family over for dinner. After I had done all I could at Johnny's place, I returned home to prepare the food. I asked Johnny's family to come; however, Betty and her children, Johnny, his wife, and his children, Cathy, her husband, and her children, and Cynthia, her husband, and daughter came. It was then that I understood Betty's remark about Cynthia being a part of the family. I was living in my trailer by then, and don't know how all those people managed to squeeze in, but they did. I had only told Johnny that "the family" was invited to dinner. I was referring to Johnny, his wife, and his children—but they brought the whole clan!

Johnny received money and clothing from his employer because of the fire. Clara was also given furniture by the factory where she worked. Other people also contributed things. A couple of nights after the fire, I got a phone call from Betty. She said that Johnny was coming over to see me. She wanted me to persuade him not to go to the pool hall. She said it wouldn't look right for him to shoot pool and make bets, after so many people had been so nice to them. When Johnny came by, I tried to ply him with enough whiskey so that he wouldn't go out. I managed to keep him with me for over four hours. He kept insisting that we should go to the pool hall. I kept telling him, "After the next drink." I didn't know how long I could hold out. He was so drunk by the end of the night that I had to drive him home. I really didn't know if I was able to make it, because I was also drunk. I managed to drive his car to his apartment; and after I had seen him home I walked back to my place. The next day, Betty called to thank me for keeping Johnny away from the pool hall. Clara also telephoned to thank me.

The family invited me to one of their parties. The party was at Cynthia's apartment—upstairs from Johnny's. I took my camera and tape recorder. It was a "nice" party at the beginning. Everything was going smoothly; everyone was having fun, or appeared to be. They danced, drank, and played cards. Then, as Clara started to get drunk, she began accusing people. She accused Cynthia of "being with my man"—meaning her husband. Cynthia had invited a "girlfriend," and had gotten the girlfriend a "companion." Clara said the girlfriend had a husband in the military and should not be "fooling around" with another married man.

As the party progressed, Clara became worse. Betty said she would leave, because she didn't like the situation. In time, all became quiet again. Clara was dancing and falling on the floor. Johnny didn't like this. He told her to sit down many times, but she refused. Finally, Johnny said, "Why don't us men go out, we can have more fun." I was asked to come along, but they had been drinking too much and I didn't want to chance a car accident. I really wanted to get home, so that I could record some of the information from the party. Once the men decided to go out alone, Clara encouraged the women to go out by themselves also. So, they took separate cars and left. I packed my belongings, and returned to my place.

The following day, I received calls from everyone at the party. They all apologized for their behavior, but especially Clara's behavior. They were all concerned about the pictures and tape I had made. I told them not to worry, that I had played the tape and the music had obscured most of the conversations.

I also said I would destroy the film. Some were satisfied with my statements; others came over to check with me again.

This party gave me a deeper understanding of the lives of the family members. I felt that I had reached a position of trust with some people, for example, those who took my word that the conversations were obscured by the music and that I would destroy the film. Those who came to check and make sure I had indeed destroyed the tape and film had not yet learned to trust me. But we can't jump to the conclusion that the ones most worried had the most to "lose," should the information go beyond me. If that were the case, the girl and Clara would have come to my place also. What went on at the party seems to contradict information that other members had given me about Cynthia and her relationship with the rest of them.

Later, Johnny came over because he said he wanted to assure me that he hadn't had any sexual relationships with Cynthia. Then he said, "although I've been tempted. She wants it. I know she do, and I want it too; but I respect Clara. Clara and Cynthia are too close. Cynthia is too tied up in the family for me to be 'messing round' like that."

Cynthia was concerned about her girlfriend, who felt that if I had pictures or conversations on tape they might get back to her husband. Cynthia said, "God knows I don't know what got into Clara last night, 'cusing me of messing round with her old man. As long as we've been together, she ain't never said something like that to me. She apologized this morning for what she said. They say that when you're drunk you come out with what's really on your mind. Well, if she think that of me, after all I've done for her, she can just forget it."

Charles, Cathy's husband, came by with Cynthia's girlfriend's companion. They wanted to be sure that I had destroyed the information, because the companion was also married, and afraid that his wife would find out about the party and the other woman. He said, "My old lady is a mean woman, and if she found that I was at a party with another woman she'd come over here and turn out this place. See this scar here. She tried to scald me to death by throwing hot water on me when I walked in the door one day. Lucky for me I turned my head in time, or my whole face would have been messed up. All over something she heard too."

I played the tape for all of them, and showed them the roll of film that I had taken from the camera and exposed. They were all satisfied, and I heard no more from any of them concerning the party.

Only four households are a part of this family. Most of the members live in the same project complex. None of these members attended school beyond the twelfth grade. They are employed as a telephone operator, factory workers, and in other occupations that do not require any skilled labor. Two members of this family live in other states; the rest live in close proximity to each other in this apartment complex. One lives two blocks down the street from the apartments; another lives in the original black district of section B.

Cynthia and the others who live in her apartment perform important services within the household. Cynthia makes sure that all the children—Johnny's, Betty's, and Cathy's—are ready for school in the morning. She receives no money for her work, but her daughter is kept and fed by the other parents. Betty stated, "We had our falling-outs, but when push come to shove, we're right there—standing by each other. Clara was just drunk that night when she started all that mess about Cynthia fooling 'round with Johnny. She always 'cusing somebody of doing something with him."

Johnny and Clara leave for work at seven o'clock in the morning. Cathy and Betty both leave for work at six-thirty. The husbands, depending on who drives, usually leave at the same time. Any of them may eat at the other's apartment. Sometimes those in one apartment prepare food for all the others; at other times, they pool their food-dishes and eat together in one apartment. They also all eat separately. On weekends, Clara's mother, Willie Bell, may take care of Clara's and Johnny's children.

Even though Clara's mother is said to be a part of the household, the relationship between Willie Bell and other household members extends only to Clara and her two children. Willie Bell is considered a member of the household because of the services she provides and because of her relationship to Clara and Clara's children. Willie Bell's services are vital to Johnny's house; therefore, to the household as a whole. Johnny gambles. Often there isn't enough money for him to pay the bills, the rent, or buy the food. However, Willie Bell often gives money to her daughter, Clara, and her grandchildren, and brings food to them.

Willie Bell has little or no interaction with other members of this family. Therefore, if Clara leaves Johnny, as she so often threatens, she will take with her the services provided by Willie Bell. Willie Bell and Johnny don't get along. Betty said that this discord is Johnny's fault. But Johnny told me that their "fallin-out" was Willie Bell's fault. He said, "Me and Willie Bell used to get along fine until she started dipping into my business all the time and trying to tell *me* how to live *my* life."

Betty said, "Clara is a good woman, and Johnny oughta treat her good. Her mama is in a position to really help them out a lot; but he won't listen to nobody. He got a hard head."

Betty has managed to maintain a "good" relationship with her in-laws. Betty made Sally, her ex-husband's mother, the godparent of three of her children, and Martha, her ex-husband's sister, the godparent of the other two. Betty said, "If anything, our relationships is stronger since I got my divorce. I keep it going. In that way, if anything happens to me, my children will be well provided for."

Johnny says that he just can't get along with Willie Bell because she is frequently "butting-in" his business and trying to tell him how to run his family. Willie Bell doesn't like the way Johnny treats her daughter. She says Johnny should be more responsible, and not spend all of his money playing pool and cards. She blames a lot of her daughter's sickness on Johnny's behavior. She said, "Clara has to struggle so hard. She's a good woman—not just because she's my daughter. She works eight hours a day, six days a week, to keep her family going. Johnny works; but he spends all of his money on foolishness. I don't say that he runs 'round with other women—like some men—that's one good thing I can say about him—but he takes money that he oughta be using on his family and give it to them men down the street shooting pool and playing cards."

Betty said some negative things about Clara. For example, "She should behave herself in a certain way that's becoming to a lady, and not act a fool like she did that night at the party." She didn't mean that Clara was a "bad" woman. On the contrary, Betty told me that "Clara is a good woman. Johnny ought to treat her good. He shouldn't waste his money in the pool hall when his family needs food or the rent need to be paid. Johnny should not go 'round beating on Clara the way he do. He shouldn't drink so much and cut-the-fool the way he do."

As Cynthia said, everybody has problems, and: "We ain't so different from everybody else, but we can solve some of our problems. Yes, we get mad at each other now and then, and sometimes we say things we don't mean; maybe we mean them at the time, but we ain't so dumb that we don't know how to say we are sorry and then things go on as usual."

Cathy is the quiet one. She only recently got married. She married after she had the baby. They all treat her "like our baby sister." Her husband is the father of the baby. His mother didn't want him to marry Cathy, and tried to convince him that the baby wasn't his. He said, "One of the reasons I marry Cathy was because I didn't like what my mama was saying about her. Also, I love her."

Betty acts more like a mother to both Johnny and Cathy. She told me that she had to teach both of them about life. Betty said, "Cathy, she don't seem to know much about life. She don't know much about woman's problem. I had to tell her everything. She still comes to me when she has her period. She was real scared when she got pregnant. I had to nurse her through her pregnancy. I felt like I was having the baby."

In one of my conversations with Johnny, he told me that

Betty had to teach him about "girls." He said, "Betty came into my room—I was about fifteen. She said, 'Johnny, don't you have a girlfriend?' I told her I didn't like girls. She said that it was time that I start liking girls. I told her I didn't know what to do. She said, 'You will—talk to some of your friends.' Well, I tried to talk to some of my friends, but I felt embarrassed to ask them questions about sex—you see, I never played with the fellows when I was growing up. I always had to come home after school and do housework, or other things my mama made me do."

Johnny told me that after Betty told him he should start liking girls, he tried; but it didn't work. He said, in his own way, that one night when he was sleeping Betty came into his room when she thought he was asleep. "She started playing 'down there' with me. I pretended I was asleep—I got excited. As soon as I got excited, she stopped. She did this for four nights in a row. The next night, one of her girlfriends stayed with her. This night, the girl came in the room. She thought I was asleep, and she started playing with me. She got me excited; only she didn't stop. She started to unbutton my pajamas, and that's when I got scared. I rolled over and laid on my stomach. She stopped. After she did this two nights in a row and I didn't do nothing, Betty talked with me the next day. Well, anyway, she made me sleep with her girlfriend, and that's how I got started."

Betty told me how she had to fight Johnny's fights for him. Even when their mother lived with them, "she never stayed at home," Betty said. "So I had to be the mama and the daddy. Our daddy left when Cathy was just a baby. Even today, when Johnny or Cathy have problems they come to me—just like I can solve them. I keep telling them they are grown, and that I have my own problems. Then, there's Mama."

The one person who really is a problem for all of them is Ludy, the mother. They don't know what to do about her. Ludy is the biological mother of Betty, Cathy, and Johnny. Betty has talked about her to me on many occasions. They all are concerned about her, but there doesn't seem to be much they can do. Betty said, "She's stone gone. I had said I would go down and talk to the Reverend about her. I was going to see a doctor, to see if I could talk to some of the authorities downtown about her. She is about the size of a pea. She's always high—drinking too much. She's one foot in and one foot out of the grave. I can't talk to her no more. I've tried to get her in the hospital; but she won't go. I can't force her to do nothing. Meanwhile, she's running 'round just dying off for the lack of attention. I know she's half eating. We told her we wouldn't bother her about her drinking if she would just stay here so we can look after her; but she won't stay. It don't do no good."

Shortly before I had completed my study, the family members had decided that Ludy was hopeless, and that they couldn't afford to continue to straighten her out. Betty said, "She don't exist as far as I'm concerned. We have tried our best to straighten her out. It don't do no good. I can't keep getting upset about her. I'm causing my own health to go bad. Neglecting myself as well as my children, worrying about Mama."

Every attempt had been made to keep the mother within the family; but when her behavior began to jeopardize other important relationships, she was rejected. The mother wasn't performing the "way she ought to." But, though they had decided not to worry about her, they were prepared to accept her fully, "the minute she decided to act right."

Betty seems to be the pivotal member of this family; all the rest of the members look up to her for advice. She is the oldest. She said she has had to make many decisions for the family and she wishes everything didn't fall on her shoulders. She said that when everyone looks up to you, it is a "terrible responsibility." She has to make decisions constantly, and sometimes they are wrong and she must live with the consequences. She recalled the hardest decision she ever made, what she called "the worst decision of my life." It pertained to her marriage. She said, "I had a child before I was married. Then, after I was married, my husband began to quarrel with me about that child. We didn't get along too good simply because of that. If I had given in to him then, where would my child be today, see? So, I was thinking, I would be less than a mama if I held my child back in order to stay with that man. Later in life, me and that man would probably have separated anyway. Nine times outta ten, if something happened to me, that very child I neglected would probably be the one that would have to come and pick me up. So, I ain't never going to hold nobody back—sending him away to my mama—on the 'count of another person misbehaving."

Betty has a boyfriend. There are no legal ties between Betty and her boyfriend, Louis, although he sends her money every month to help her support herself and her children who don't belong to him by birth. Louis provides important services that help the whole family, besides the monthly money to Betty. Betty said, "With this money, I am able to make it. I wouldn't be able to make it otherwise. I don't make enough to pay the rent, food, and all the other bills I have."

Louis also sends clothes for the children. When he visits them, he spends anywhere from two weeks to a month at a time. Betty said, "When he's here, I don't have to worry about nothing. He won't let me spend a penny of my money. Now, that's a good man for you."

The relationship between Louis and Betty is helped by all her children, as well as by other members of the family. I have been at Betty's house when Louis telephoned. He talks to Betty and every one of the children before his phone call is completed. Once, when he called, some of the children were outside. Betty's oldest daughter answered the phone. She called her mother to the phone, then ran outside to get the other children. They hurried in and waited enthusiastically for their turn to speak to Louis.

When Betty writes to Louis, she asks all the children what they want her to tell him. Once, her older son said, "Mama, why don't you marry Louis, so he's here with us?"

The other children yelled wholeheartedly, "Yeh Mama! Yeh!" Betty asked my opinion about the marriage; I told her that it was something she had to decide for herself. Her reason for having hesitated so far, according to Betty, is: "I have a good thing going just the way it is now. If I get married to him, things may change. That's the way it went with my first husband. He was the best person you ever wanted to meet before we got married. He told me that it wouldn't make no difference that I already had a child. Shortly after we got married, he began to change. Now that's why I haven't married—or made up my mind to marry Louis."

Once, when I was at Betty's house, Louis was there on one of his visits. He brought presents for everyone in the family. Betty said that he always did that, every time he came to Vera Ridge. Johnny called Louis "Bro," and Betty said, "Everyone feels like he's already in the family."

FAMILY
NUMBER FOUR

M R. Smith (no relation to the Smiths in Family Number One) was the second person Mrs. Walker introduced me to on the day I arrived in Vera Ridge. He was sitting at a table in his establishment, talking with two older men. After we were introduced, Mrs. Walker went to the counter and began talking with a lady who worked there. During our conversation, Mr. Smith said, "I'm glad you don't wear that Afro, or whatever they call them things. I go to the barber-shop three times a week."

He told me that he had a son, Ronald, who was away in college, and that his wife, Bertha, was a teacher. We talked about my work, and he said, "If you want to know about anything and anybody in Vera Ridge, just ask me. I can tell you everything. I've been right here in Vera Ridge, in this same spot, for over twenty-five years."

Mr. Smith saw me looking around his shop, so he said, "Oh, this is a new shop. I got a new house too; but the old one stood right here, right where I'm standing now."

Mrs. Walker said that she had to go home and get supper ready. Mr. Smith told me that anytime I got ready I could come by, "for the low-down."

The next day, I walked over to Mr. Smith's shop. He offered me a cold drink. Then he began telling me about the layout of Vera Ridge. I asked him if black people supported his business and he said, "I hate to say it, but you are looking for the truth. They'd rather go down there and give their money to them white folks than spend it in their own community."

"Aren't they interested in helping other blacks?"

"No! They don't want to see another colored man have a dime. Things aren't as bad as they used to be. I get more business now, but that's the trouble with our people. They don't help each other out."

After listening to Mr. Smith talk about people who owed him money, I decided to go for a walk around the area. As I left, he said, "Hurry back; you're always welcome—any time."

The following day, I again visited Mr. Smith's shop, because I had a check to cash. He was talking to the same old men I had seen in his shop the day before. They spoke of the problems children get into. One of the men said, "They have no respect for their elders."

The other man said, "If we did anything wrong, when we were growing up, our grandmama would take a broom handle to us."

They all talked about how they grew up, and how the children today were "having it easy." One of them said, "You know what, one day our grandmama found a whiskey bottle under the bed. She came through the door, after all of us were in bed and asleep. She woke us up with this broom handle. She didn't ask which one of us did it. She just went to beating all of us. I'll beat my children too, as long as they stay in my house and eat my food. If they feel like they're too grown to get a beating, then they can move out."

The other man responded, "We had respect for our folks. I remember how we used to hide our cigarettes too—being careful not to let our folks see us smoking."

Mr. Smith said, "The trouble with the kids today is these old folks. They arrested two sixty-nine- and sixty-five-year-old-men just the other day for selling dope to some young kids. It would be all right if they sell it to their own age, but not to kids."

One of the men said, "I saw a woman with her children and she had on a shorter dress than her daughter, who was with her. I tried to hold my tongue, but I just couldn't. I had to say something to her."

The other man responded, "These dresses women are wearing now-days is somethin' else. I saw this woman wearing one of these long dresses, and as long as she was still—not moving— you couldn't tell nothing, but when she moved, you could see almost everything."

Mr. Smith said, "Yes, these dresses, some have splits on the side and others have splits in the front and back."

Mr. Smith's helper came from behind the counter and she demonstrated how the dresses were designed. They all said how shameful it was for older women to wear those kinds of dresses. There was a brief discussion of "hot pants"; and Mr. Smith said, "I wouldn't wear them things if they paid me, and my wife better not wear them either. If she wore something like that, I would throw her out of the house. They say that the wife owns half of what you get after you marry. Well, she can have her half, but I'll make my half so hot she won't want to stay over in her half."

While we were talking, a car pulled up to the shop. Mr. Smith remarked, "They must be going to a funeral."

"How do you know that?"

"You can tell from what they're wearing. Nobody go 'round all dressed up in black unless they're going to a funeral."

They all tried to figure out whose funeral the people were going to. Mr. Smith said, "They brought a lady here from California to bury; maybe that's the funeral they're going to."

A woman from the car came into the shop. One of the men asked her whose funeral she was attending. She told him; but he didn't seem to know the person. Mr. Smith knew and tried to make the man remember the person. While we were talking, the postman came in. Mr. Smith received his mail. One of his letters had been returned with the notation: "No longer at this address" stamped on it. He examined the letter, then said, "I'll take care of this. I'll find him, wherever he is."

He checked his files. Then he said, "The address and the initials are right. She just sent it back so that the bill wouldn't be paid; but we'll get them."

I decided to walk to the laundromat I had seen down the street. There were people in there all during the day and I wanted to see if it would be a good place to learn about some of them, as the men and women talked while they were washing their clothes. I always carried my pack with me. In it I had a tape recorder, movie camera, Polaroid, pads, and pencils. One of my techniques to attract the attention of people I didn't know was to use my Polaroid. I walked into the laundromat. People who were washing and talking looked at me as I came in. Some took a quick glance and resumed their work, while others continued to stare.

I found a seat, and set my pack on the floor beside me. I wanted someone to come over, because of their curiosity, to talk with me. However, no one did. There were many people washing and all the machines were being used. They had bundles and bundles of clothes. Some machines had suds spilling from the top, and the person who managed the laundromat criticized the people for using too much soap. He also told them they were putting too many clothes in the machines. One woman complained, "These machines are so small and you charge so much money. What do you expect us to do?"

I took out my Polaroid, pretending to examine it. Usually this causes some concern with the people, and often someone wants me to take his picture. This gives me my entry, and I can begin talking with the people. However, these seemed to shy away, as if they didn't want me to take a picture of them. Two young girls ran into the laundromat, crying, "Mama, Pat stepped on our mud house." The mother yelled for Pat to "come in here, and I mean now!" She slapped him in the face, and said,

"Didn't I tell you about fighting with your sisters? Now y'all go on out there and play and I don't wanna have to tell you again."

As Pat, the little boy, was leaving, he spotted me and came over. He was very curious about my camera and wanted me to taked a picture of him. His mother yelled for him to "stop bothering that man and gone outside and play like I told you."

I said to her, "He wants me to take a picture of him. Is it all right by you?"

"It's all right with me; but you don't know whatchu doing. Them children will worry you to death."

I told him to come outside and I would take his picture. I used the Polaroid camera and gave him the photo. He went around showing all the other kids; they all came over, wanting me to take their pictures. I suggested they group up and I would shoot all of them together. At first, they insisted on individual pictures. I said I didn't have much film left, took three pictures of the group of eleven children, gave them to the first three hands, and told them to pass them around.

I returned to the inside of the laundromat. Pat was there, showing his picture to his mother. When she saw me come in, she told him to go over and thank me, which he did. I walked over and asked her if she would mind if I took a picture of her and she said, "Like this? I don't want a picture of me looking like this. Why do you wanna picture of me like this?"

"I like to have pictures of people in their natural setting. If I tried to talk about what was going on in the laundromat, it would take me a long time, but one picture could say so much more."

Other women began to come over and I got a chance to tell them what I was doing in Vera Ridge. Some of them, on finding out who I was, immediately returned to their duties; others stayed and listened to what I had to say. I made several contacts and the woman who didn't want me to take a picture of her decided that it was all right. So I took several pictures of her.

I offered her one, but she said, "I don't want no picture of me looking like this. I tell you what, when I get dressed up, I want you to take a picture of me."

I agreed, and also agreed to take pictures of some of the others who were there. I collected my equipment and continued investigating the area.

The following Saturday, I was at Mr. Smith's shop again. His son, Ronald, had come home from college for the weekend. He was working in the shop. He had a big Afro and a beard. Mr. Smith turned to him as I came into the shop, and said, "Now look at that young man; he doesn't have all that mess all over his face and on his head. Tell him, Reggie, that looks like hell. A man's appearance is the thing that counts, these days. I don't care how much education he's got."

Ronald continued working, as if he wasn't concerned with what his father had said. Remembering that he hadn't introduced us, Mr. Smith told his son to come over and meet me. He said, "This is Reggie; he's from a college out East, and he is here in Vera Ridge doing a study on the Negro family."

Ronald came over and shook my hand; then he said, "Tell him, Reggie, they're wearing these everywhere. This is the latest style."

"Latest my butt," Mr. Smith said, "it's a style, all right. Look like you just came out from behind a bush or something. It's not the way Africans wear their hair, anyway. That's them Muslims."

"He don't even know what he's talking about. Muslims! You're old-fashion, daddy. This is the Black look."

"Black, hell! If anybody called you black a few years ago, you would be ready to fight him. Now, everybody's going 'round calling themselves black. I ain't black. I'm Negro. All Negroes ain't black. I don't mind being called colored. I hate being called black!"

It was time for me to leave, I thought. I didn't want to get into a family argument until I knew Ronald and Mr. Smith better. I could see that Ronald wanted me to take his side of the argument and Mr. Smith wanted me to take his. I took my side, and left.

During this period, I visited Mr. Smith's shop almost daily. Eventually, I began spending time at his house, which was adjacent to the shop. The Smiths' house is one of the best homes in the black community of Vera Ridge. It is the only one in the immediate area that is built of stone and brick. Mr. Smith told me he normally enters his home through the door that leads from the shop; however, he said it would be all right if I came in from the front entrance. The outside of the house was well kept. There are hedges almost six feet tall around the front and side of it. The grass is always cut, and the hedges always trimmed.

The front porch, although not completely enclosed, contains some iron cast leaf (wrought iron) furniture that had been painted white. There is a large swing attached to the ceiling of the porch, taking up one-fourth of it. Just over the door hangs a lantern-style chained lamp. It hangs so low that one has to step to the side of it, or duck, to avoid being hit on the head.

Once inside the house, you are immediately impressed by the way it is decorated. You first come into an entrance hall. There your coat is removed and placed in a large closet. You then enter the living room, after fighting strings of beads hung in the doorway. The living room is more narrow than wide. There is a large piano occupying an entire corner of the room. Two long, low-backed sofas sit against the east and west walls. Behind the sofa on the east wall is a large picture window with sliding drapes. Behind the other sofa is a large mirror that runs the length of the sofa.

A huge chandelier hangs from the center of the living room. The oak floor has a Persian-like rug laying in its center. There are end-tables to match the sofas—four of them. In front of the sofa, against the west wall, is a long coffee-table. As you enter, on both sides of the door, there are chairs upholstered in leather, or a leather-like fabric. To the left of the piano is a reclining chair that Mr. Smith calls "my chair."

Mr. Smith asked if I wanted to stay in the living room or go into the family room, "where we can relax and feel more comfortable."

I told him that I thought that would be better, because of my tape recorder and other equipment. I didn't want to litter his front room with the many things I used, and was concerned that I might damage his furniture. As we made our way to the "family room," we passed through the dining room. The floor was carpeted wall to wall with a deep-red carpet; you sank down as you stepped on it. In the center of the room stood a long, chrome dining table with a glass top. The chairs that sat around it were also made of chrome. A larger chandelier hung over the table. There was a wood cabinet with partially glass doors, storing plates, glasses, and other dishes. A buffet stood along the north wall; on top of it was a large punchbowl with glass cups hanging around its rim. Artificial flowers, in vases, sat on both sides of the bowl. There were two entranceways, one leading to the kitchen and another to a hallway that gave access to three bedrooms and a bathroom. You could enter the family room from either way. We went through the kitchen.

As we walked through the kitchen, Mrs. Smith asked me to excuse its appearance, because she hadn't had time to clean it. I remarked how beautiful I thought her entire house was; and Mr. Smith said that it was only three years old. The kitchen had two exits; one led to a breakfast room and the other to the family room. In the family room, there was a pool table, a Ping-Pong table, a juke-box, and a pinball machine. There were also a leather sofa and chair in this huge room, and a bar in one corner. The entire oak floor was bare and highly polished. Next to the sofa was a round coffee-table. Mr. Smith told me I could set my equipment down there. He sat in the reclining leather chair; Mrs. Smith, Ronald, and I on the sofa.

The income of this family is approximately twenty thousand dollars a year. Mr. Smith says he earns anywhere from eight to twelve thousand a year. "That depends on the people paying me. You see, I give credit, and sometimes people don't pay me."

Mr. Smith told me angrily that he can't understand why

colored people don't pay him. He said that if it was a white man, they would pay him. His wife, Bertha, says she makes from eight to ten thousand dollars a year. Neither Bertha nor Mr. Smith was eager to tell exactly how much they made. It was as if they were trying to keep it a secret from each other. Ronald goes to college and works in his father's shop on weekends. His father gives him an allowance and pays for his schooling. The Smiths are financially "well-off," as Mr. Smith told me. "But I made it that way. I've worked all my life; and I never asked nobody for nothing."

Mr. Smith and his family members seemed to constitute a typical nuclear family. Mr. Smith had his own business, and had gone to college. Bertha has been a grade-school teacher for fifteen years. She received her Master's degree by attending summer school over the years. Ronald, his son, attended college during my study. They live in a big house that "is paid for because I used cash," said Mr. Smith.

Mr. Smith's background was very interesting to me. He said that once he left home to go to college, he never returned during the school year. He only saw his "family" at the end of each school year. "And, I worked my own way through college. I didn't ask my folks for nothing. They didn't have it, anyway."

Ronald asked, "Daddy, are you trying to give me a hint?"

"If you don't straighten up, I might be telling you—not giving you a hint. But no, I planned for your schooling. I didn't want you to go through what I had to go through. I just wish you would respect that."

According to Mr. Smith, he pretty well isolated himself from the rest of his "family" while growing up. It was Bertha and Ronald who have kept Mr. Smith in touch with them. Mr. Smith wouldn't tell me much about them. However, Ronald said, "My Daddy knew one of his first cousins on his daddy's side. When my great-granddaddy died, we didn't even know him until he died. We knew one of his nephews. He had said he had some brothers; but he didn't know anything about them until one of them died."

Mr. Smith didn't think that he had made a deliberate attempt to separate himself from other members of his family. Rather, "that's just the way it was, the way it happened."

When Mr. Smith did give information about his family, I was often confused about its meaning. For example, I would ask, "Who are the people you consider a part of your family?"

He would respond, "My son, my sister, and my brother. I should have said, 'my son and sister'; leave the brother off."

At first I thought it was the way I had phrased the question that produced this response. However, he insisted, "My family is my son and my sister; and that's all."

He didn't include his wife, or any other kin or relative. Bertha and Ronald constantly reminded him of, or corrected him about, members of his family. He didn't seem to know (or want to recall) how many children a certain relative had, where that relative lived, or how that relative was connected to the family. For Mr. Smith, his "family," his "kin," were his son and his sister— not even his brother. At first, I thought he was not including kin because they were dead; but he had two brothers and another sister whom he didn't consider a part of his family. Of course, he didn't refer to these brothers and sister as "kin." Only those he referred to as "kin" did he include as members of his family. Even when Bertha and Ronald reminded him of people who were related to him, he would say, "Oh! Those relatives! But they're not my family."

Ronald said, "Daddy, you got more than one brother. What about Uncle Will? We just saw him last year. Daddy, you must be forgetting or something. Mama! Did you hear Daddy say he only got one brother? He had three brothers: Tommy, Gerald, and Will."

Ronald continued his account of his father's family. Mr. Smith didn't seem upset, one way or the other. I got the feeling he didn't want to talk about his folks, and that it had little to do with not remembering them. Ronald said, "Well, I'm the only child. My mama comes from a family of twelve. She has six brothers and six sisters."

"No, Ronald," Bertha said, "I only have five sisters. I'm the sixth."

Ronald didn't seem to be concerned about telling me what he knew of his relatives; and Bertha would assist him. I thought I wouldn't ask any more questions about the family since Mr. Smith seemed uneasy; but Ronald insisted and said, "My daddy comes from a small family of four: one sister and three brothers."

"No, Ronald," Bertha said, "He came from a family of five— he makes the fifth."

"That's right, Mama. My Daddy didn't know he even had any uncles until he was grown. My Mama had twin sisters. One of them died. My second auntie, the other of the twins, had a kid when she was young. She wasn't married. My Grandmama raised it; and she grew up with me. She is more like a sister to my Mama and her Mama. She is really my Mama's niece."

As you can see, Ronald wasn't always right in his account of family history, but his mother corrected his mistakes. His father's main concern was the impression he wanted his son to have about him as a father. This overshadowed his accurate reporting of information concerning his family. Even when he talked alone with me, he wouldn't go into any details about his family. It was not until my last meeting with him that he began to talk about the influence his family members had had on him.

During the week, I would talk with Bertha and with Ronald when he came home for weekends. I accompanied Ronald to school on several occasions. He often explained his father to me. That is, he would say that his father was trying to "blackmail" him by threatening that if he didn't "shape up," he wouldn't inherit the business. A young man named Steve worked in Mr. Smith's shop. He was Ronald's age and had worked there many years. Mr. Smith said he would get the business if Ronald didn't "shape up." Bertha spent hours talking with me about Mr. Smith. She said that he had had a hard time when he was coming up and, "That's the reason he act the way he do toward Ronald."

I asked her, "Why didn't he consider you to be part of his family?"

"He's a funny person. I don't think I know a nicer person; but he is very old-fashioned. He won't let you know if he loves you or not. How you do is by what he does—not what he says. I think Ronald is the only one that he comes close to telling him he loves him as a son—even then, it comes out funny. But, if you don't think he cares about me, just let me be one minute later than when I'm suppose to be in. Just let me seem to be looking at another man, or have a man say something about how I look—you'll see him in action."

I got to know the members of this family to the point where I didn't have to call before visiting their home. While Mr. Smith tried to use me as a model for his son, Ronald did things that his father wouldn't have approved of. Ronald translated this as doing things "his" way—being black. When he wasn't around Mr. Smith, he went out to bars, parties, and had good times with girls.

During my second interview, Mr. Smith tried to talk me into convincing his son to "do something" about cutting his hair. Many times, in the presence of his son, he would refer to me as "a nice young man." He would say, "You don't see all that stuff on his head and all that mess around his face."

His son would look at me, then at his father. He would shake his head and leave. The relationship between Mr. Smith and Steve, the young man who worked in his shop, seemed like a father–son one. Steve had worked in Mr. Smith's shop from the time he was a child in grade school. Now he's in college, studying to become a doctor. Mr. Smith keeps a close watch over him—even more so than he does with his own son. That is because Steve pays attention to what Mr. Smith says, whereas Ronald "does his own thing." Mr. Smith makes sure that Steve does his schoolwork, and if he has problems with it, Mr. Smith assists him.

Mr. Smith is able to help Steve in his schoolwork because he too had studied to become a doctor. But he didn't go on to medical school, "because I didn't have enough pull to get into medical school. You see, you had to know somebody important; and I didn't."

Mr. Smith still hopes that Ronald will go to medical school; but Ronald has told him that he isn't interested. In the presence of his son, Mr. Smith would say to me, "Steve, that's a smart boy. He's going to take over the business when I retire, if my son don't get on the ball, Steve gets it all."

I asked Steve about his relationship to Mr. Smith's family and he said, "We're very close; they are all very close to me. It's just the same as my second family. I never really knew my daddy. Mr. Smith is the same as a daddy, and Mrs. Smith is the same as a mama to me. They treat me the same way they treat Ronald. Mr. Smith is sending both of us to college. He buys my clothes and my books, and lets me work in the shop to have some money to pay for my food and stuff like that."

Mr. Smith often told me that Steve was the same as having another son. He said, "Sometimes he acts more like a son than my own son, and I gotta tell the truth. He's smart—at least it seems so—so far."

Mr. Smith spends a lot of time with Steve; on the other hand, Bertha spends a lot of time with her godmother. Thus, both Steve and the godmother are important to this family. As Bertha said, "Annie May, my godmother, is the same as a mama to me. She bought me all of my clothes for school. I never lived with her, but she raised one boy and three girls that didn't belong to her. She had one girl of her own—she was never married, though. She treated us all just the same as we were her own children. I just saw her the other day."

Bertha is attempting to maintain her relationship with Annie May. She got Annie May's daughter to be Ronald's godmother. Mr. Smith and Bertha have introduced nonbiological, nonmarital relationships into the family. In addition to family relationships with people unrelated to them by blood or marriage, the family included other people as part of its household. Shortly after I began my study, a cousin of Ronald's married and moved out of the Smiths' home. He had lived with them for seven years—"even when we had the old house," Ronald said. He was the nephew of Bertha. According to Ronald, at different times, different relatives lived with them, either because they were going to school in Vera Ridge or "just came to live with us like I lived with my grandmama," Ronald said.

Ronald said that he was raised by and lived with his grandmama. He said, "One of my mama's younger brothers stayed with us for three years. He and I was more like brothers than he was my uncle. I also stayed with my grandmama when I was young. I went to school up there. My youngest aunt used to keep me. I only started living permanently with my mama and daddy a few years ago. Most of my life I lived with my grandmama, who I called 'Mama' too. My mama and daddy had a terrible time taking me away from my grandmama. My youngest aunt, who kept me too, acted more like a mama to me; but I called her by her first name. My mama and daddy had to fight with her too, to get me back. She didn't want me to leave. My grandmama didn't want me to leave; and I didn't want to leave. That's why I spend all my summers with them, and every time I get a chance I'm up there with them."

Bertha spent only her last years of high school living with her mother. She said, "My grandmama raised me. I grew up with her youngest daughter. She is like a sister to me. All of us think of her as our sister. Actually, I only have four sisters. I said six, but one died, and the other one is really my aunt, the one I said is like a sister to me—nobody thinks of her that way."

Mr. Smith left home at an early age. He worked his way through school, and then college. He spent time in the military, and sent money home "to support my mama, sister, and brother." He has several sets of brothers and sisters. He attempted to shield or keep this information from me, but Bertha and Ronald, who know, told me. His mother had children before she was married; children by the man she married; and children by another man after her marriage broke up. I was able to gain this information—to verify it—when I went to Savory, where Mr.

Smith was born and his family still lives, and talked with some of his "family" and people who knew the family there.

Both Bertha and Ronald can name "kin" and "relatives" on either side of the family. They know the number of family members, when they expect to see them again, and the number of children each of them has, as well as whom they resemble.

THE BLACK
FAMILY UNIT

IF it wasn't for mama
and mama's mama
I would be unhappy
If it wasn't for daddy
and daddy's daddy
I would be sad

No one can ever take my feelings
the feelings for my daddy's daddy's sister
away from me
cause she's my mama too

I'm now in Vera Ridge
Tomorrow it may be California
I'm home in New York too
My daddy's daddy's brother's daughter
she live there
I'm home in Michigan
in Florida where I was born
Who can give me so many homes

There's kinfolks and kinfolks's folks
there's relatives and relatives' relatives
these too have homes for me

For I am a Willis
and where there's a Willis
should he recognize me
so I will be

For I am a Jones
and where there be a Jones
should she recognize me
I too will be

Where my sisters marry
I will have more brothers
my brothers will give me sisters

My aunts—they give me uncles
and my uncles give me aunts
My brother's children
are my children
my sister's children
are mine too

My cousins
Oh! My cousins
they are everywhere
So! I will be there too

My family

An analysis of these four families provides a comprehensive study of black families in general. This analysis begins with the questions that must be asked regarding the controversies surrounding the overall structure of the black family. And these controversies begin with the name of the family itself. Early works referred to it as the "Negro Family." This nomenclature has been superseded by "Black Family" and "Afro-American Family." I will later term it the "Black Domestic Unit" (BDU).

There are even more problems concerning its composition and structure than regarding its naming. I will begin by calling it the black family, for no other reason than personal preference. Later, I refer to it as the BDU because I feel this nomenclature best describes the configuration of its kinship structure.

The important questions for understanding the black family are:

1. Are there two kinds of black families—middle-class and lower-class?

2. Why are lower-class black families compared and contrasted with middle-class white families instead of with lower-class white families or middle-class black families?

3. Can the concept of "family" be applied in an analysis of black families?

While these are not all the questions surrounding some of the misconceptions about the structure of black families, they do address the basic issues.

To respond to the first question, one must first define what one means by black family. The black family written about here does not necessarily represent all black people in the United States. In an isolated community in New Hampshire it is possible to find a few families of blacks whose structure is similar to that of the white middle-class nuclear family. In some of our large cities and suburbs one may also find blacks whose family structure resembles that of the white middle-class. Some of these blacks may be descendants from generations of blacks who came to this country upon its discovery (but not as slaves). Some may be immigrants, old or recent; but neither they nor their descendants experienced slavery in the United States. Or, some may have originally come as slaves, but eluded the lifestyle of slavery produced by the plantation system. They escaped to the North and occupied small communities where they were isolated from any sizeable black population. For these blacks, their family structure may have been greatly influenced by and developed along the lines of the white families for whom they worked.

Where these family members became upwardly mobile they

may have created a middle-class nuclear family arrangement. Where they remained poor, their family structure may have developed an extended or stem arrangement—with a nuclear base, however. Although these are black people, they do not necessarily belong to what I refer to as the black family. At the same time, when these blacks were no longer isolated, and with the migrations from the South to the North and from the rural areas to the urban areas, marriage and other forms of unions and exposures between the two groups—especially those who were poor—produced families I refer to as the black family.

The black family is composed of people whose ancestors were brought to this country as slaves and whose conditions and situations were influenced by the environment of plantation lifestyle. The black family today is a product of the plantation system. Its strength lies in its ability to maintain and survive under the slavery system. It is the outcome of a determined people who sought to function, maintain, and perpetuate under the adverse conditions of slavery. Du Bois (1909), Frazier (1939), Pinkney (1975), Gutman (1976), and Haley (1976) are only a few writers who have spelled out the conditions under which the present black family developed as a result of slavery.

This leads into the second question: why are lower-class black families compared and contrasted with middle-class white families instead of with lower-class white families or middle-class black families? First, there has been little research on lower-class white families until most recently. Although social scientists are beginning to do extensive research in this area, for some reason they previously concentrated on lower-class blacks or other lower-class minority groups. However, most of us can speculate that lower class was a label reserved for blacks and other minorities. The stigma that goes with being lower class would lose its importance if it were shown that a significant number of white families were also of the lower class. This is analogous to being on welfare. When one speaks of welfare, the first people one thinks of are blacks. It does not seem to matter that a much greater number of whites are also on welfare; welfare has become associated with blacks, so too has lower class.

Second, most social scientists assume that the nuclear family is the basis for all other family types in the United States. Therefore, one only has to analyze class differences in order to account for family differences between minority groups and the white middle class. These social scientists assumed that the white middle-class family was the ideal representation of the nuclear family. Therefore, any other class of people would simply have a family structure that was an extension of the nuclear family. Consequently, there should be no reason why one could not contrast black lower-class families with those of the white middle class.

In the black family as I have defined it, class distinction does not become a problem in the sense that there is a black lower-class family and a black middle-class family. The basic family structure is the same regardless of its members' upward mobility or economic status. This can especially be seen in Family Number One of this study. Most of the members were self-sufficient; however, two were especially successful: Peggy and Terry. Still, they maintained the basic relationships they had formed prior to their success. With the exception of members in Family Number Three, some of the members in other families could hardly be considered lower class; however, the basic family structure of all four families is the same.

As material wealth becomes more accessible to members of the family, they do not abandon what is already of value. What upward mobility produces is a quantitative rather than a qualitative change in the relationships between members. Members retain previously held values that are deemed necessary to one's lifestyle and they build on to these values. This is shown in Peggy's (of Family Number One) remarks when we were discussing her social situation as a result of her career. I asked her if she saw herself as middle class and she said, "Honey! I'm any class (snapping her fingers). High, low, or in the middle, take your pick. 'Cause what you see is what you get."

"Maybe I don't understand. Could you explain to me what you mean by that?"

"Honey! You have to excuse me (laughing as she sat down), but I've been asked that question before, especially by reporters and I tell them anything just to get rid of them. Honey! I'm me! And, I'll always be me. Some people think they have to change just because they become famous or run into lots of money. That's their problem."

"What do you mean by change?"

"Well, they don't want to speak to you and you've known them all their lives. They no longer want to associate with you; I guess it's because they think they're better than you now. They even act funny with their own folks. Me, I couldn't have gotten where I am today if it weren't for all my folks standing behind me all the way. I'll never forget where I came from. All these wonderful people. How could I forget?"

This was the attitude of most of the black professionals I interviewed throughout the country. These professionals included entertainers, from opera to rock music; athletes; teachers, from grade schools to universities; lawyers; doctors; and business people. Their ages ranged from upper teens to early seventies. In many cases their profession had been in the family for several generations. For more than ninety percent of the professionals interviewed, the first person to be rewarded upon their success was "Mama." Where both parents were still living together (and this was well over half of those interviewed), rewards went to both parents. As we will see, parents are not the only people to whom recognition upon success is awarded. For Peggy and Terry in Family Number One, the mother and father, the next-door neighbors, and the cousin Alice were equal recipients. Bertha, of Family Number Four, acknowledged Annie Mae, her godmother.

Preference in acknowledgment and reward had nothing to do with a person being married or even having children of his or her own: "The first thing I'm going to do is build my mama and daddy a house." Even if members of the family thought

about changing their attitudes toward members with whom a
relationship had been established, "Mama would always be
right there telling you wherever you go, 'remember cousin so-
and-so lives here or aunt so-and-so lives there.' "

The majority of the professionals interviewed remembered
mama, daddy, sisters, brothers, and everyone responsible for
their success. However, a few professional blacks indicated they
had changed their style of living: acquired new friends, became
Presbyterians, read the *New York Times* and don't see so-and-so
any more. Sherry, a successful entertainer, told me, "I don't
like it when mama sends people to see me just because they are
relatives or people I used to know. Every time I go home she
has all the neighbors and people I used to know coming by to
see me. I don't want to see those people. We don't have anything in common any more. It took me awhile before I got her
to understand. Now when I go home, which isn't too often, I
spend a quiet time with Mama and my brothers. I don't have
to put on an act just to please my mama any more."

"Can you tell me what you mean by putting on an act."

"You know, you smile when people you used to know come
up and greet you. You listen to them talk about old times and
pretend to remember. Half the times you can't remember what
they are talking about, but you agree with them any way. You
can't wait for the time when you can tell them you have to get
some rest because of an up-coming performance."

"You mean you didn't make any friends or know any relatives you liked well enough to continue relationships?"

"I have one childhood friend that I see when we cross each
other's path, and an aunt that I'm very close to. But for the rest
of them, except, of course, my mama and brothers, since my
daddy's dead, I just don't feel comfortable being around them
now. The things they like, the things they do, the things they
talk about just don't interest me any more. People say I'm
snobbish, but I really don't care. I have my future to think
about. It's my career and they just don't fit in it."

One lady, of the community where Sherry spent several

years in preparation for her debut, commented to me, "Sherry acted like she didn't even know me when I went backstage to see her after her performance. When she first came to our community she didn't know anyone. I am the one who found a place for her to stay. I even found a place for her mother to stay when she visited Sherry. I was like a mama to her. I introduced her to Arta, a bleaching cream to get rid of those bumps on her face and to smooth out her skin. Now she acted like she don't know me. Everyone here is upset with her, after all we did to make her welcomed—now she don't seem to know us."

Once while interviewing Sherry's mother at her home down South, I asked the mother when was the last time she had heard from Sherry. She said, "I'm expecting a call from her today, but I know I have to wait until she's had her afternoon nap—that's the way she is now."

While the mother seemed to be proud of her daughter's success, she often talked about Sherry before her success. For example, the mother seemed most happy when she told me about Sherry's church activities when she was a little girl growing up. She talked about the people in the community and how much they admired Sherry. She said that Sherry used to attend church every Sunday and sing in the choir, but "she doesn't go to church any more." Once in New York we sat next to each other at a performance given by Sherry. I talked about the greatness of Sherry's performance; she talked about her return trip to the South—home.

Whereas Peggy's attitudes toward "people who stood by me and are responsible for my success" is characteristic of most of the professional blacks I interviewed, Sherry's attitudes exemplify those few blacks who "have a different lifestyle from people you used to know." I think the comments of one such successful professional black sums up the feelings of people who abandoned or attempted to abandon those who were once important in their lives. This professional told me, "I have all the money I can spend the rest of my life—they know me all over the world, I have a large home on the West Coast, an apartment on the East Side in New York, a home in Maine, but I'm the loneliest person in the world."

"You have all of that and you say you're lonely. How can a person with all of those things be lonely?"

"My husband died. One of my children died a month later. My only living child is married and leads his own life. That's the only reason I'm still in New York, so that I can be near him. I would like to live on the West Coast."

"But don't you have other relatives and friends?"

"Friends, I have, but I left my people when I broke into show business. I used to see some of them some of the times, but after mama died, I lost all touch with the rest of them. They still know of me—I guess, but I don't know where they are. Let me tell you something, and listen to me well, keep in touch with your family, all the time, always. No matter how big you become, how famous you are, never forget the people who got you there. Friends may love you and may care for you very much, but there's nothing like being loved by your own flesh and blood."

The process whereby previously held values are maintained can best be understood through a discussion of reciprocity. Anthropologists have used this concept for many years. Radcliffe-Brown (1950), Gough (1959), Fortes (1958), Levi-Strauss (1969), Rappaport (1963), Fox (1967), Buchler and Selby (1968), Sahlins (1965), and Stack (1974) have shown that exchange between family members is an important function of the family.

When I speak of reciprocity, I am not only referring to material exchange I am also referring to the idea that obligations may include "looking out for me when I get old and need help." Leach (1961) pointed to three types of exchange:

1. Relationship between social groups is expressed by the simultaneous or nearly simultaneous exchange of goods.
2. Relationship between social groups is expressed by the simultaneous or nearly simultaneous exchange of women.

3. Relationship between social groups is expressed by exchange of women for goods.

If you add the exchange of emotions, comforts, security, and love to Leach's three types of exchange, then you have what I mean by reciprocity in the black family.

As Stack (1974) reported, "People exchange . . . new things, treasured items, furniture, cars, goods that are perishable, and the services exchanged for child care, residence, or shared meals" (33–34). Reciprocity goes much farther than the exchange of material items. Respect may be a critical content of an exchange from a child to the parents in return for what they have done for the child.

For example, respect, though not always exhibited as an overt emotional response, may be expressed through the exchange of material items; thus exchange implies a message about how someone "acts" to another person. Davenport (1961) pointed out that "The greatest assurance against the threat [of growing old and living alone] is to have been successful in establishing a large and prosperous household which contains all one's children and grandchildren." This is a very important aspect of reciprocity in the black family. As I have had informants tell me, "I don't care about gifts, or about him bringing me something. I just like to know that he remembers me."

In assessing the concept of reciprocity, one must be aware of several aspects of commitment in the black family. Reciprocity includes taking care of those who took care of or raised you. It is also a form of respect that involves communication: "Keeping in touch with me." Visiting and remembering special occasions are also a part of this respect. Role reversal, where a child grows up and then provides services for his parents, is an important feature of reciprocity.

In the black family, a parent-child relationship becomes symmetrical over a period of time. The child, when he grows up and his parents become old, may assume duties that are similar to those done for him once by the parents. For example, providing and taking care of the person is one such reciprocal act. He is concerned with the welfare of the parents as the parents once were concerned with his. At a given point, the parent-child relationship represents an asymmetrical relationship of exchange when one gives more than the other. With reversal of certain roles over time, there really is a symmetrical exchange evolving because the parent had provided earlier in his life. Where the parent did not require material things, he or she received love, respect, and other emotional exchanges.

Where reciprocity is concerned, sex roles are not strict. This nonlimiting sex role performance is instrumental to the functioning of the household: services that are necessary to maintain a household are not restricted by sex if the household would be deprived because of its sex composition. Some households, as in Family Number One, may contain mostly women; others may contain mostly men. However, if members are expected to perform according to ability rather than sex, then no combination of males and females will disrupt the functioning and maintenance of the household. According to Gonzalez (1970), "as societies develop, the sexual division of labor becomes less rigid, and roles are structured more on the basis of ability, training, and personality than on sex" (240).

Sex roles and the division of labor allow any member to perform in almost any role that involves commitment to other members. For example, when the need arises for a child to take care of a parent, or anyone who "raised him" or "took care of him," he must be prepared to do so or relegate those duties to persons with whom he will exchange services. Often if there is no female, a male will perform duties such as cooking, washing, or cleaning the house (Hill 1972).

Reciprocity is also the basis of special relationships denoted by "I did you a favor and now it's your turn to do me one." Such relationships play an important part in the member's maintenance of connections. The only reason why the member has to ask for a return of service is because the requested service is for someone else; otherwise, those whom he or she asks would probably have already known and responded without being asked. Reciprocity does not always involve direct exchange between persons.

A member of the family receives services from another member. The services, however, may be reciprocated not necessarily to the person who rendered them, but to the person's child. Two features come to light here: the asking for favors in return and the indirect payment of a favor. In the former, the behavior is most noticeable where a person is not able to provide services expected at the time of the request. In the latter, a person may have lived with another person for several years, "But after he got on his feet and was doing good, I sent Mary Joyce to live with him so she could go to school up North."

Therefore, members are locked into relationships that are perpetuated throughout their lives. When they get married and have children, the foundation of the married couple and their children have already been formed. They simply produce another link in the growing kinship network. It does not matter how successful they become, they do not abandon relationships already established. To do so is to be excluded from the family, and this rarely happens among members of the black family. For they know that someone is depending on them as they had depended on someone.

The third question to address is: can the concept of "family" be applied in an analysis of the black family? Obviously the answer is a resounding *No!* The organization of these families can best be represented as a complex pattern of relationships between a wide range of people. These people may be related by blood, marriage, and mutual consent. Their relationships involve people's day-to-day situations that are shared with each other. Every member shares in each other's joys, hardships, and needs. They become familiar with each other so that they know *how to deal with* any situation that may arise.

Sharing is very important among all members. It is this sharing that maintains and assures the survival of these family members as a unit. According to Fox (1967), "Nature had already provided within the structure of the primate bands, along with the principle of 'dominance' . . . the ideas of 'sharing' and 'cooperation'; the basic idea of 'reciprocity'—give and take" (117).

Therefore, the role that people play will be determined more by their ability to perform in those roles, rather than their biological or marital connections. Performance is of paramount importance, because it is the means whereby members communicate with each other. This communication is not so much what a person says, but what a person does, and how well he or she does it. Therefore, personal relationships at a given time may never be explicitly discussed by the person involved.

People may confront one another about the way he or she is not behaving, but they do not explicitly delve into the implications of the behavior for their relationships. What people know about their relationships with others is realized when a person performs or fails to perform in his or her assigned roles. Members may ask and receive services; however, it is more important for a person to know what is needed from him or her and to provide the services without having to be asked. Failure to perform in these relationships is a serious matter. It is the failure to *act*, not the failure to *ask*, by which a member's performance is assessed by other members of the family. To have a "close" relationship with other members is to perform in one's role as expected.

This complex structure provides for an elasticity of function within the black family. Thus, the black family need not be restricted to a "fixed" set of consanguinal and affined members. This is why we see in these families people who are not related by blood or marriage. For example, in Family Number One, Phillis, Jim, and "Sister Child" are not related to other members of the family by blood or marriage; however, they are considered members of the family. In Family Number Two, Sue, Billy, and Mayola were considered family members, and they also were not related by blood or marriage. In Family Number Three, Cynthia, her husband and child, and Louis were considered family members; however, none of these members were related by blood or marriage. Therefore, another factor that must be considered in assessing these four families is *mutual consent*. Here people can become members when there is an agreement based on friendship.

In the black family there is potential for reorganization, unlike the white middle-class nuclear family where mother, father, sisters, and brothers may turn into strangers after the children are grown. In the black family they do not become strangers. The members remain an intricate part of the family so long as they perform in their roles as expected. One cannot discuss the black family in terms of individuals, because there are no "specific" roles tied to "specific" people. The father may or may not be the provider, and, if he is, he may not be the only person providing for a given number of members. For example, in Family Number Three, although Johnny is the father to his children and he provides for them, Willie Bell, his mother-in-law, also provides for them. Her services, as described by Betty and other members of the family, are extremely important, for they not only supplement the needs of the family, but in many cases become primary when Johnny gambles his money away. Activities centering around the black family must be discussed in terms of households—not individuals.

These households provide necessary services for the benefit of the family as a whole. For example, a mother does not have to worry about all the responsibilities of rearing her child. Some of these responsibilities may be shared by her mother or other members of the family with whom the mother has a relationship. There are no responsibilities that are delegated exclusively to any family member. Responsibilities fall on the person who can best provide the services necessary. Getting assistance in rearing the child allows the mother freedom to carry out other tasks vital to the maintenance of the family. The mother may have to financially support the child; therefore she must be free to work. Still, the child must be cared for, and other members of the household can fulfill these duties.

For example, once while I was talking to Ola May, of Family Number Two, a young lady came in with two children. She said to Ola May, "Mama, don't forget to give Jean her medicine." Then she left. I asked Ola May about the children, and she said, "These are two of my grandchildren. This house has raised many children. Some not even my own. Now let me see just how many children I have raised in this house."

She began counting, using her fingers; then she said, "There was seven. . . . No! Wait a minute—eight. I forgot about Barbara. Yes, I raised eight children that wasn't my own, and right today all of them will come and see me at certain times. None of them have ever forgotten about me and what I done for them. Some of them are married and have their own children; but they still mind me and do what I tell 'em to do."

The relationship between the mother and the person or persons caring for the child determines to whom the child will be entrusted. There is very little, if any, verbal request from the mother to other members for assistance. For example, while I was talking to Betty, of Family Number Three, the phone rang. Betty answered it and said, "Yes, Johnny, I called you. I want you to tell Clara to go by Cathy's apartment and pick up Shelly and bring her home with her. Cathy is supposed to go and look for a job today. See that she gets to where she has to go."

The network of relationships are such that people know conditions and situations of each other at almost any given time. If someone has to ask for help from another member, these people are said not to have a "good" relationship. People are supposed to be aware of each other's situations. For example, Betty said, "Johnny and Cathy fight like cats and dogs sometimes, and they are sister and brother; but you let somebody else try to bother one of them—holy hell will break loose. Now Cathy and Johnny had a falling-out, but it won't last long. Today Cathy has to go to work and her car broke down. Wait and see who takes her to work. She ain't even gonna have to call him. Johnny's gonna be right there waiting for her to come down them steps."

Where a person has to ask for help indicates something about the relationship between the person and the one who's asked. An example of this can be demonstrated by a conversation I had with Ola May. She said, "Essie Bell will be bringing those kids by my house first thing in the morning, but I done told her I ain't gonna take care of them. Just because she's my niece she thinks she can run over me. She's been foolin' 'round all weekend, and she ain't going to work come Monday. I know what she's gonna do. She's gonna bring them kids by here and pretend she's going to work, and she's going right back to that house and lay-up there in that bed all day, trying to get rid of a hangover. But I'm not gonna keep them kids, because that kind of stuff don't make no sense—now do it? As long as I put up with it, the longer she's gonna try to get away with it. But I'm gonna put my foot down this time. You just wait and see."

The household arrangement of the black family allows for the family to group its members into smaller units. This grouping serves to create a home base where a member may expect certain types of immediate assistance. For example, a person knows that he can go to his home for food, comfort, or protection. He learns that these people are immediately accessible to him. Even though the person is aware that many people in his household provide for him, he knows whom he can count on when these people are not available to him. The members he will or will not go to are not always determined by biological or marital connections. A household that is a part of the family may contain people who are not related by blood or marriage. For example, in Family Number One, Phillis and Jim provided services to Peggy and Terry; however, they were not related to them by blood or marriage. Nevertheless, they are considered "family," and therefore they form a household that is a part of Peggy's family.

As Peggy said, ". . . from what I just told you about relatives, the people next door, Phillis and Jim, are more than relatives to me. To be a relative doesn't necessarily mean that you love someone. But the people next door, I do love. And, I think they love me. What I mean is that they are closer to me than some relatives. . . . Phillis is the same as mother to me, I consider her to be a member of my family. I consider Cousin Jim, Phillis' husband, also to be a member of my family by virtue of the fact that I have no hesitations in going to their house whenever I'm in town and feeling the same warmth and relaxation as I do in my own mother and father's home. This includes food, words of inspiration, faith, opinions, just the same as I would my own family; and we aren't related by blood."

These households provide for an orderly system that prevents a person from being confused or frustrated because so many alternatives face him or her. Households keep the person from having to negotiate relationships entirely "from scratch," and serve as a hierarchical structure within the family. Here the pivotal household is very important. The oldest generation of members is usually located in the pivotal household, for example, the grandparents. This is not to say that some people are ranked above others; rather, households may have priority over other households. The importance of the households is that their members work together for the "good" of the entire family.

Each member performing in these households is viewed by himself or herself and other members as "family" members. They are also referred to as being "family" or "part of the family." For example, Betty, of Family Number Three, has a boyfriend who lives in Michigan. He sends money to her monthly. This money helps pay the rent for the apartment. Betty stated, "If I didn't get the money from my boyfriend, I don't know how I could make it. The money I make barely pays for the food we need. My boyfriend always comes through. He ain't let me down yet . . . and I don't expect him to. He treats me better than my husband did."

The relationships between people who are connected by blood and marriage may be important; however, those people who acquire membership through friendships are just as important as if they were born into the family. These relationships should not be confused with "fictive" or "created" relationships that refer to temporary or convenient associations between members and nonmembers of a family. In these latter relationships, the people are not considered members of the family—they may be referred to as a "friend" or a "good friend" and in some cases just plain neighbors. For example, Ola May, of Family Number Two, talked about a school teacher who provided services for her daughter. She said, "Miss Williams, the school teacher, she is the reasoning of my daughter finishing school. When my daughter graduated, Miss Williams bought her graduation things for her to graduate in. She was just a friend of the family—a good friend. She helped my daughter through high school. The things she needed, she got."

Thus, the black family is composed of two or more households; each household contains one or more members of the family. Each household provides not only what we think of as "domestic services"; it also provides "words of inspiration," "faith," and "opinions." None of the members is confined to any one household. Social scientists have attempted to discuss black family structure based on its household configuration. For example, these households have been characterized as containing predominantly female adults and children, with an absence of most male adults. Moynihan (1965) saw the absence of male adults as a result of abandonment or desertion. Gonzalez (1970), on the other hand, saw the absence of male adults as a result of migration in quest for employment. For the most part, any attempt to account for black family structure based on a configuration consisting of predominantly female adults and absent male adults would be only representative of a few households within the total black family structure. Such representation does not hold true for the majority of the poor blacks, nor does it hold true for a significant number of blacks in any other economic category.

Any attempt to collect census data as to the presence of female and male adults would produce a different configuration no matter how often a census was taken. Several factors are responsible for this inconsistency: (1) the census taker; (2) secrecy in revealing information; (3) temporary absence; (4)

residential patterns; (5) marriage customs; and (6) nonbiological, nonmarital relationships.

Census takers are basically concerned with individual houses and the biological and marital members residing there. In many cases, informants will not reveal who resides at their dwelling because they do not trust such information falling in the hands of someone they do not know. Often members may be away for a period of time and are not included in the figures given anyone who seeks the information. Since members may eat and sleep in any household that is a part of their family, they may be present in one household at a given time, and still another household at a different time. People live together but may not be legally married; therefore, they will not always reveal the presence of their mates. Finally, people who are considered members of the household may not be related by blood or marriage, and therefore the researcher does not include them in his survey; or if he does, he does not consider them to be members of the family.

With all of these possibilities, any attempt to describe household configuration on the basis of who is present and who is not would be counterproductive and shed little light on the true nature of black family structure. For example, in Family Number One, Peggy said that relatives constantly moved through their house. That is, they came to live with her for periods up to eight years. Alice talked about residing at Peggy's house until she went to work for some white folks where she stayed. In Family Number Two, Ola May raised many children that were not her own. She said that many people stayed with her. Today, she reserves a room for "any of my people who want to come and stay with me." Ronald, of Family Number Four, lived with his grandmother, then his aunt, and finally his mother and father. He said that he still returned to live with his grandmother at least three months during the summer. Ronald said, "One of my mama's youngest brothers stayed with us for three years. He and I was more like brothers than he was my uncle. I also stayed with my grandmama when I was young. I went to school up there. My youngest aunt used to keep me, too." His mother, Bertha, first lived with her grandmother and then her mother. Even when she was living with her mother, her godmother—Annie Mae—provided her with most of her necessities.

A member's performance is very important to the relationship, and therefore the process for entering the black family, as well as remaining a member, is based on the member's ability to perform in his or her roles. A lack of performance in role assignment makes it possible for any member to be terminated from the family. Therefore, it does not matter if one is born into the family, marries into the family, or enters the family through mutual consent; one remains a member of the family so long as he performs his expected duties.

For example, Betty and the rest of her family have excluded Ludy, their mother, from the family. Betty said, "She's running 'round just dying off, for lack of attention. Well, you see I work every day. I know she's half eating 'cause half the times she come down here, she don't even have a cigarette. Well, she's with this man. He can't buy her food. He can't buy her cigarettes. In fact, she comes here and eats a meal and gets a pack of cigarettes. Then she's gone again. I can't keep her here. She comes and says she is going to stay. Soon as we're gone to work she take off. We may not see her for a whole week. When you go down there to get her, she rears-up at you and say, 'Don't come lookin' for me. Go on, leave me 'lone.' So, what can you do? We told her we wouldn't bother her about her drinking if she would just stay here so we can look after her. We all work, but there's always someone 'round. Sometimes she come here and say, 'I done quit that,' meaning drinking; and maybe for a few days she won't drink. That's because she don't have no money to buy it, and we won't give her no money for it. We know what she will do with it. If that old man don't take it from her, the man at the whiskey store sure will. That's why we can't depend on her doing anything. She's not dependable at all. She's subject to come here and say, 'Well, I'll keep the children while you go to work.' Well, if she got a drink in her hand, or have a mind to, she'll tell the children, 'I'll be back.' And who knows when she'll come back. . . . That was our problem."

Shortly before I left Vera Ridge, the members of Family Number Three had decided that Ludy, the mother, could not be helped and could offer no help; therefore, they would try no longer to "straighten her out." Betty said, "She don't exist as far as I'm concern. God knows I have tried. She just don't look to me. I mean, she look to me as if I'm trying to run her life. She won't listen to me at all; so, I don't know. . . . She kinda make me feel that she just looked over me as being her daughter. But I don't let that take no effect on me. I know that I might get on her about the way she lives; that's why she feel the way she do toward me. I mean, it don't bug me one bit. But I can't keep getting upset about her. I'm causing my own health to go bad. Neglecting myself as well as my children, worrying about Mama. Any time she want to act right, she can come back."

As we can see, blood members do not automatically have a permanent position in the family; therefore, blood is not the most important factor for determining and maintaining one's membership. Performance as a member becomes the most important factor in the black family. This is also borne out by Harry (the boxer who wanted to protect me from the four men) and his brother. He said, "Every time I'm ready to give up on him, he comes by the house and throws me a few bucks. . . . But I'm getting tired of his shit. Man, I don't know how much longer I can take him. None of the other folks will have anything to do with him. I'm the only family he's got."

Once, while attending a basketball game, a fight in the stands broke out. Harry was in the middle of the fight. He was "taking on" three men. It took several people to calm Harry down. Once they pulled him off, he was hustled outside. I walked out to where he was standing and asked him what had happened. He said nothing, but stood there frothing at the mouth. His brother walked out of the door and started off. Harry rushed up to him and grabbed him by the shirt. He slapped him twice in the face, told him that was the last time he would defend for him, and said he didn't ever want to see him again. To my knowledge, the end of Harry and his brother's relationship came shortly after this. His brother got into another fight and was badly injured. He wasn't expected to live. I talked with Harry about his brother's condition, and he said, "I don't care what happened to him—I don't care."

Members of the family know what is expected of them. They also know when their behavior is "wrong." Other members will begin to alert the member who is not performing as expected that "he better straighten up." Often this warning is not direct; it is a shifting of attention from that member to other members. For example, John told me, "People all the time are accusing me and Dot, Billy's wife, of 'doing it.' That's just because they see us together a lot of time, and doing things together. I'll be honest with you. I do like Dot, but not that way. We get along good together. My brother never said anything to me about Dot and me 'cause he knows better. It's my sister who's doing all the gossiping. She said, 'Why you and Dot all the time laughin' and jokin' together? Every time I see one of you, I see the other. Must be somethin' goin' on. I ask you for somethin', you ain't got it. She ask you for somethin' and you give it to her, just like that!' My sister is just jealous 'cause 'um not always doing things for her. She's all the time, 'givema this and givema that,' but she don't have nothin' to give you when you ask her for something. She keeps my mother in a bundle of nerves. You never know, when she comes home, how long she's going to stay. You never know where she is when she's gone. She don't write, she don't call."

Members are also aware when another member cannot perform as expected. Where a member cannot perform, this does not mean that he or she will be eliminated from the unit. The important factor is that he or she is willing to do all that can be done in an attempt to carry out his or her duties, and maintain a relationship. Where a member may not be able to perform, the member does not necessarily let this be known to the person or persons for whom the services are provided. In the black family there is a wide network of communication, and "the word gets around."

For example, in Family Number One, Alice said, "Once I didn't hear from my daughter in nearly a month. But I wasn't worried. I had already heard from my aunt up North, and she said that my daughter came by to see her. There was twenty dollars in the letter I got from my aunt; she said my daughter gave it to her to send to me, but I know that ain't true. You see, what she did was ask my aunt to send me twenty dollars and she will pay her back. See here, I know my child. Now she must be outta work, 'cause when she's working and doing fine, I hear from her every week. She just don't want me to know about how she is doing 'cause she knows I worry about how she is. You see, Aunt Lisa told me she lost her job—so I know about these things. But, soon as she get back on her feet, I'll hear from her. It may just be that she'll walk through that door and surprise me. She likes to do things like that."

Not all people living in a household are members of the family, yet it is possible to see people performing tasks that are like those of family members. Therefore, mere performance in certain roles does not necessarily mean that a person is a member. In Family Number Two, Ola May has a boarder who has certain chores; however, he is not a member of the family. The boarder is not related by blood or marriage. However, there may be people living in the household who are related by blood and marriage and are still not considered family members.

For example, in Family Number Two, a cousin named Gracy Lee stayed with Ola May for several years. Ola May said, "Her mama forsake her and I took her in. When she left to go where her mama was, she had to hustle up on the street to get enough money to go where her mama was. She wasn't but fifteen years old." Gracy Lee was not considered a member of the family, even though she was related by blood.

Therefore, the criteria for determining who is or is not a member of the family are: If one is in daily or continual interaction with others in the family, then one is usually considered a member. If one performs necessary tasks for the maintenance of the family, such that his or her absence would jeopardize the existence of the family, then one is seen as a member of the family. If one's relationship with others in the family is perceived as that of a "family" or "part of a family," and talked about in such a manner, then one would be considered a member by others and by oneself. Frequency of interaction, performance of tasks, and personal relations combine to form most of the criteria of eligibility for membership in the black family.

In conclusion, the black family is composed of households. The interaction taking place between members in these households is based on the relationship established between them. The type of relationship will determine how one performs toward other members. The most singular aspect of the black family is a member's performance in his or her roles, since lack of performance is cause enough to eliminate a member from the family. Thus, the black family contains a wide range of people connected by blood, marriage, and mutual consent, working collectively for the benefit and survival of the family.

I ain't never had no family—no people
Some time, way back they snatched them away from me
I can't even remember when it was
it's been so long ago
You know why I walk with this here stoop?
Pickin' cotton—from pickin' cotton
Looka these hands
They done picked so much cotton
everytime I reach fur somethin'
I think 'um reachin' fur cotton bows
Ma back's full of scars where I've been whipped
a many a many a times
I can see him comin' now
I can feel maself in pain

I can hear that voice a yellin'
so, I start shakin' all over
Sayin', laughin' his teeth so white,
"Pick that cotton!
Let me see them assholes reachin' fur the sky!"
He'd git off his horse and walk ober to the babies
tuggin' on they mama's sack
and then he'd lift up they dresses
and say
"You comin' long fine—just fine
You gonna make lots of nigger babies
when you grow-up"
That's all our women-folks was good fur to dem
birthin' babies
All dem babies
and I don't have none—not a one

These are the words of an old man I met
he said to me
"I'm a hundred and somethin', I don't
know how old Jest exactly when I was born
I can't tell ya
But I can remember when all of this land
where we're sittin' right now
was covered with water
I never thought I'd see the day
when I'd be sittin' here
eatin' with white folks"

GOOD-BYE
VERA RIDGE

*T*HE last day I spent in Vera Ridge was hot and humid. The temperature was in the nineties. There wasn't wind and no way to cool off. I was cleaning out the trailer and wondering about all the extra furnishings I had acquired when John came by. He asked me what I was going to do with the furniture and other household items I had bought. I told him I was going to give them to some needy family. He said he knew of a needy family. I asked, "Who is this needy family?"

He said, "My own." He wanted the furniture and offered to pay for it. I told him I'd rather give it to someone who really needed it, and that it was the least I could do for the community of Vera Ridge. He told me to think about his offer and that he would return later. I felt badly that I didn't immediately give everything to John, but I also knew that there were people who needed it more than he.

I continued to clean my trailer-house. I had packed everything in my car I thought I would take, but whenever I turned around, there were additional things to pack. While I peered into my car looking for extra space, Mrs. Andrews, the lady across the street, came by. She asked me what I planned to do with my furniture. I told her I was going to give it to a needy

family. She told me that she needed it, and that she was willing
to pay for it. I told her, as I had told John, that there were people who were more in need than she, but I would think about
her offer. She said that after I had made up my mind I should
come to tell her. Meanwhile, she would be waiting in her house.
As she walked to her house I also regretted what I said to her.
She had been so careful to watch over my trailer whenever I
was out of town. I thought I had better get rid of these things
quickly, before anyone else asked for them. Otherwise, I was going to leave Vera Ridge the way I came, with people angry at
me. I didn't want a crisis on my hand. More than likely I would
have to return to Vera Ridge; therefore, whatever my choice, I
had to leave in good grace with most of the people here.

But Mrs. Andrews wasn't the last to ask for the furniture.
Betty, from family number three; Billy, the person John referred to as 'Bro'; Tessie, the woman John had a baby with before his marriage; Lee Ola, the woman who said that she would
let me adopt her two children if I would marry her; and Mrs.
Turner, the lady from whom I had rented the trailer-house—all
wanted the furniture. So, I had a problem on my hands. Actually the furniture should have gone to Lee Ola because she,
without a doubt, was the most in need of it. In my eyes, this was
a serious issue because I did want to leave the community in
good standing—especially if I should want to return.

A thought flashed through my mind: give each of the people
who had asked a piece of furniture. I could divide it among
them. I was happy with my decision but the people who wanted
it were not. Then I remembered a lesson that Vera Ridge had
taught me: how to deal with situations. I was not going to let
them back me into a corner. I was going to deal with it! If they
accepted my plan, well and good; if they didn't, it would be
their problem—but maybe mine. Anyway, I told them I would
divide the things among them, and that I would decide who gets
what. I further stipulated that I was going to charge a small fee,
and if I detected any signs of disapproval, I would return to my
original plan and give it to a needy family of *my* choosing.

I felt firm, and hoped that I had sounded firm in presenting my decision. Everyone seemed to accept my plan because they knew if they didn't they'd get nothing.

I returned to the trailer and began to divide up the furnishings and other things according to who I felt needed them the most. I knew no matter how I divided the items there was going to be suspicion that I've been partial. Still, I believed my way was the best, and so I stuck to my guns.

I had them come over one at a time. As I sold the things, each person wanted to pay less than agreed and to acquire more furniture than I had included in the lot. But I didn't let them sway my decision. I told them they could take it or leave it for the others. Some of them, in trying to get me to reconsider, reminded me of the favor or favors they had done for me, but I didn't change my mind. No one seemed particularly happy as they took their newly acquired possessions. I got rid of everything except the things I needed to finish cleaning the trailer-house. I said I'd give them to Mrs. Andrews after I was finished.

I felt good about the way I had handled the situation, and I think, for the most part, they are still my friends—I had dealt with it!

Later that evening, after I had distributed all the furniture, cleaned the trailer, locked its doors, and returned the keys to Mrs. Turner, I began my rounds of good-byes. I really felt rather sad about my leaving, and I felt sadder as I told each person of the households good-bye. It seemed so final—too final. They really made me feel they were sorry that I was leaving, even those who received some of my furniture. They reminded me of the good times we had shared. It pleased me that they spoke of good times because I remembered so few.

Perhaps, I thought to myself, they were referring to the Christmas party I had given for the children of the community. I had spent several hundred dollars buying gifts for most of the community people with whom I had particular relationships. I gave special gifts to the families with whom I worked, and/or the people with whom I was especially close. For me, the happiest part of this event was that I was so thorough in giving gifts that no one complained that I had neglected them at Christmas; nor did anyone criticize their gift from me. Yes, that was a good time.

Another good time was the party I held for the young people. Over a hundred people crowded inside and outside my trailer-house. All had fun and there were no problems. The basketball players of the community college stood guard in case anyone started trouble, but no one got out of hand. People danced on the patio and even though the music was loud, none of the neighbors complained. Everyone made me feel special, because they considered my party elaborate—certainly something they wern't used to. Many people whom I didn't know came, but somehow everyone seemed to know me. They also seemed to respect me. I told them I didn't want any "pot" smoking on the premises and although I knew they had it with them, and it would be smoked; none was smoked in or about the trailer. The party had lasted until four o'clock in the morning. The next day some who had helped to organize the party came by and helped clean the trailer. For days afterward people talked about the good time at my place. There were a few items missing from my equipment, but I didn't report it to anyone.

Everyone in Vera Ridge knew that I was leaving and some gave me surprises. Perhaps the most rewarding and unexpected was given by Betty and her family. When Betty was picking up her furniture at my trailer-house, she said to make sure I came by before leaving. So, this family was the first I said good-bye to. I knocked on Betty's door and she invited me in. I thought it strange that no one else was present when they all knew I was coming to say good-bye. She said to have a seat and that she would be right back. She walked outside as I sat there waiting. Shortly, she returned and told me to come with her. We walked over to Johnny's apartment. And, there they were—all of them. They yelled "Surprise!" Betty said that she knew I didn't have much time so they would make it short. All the women kissed me and gave me pastry they had baked. I received a sweet potato pie, a fruit cake, some cookies, and a bread pudding—all my favorites! Just as I was learning about their behaviors, their habits, and lifestyles, so were they learning about me. I received a wallet as a gift from all the men. I didn't know what to say except "Thanks!"

As usual, Betty came to my rescue. She said, "All right now, let him go. We just wanted to show our appreciation for knowing such a swell person, and we hope you come back. Remember you're always welcome at my place."

I said I certainly would. They helped me carry the gifts to my car. I put them on the front seat and some on the floor. I got into my car and told them I would never forget them. Then I drove away. I was very moved as I looked back and saw them waving.

I drove over to Mr. Smith's shop. He was the only person there. Ronald, his son, and Bertha, his wife, were away. I didn't have much difficulty saying good-bye to him. He said it had been a pleasure knowing me and he wished me well. He told me I was always welcome at his home, anytime I was in the area. I shook his hand and then I returned to my car. Finally I reached John's house.

John and his family were the last I would say good-bye to. Leaving John's household was difficult for me. Sammy cried when he found out I was leaving permanently. He jumped into my lap and cried, "Uncle Reggie, please don't go."

I told him I would be back to see him and that he would always be in my mind and in my heart. Then both John and I said to him, as if our minds were together, "Big boys don't cry." John further added, "You don't want Uncle Reggie seeing you looking like this. Now stand up and be a big boy."

Sammy crawled down from my lap, wiped his eyes, and ran to his mother. I told John that I had had many rough times while being in Vera Ridge; however, I really appreciated him and his family for their help and support. I told them that knowing them far outweighed any of the hard times I faced. He said he was glad he was able to help me and he added that his

house was always a place where I could stay. Sarah followed
with similar words. As I was leaving, he said, "Reggie, come
back to see us now."

I told them to count on my returning. He said he would be
eager to have a copy of my report on Vera Ridge. I said a final
good-bye. He walked me down to my car and Ola May came to
her window, yelled good-bye, and added that she expected me to
return. I told her that I would—soon. I shook John's hand, got
into my car, and drove away.

I headed for the highway, passing houses I had visited many
times, wondering what the people inside were doing at that moment. I passed the Walker's house, but I didn't stop to say good-
bye to them. I passed the empty house where Peggy used to live,
slowed down for a moment, then went onto the entrance of the
highway that would take me far away from Vera Ridge. Near
the highway entrance was the hotel where I had my first serious
encounter with the four men. The incident was quickly remembered and even more quickly pushed into the back of my mind
as I got onto the highway and sped West. I never looked back,
not even through my rearview mirror. A few miles up the road
I saw a sign saying MUDDY RIVER—I knew then that Vera Ridge
was behind me . . .

APPENDIXES

Appendix A
A Survey of the Literature on the Black Family

Research on the structure of the white middle-class family in the United States suggests a general agreement about the putative characteristic features of this family. I am not surprised that such research, based on previously accepted universals, has depicted American kinship as homogeneous in structure. Recently, however, other social scientists have begun to challenge the application of the nuclear family concept to all ethnic groups in America.[1] For example, Schneider and Smith (1973) state that, "there has been a growing suspicion that social scientists who find nuclear families everywhere may well be importing their own cultural preferences" (1).

They hold that, while all Americans may share the same categories of kinship system, the actual family arrangement for some Americans may differ. These differences, according to Schneider and Smith, are based on the *emphases* and *stresses* placed on sexual values.[2]

As a result of depicting American kinship as a homogeneous structure, based on a nuclear arrangement, much injustice has been done in attempting to understand the subtle complexities involved in kinship patterns among some ethnic groups.[3] Some social scientists—Drake and Cayton (1945), Johnson (1941),

Myrdal (1944), Banfield (1958), Abrahams (1963), Hannerz (1969), Keil (1966), and Schulz (1969)—have directly contributed to this misunderstanding.[4] This is not to say that their studies on the black family did not have good intentions in their representations; however, their research seemed to support and perpetuate stereotypical attitudes about the black family. Perhaps even more important is that these studies were made under the guise of the black family in most cases when in fact the author was talking about "black lower class," the "poor blacks," or "black family in poverty." This distinction is crucial in any cultural account of the family. As Lewis (1966) pointed out, a segment of society may be poor, but not necessarily in a "culture of poverty." Valentine (1968), Lewis (1965), Hannerz (1969), and Libow (1967) have gone a step further and shown that the so-called culture of poverty, for the most part, is simply a definition of poverty and not of culture.

Moynihan (1965) and Oscar Lewis (1966) have directly contributed to this injustice. For example, Moynihan states, "The evidence—not final, but powerfully persuasive—is that the Negro family in the Urban ghettos is crumbling. . . . A National effort is required if the Negro family is to stablize itself." (43, 51). For Moynihan, the black family was becoming, if not already, "matrifocal." The existing literature depicts the black family as ranging anywhere from extended to matrifocal in structure. It was Moynihan's report that seemed to spur some social scientists (both black and white) to abandon the idea of matrifocality apropos of the black family once and for all.[5] I can only agree with this abandonment. Most black social scientists have put the subject matter to rest. On the one hand, they see its continual discussion as a means whereby the white man is attempting to continue to discredit the black male as an incapable father and make him look as if he is a weak man who cannot provide the basic necessities for his family. On the other hand, it makes the black female look as if she is the "Amazon" woman, the pillar of the black family. These ideas have been advanced by both Cleaver (1968) and Davis (1971).

There are several popular and widely accepted historical approaches to the black family: Du Bois (1909), Johnson (1934), Frazier (1939), Herskovits (1958), Gutman (1976), and Haley (1976), to name a few. Herskovits describes a family stripped of its culture and reconstructed on the basis of slavery. He concludes that, "The Negro is thus a man without a past" (Herskovits 1958:298). Frazier (1939) maintains that few of the previous values of African origin were still held by blacks. He stated that "Probably never before in history has a people been so nearly completely stripped of its social heritage as the Negroes who were brought to America. . . . Slavery destroyed household goods and dissolved the bonds of sympathy and affection between men of the same blood and household" (15).

Frazier does not state that blacks have no past; what he does feel is that few values have "survived" the institution of slavery in terms of the family. Both Gutman (1976) and Haley (1976) attempt a chronological account of the black family over a period of several centuries. While their accounts of the black family offer some historical insight, they provide very little on the present-day structure of the black family.

Another approach to the study of the black family has been advanced by such black writers as Pinkney (1969), Billingsley (1968), and Ladner (1971). They suggest that there are African roots in the present black family structure. The assignment of a common root cause—slavery—links this model with the previously mentioned authors; however, it is representative of the black family structure as it exists today. The former model emphasizes external "forces" as the basis for the black family structure, whereas the latter model stresses that the elasticity of imported values allowed the black family to survive in spite of the hardships slavery imposed. One model implies that slavery produced the conditions of the black family; the other suggests that because of slavery, the black family exists as it does today. Whatever the cause—economic, political, religious, and so forth—the approaches are necessarily concerned with history.

Still another approach to the black family is the view that the nuclear arrangement of family structure prevails in American kinship structure. This approach is popular with both anthropologists and sociologists. For example, Schneider (1968), Schneider and Smith (1973), Murdock (1949), and Parsons (1943) share in this view. Their studies suggest that while the black family places different emphasis and stress on various values, it shares the same kinship structure as that of the white middle-class nuclear family.

Authors that appear only to argue against the implication that the black family structure is different from that of the white middle-class nuclear family are Bernard (1966), Hill (1972), Ladner (1971) and Billingsley (1968). Here the black family is not viewed in opposition to the nuclear family structure of the white middle class. Bernard (1966) suggests that a "typical . . . family type among Negroes is one in which both husband and wife are living together in their first marriage" (Bernard 1966:40). Ladner (1971) points out that although there are "female headed households" these households constitute only a small percentage of the total family arrangement.

Current writers on the black family use the inductive method. Staples (1971), Hill (1972), Diggs (1973) and Stack (1974) emphasize the necessity of defining the black family within its own context. These writers seem to devote themselves to disproving the relevance of the nuclear concept to all family structure within the United States. They attempt to correct what is viewed as "ethnographic bias." They suggest that social scientists who did not find the nuclear family arrangement among the people they studied may have failed to do so because of their own "hang up" or personal bias. This idea has also been advanced by Schneider and Smith (1973).

The concept that the particular context is more important than the idea that all groups share a common value system as Americans has been forwarded more precisely by Ladner (1971) and Stack (1974). Ladner points out that "In every racial, ethnic, social class and religious group in American society, a standard norm prevails" (110). Although criticism of universal values in the study of different cultures is not a new debate, it is a recent development in evaluating components of complex, polyethnic societies such as the United States (Kluck-hohn *et al*. 1952:412).

The problem with most representations of American families that differ from the nuclear construct centers on the question of values.[6] Some social scientists such as Schneider and Smith (1973) feel that the differences in these family arrangements result from the varying emphases and stresses placed on *sex* values. For Schneider and Smith, these emphases and stresses occur at the level of sexual intercourse. Rodman (1965), on the other hand, suggests that there is a "value stretch" among the "lower-class" black families.[7] In other words, when people cannot share in the values of the "mainstream" society (sexual or otherwise), they upgrade their own values so that they are recognized and are acceptable to them. One example of this value stretch can be seen at the level of offspring legitimation. Children who are born out of wedlock are considered illegitimate to the mainstream society, but to lower-class blacks these children would be considered legitimate.

Still another view of value differences is advanced by Davis (1946). He suggests that there is a "dual" value system whereby lower-class people participate in both the mainstream value system (where possible) and embrace their own set of values where participation is not possible. Of course, the most scathing representation of lower-class families has been forwarded by Oscar Lewis (1966) with his concept of the "Culture of Poverty."[8] He characterizes a segment of the American population (some lower class) as having a perpetual "psychological pathology." In most cases, lower-class values are generally seen as a departure from middle-class values and the result is "disorganization," "deprivation," or "poverty."

I would contend that the black family cannot be discussed in terms of a "deviation" of, or a "derivation" from, the typical white middle-class nuclear family. I further contend that the black family cannot be discussed in terms of lower class, middle class, or any other class. To suggest so is to reify the concept of family. I intend to demonstrate that the concept of family (whether one is talking about the lower class blacks or blacks in general) is not applicable when discussing black kinship structure. My assertion is based on evidence I acquired from fieldwork described earlier in the book.

At the heart of any society's social fabric is a set of rules that are supposed to determine how its members will behave.[9] These rules are a result of the norms and values of the society, and they provide a code of conduct that members are to follow. In each social system of a society a code exists as to how members are supposed to behave in a given situation toward other members of that society. In less complex societies the code will regulate most of its members' behavior and, for the most part, the members will comply. However, where the society has a multi-ethnic make up, its code of conduct may not be followed by all the ethnic groups within the society—whether they are supposed to or not. Therefore, to understand one ethnic group's behavior as opposed to another, or to some standard code of conduct of that society, it becomes important to observe those rules that govern the behavior of the particular group with which one is concerned.

The problem with most studies done on the black family centers around their approach to the rules that govern the behavior of black members within the family. The most important aspect of black kinship structure that makes it different from that of the nuclear family arrangement can be found at the level of rules governing members' behavior toward one another. The rules that we speak of when talking about kinship are "jural rules."[10] According to Stack (1974),

> If we try to define jural motherhood by the kind of rights and duties comprising it, we are in trouble, as the societies we have already considered reveal. For the ways in which rights in children distribute socially and the very content of the rights themselves vary considerably cross-culturally. We are dealing with a jural role, then, but can identify it

cross-culturally not by its content but by some constant among the criteria by which people are entitled to the role . . . (87).

The evidence received in my study suggests that the rules that govern behavior for the nuclear family arrangement are not applicable to the black family. I suggest that the difference may appear at the level of transformation rules rather than general rules. Gonzalez (1970) suggested that the jural domain is in the hands of females and thus the mother becomes centrally important to the family. Although there can be strong ties between the mother and her children, the strength of such ties will depend on the relationship between the mother and her children.

Most noticeably, jural rights may be transferred to people other than the parents. The recipients of such rights can all be males. He may be an older brother, an uncle, or someone who is not related by blood or marriage, for example, a godfather. According to Goodenough (1970), one "of the transactions relating to parenthood [is the] outright surrender by jural parents of some or all their parental rights to someone not otherwise entitled them, so that jural parenthood is transferred in whole or in part from one party to another" (409).

The transferring of rights in the black family will override what may seem like concrete rules as a result of jural rights of the mother. However, Gonzalez (1970) suggests that the one domain where women seem to have some participation is in jural affairs, "and perhaps in this sense we could label those societies which grant women a larger or more important role as more strongly matrifocal" (234).

In the black family there is no rigid set of rules ascribing particular behavior to particular statuses because how one behaves must give way to the situation at hand and not according to some predescribed behavior.[11] In the nuclear family, one's performance toward another member of the family is predicated on one's status in relationship to that member. For example, in the black family, who provides services for other members of the family is not as important as the services being provided. Therefore, one can say that there is a rule where one is supposed to be provided for; however, who provides for one has nothing to do with one's status to the person as much as it does with his ability to provide. Witness the behavior between members of the four families. Every member had as many options as he or she had households from which to obtain services. If Peggy or Terry's mother (of Family Number One) was not at home they could simply go to Phillis and Jim, their next door neighbors. As Alice (the cousin) said, "Peggy and Terry would go over to Phillis and Jim's house and eat just like they were at home."

Neither Phillis nor Jim are biologically or maritally connected to Peggy and Terry. However, they are considered members of the family. They provide services for Peggy and Terry that are said to be the responsibility of the mother and father in the nuclear family. As the rules in the nuclear family may limit these services to that of the mother and father, in the black family a wide range of people can provide these services.[12] Just who will provide them at any given time will depend on the context of the situation. As Peggy said, "From what I just told you about relatives, the people next door, Phillis and Jim, are more than relatives to me. To be a relative doesn't necessarily mean that you love him. But the people next door, I do love. And, I think they love me. What I mean is that they are closer to me than some relatives."

As we can see, the provider is not only unrestricted to blood or marital members, but he or she may include anyone who is considered a member, whether or not the membership was accrued through a relationship stemming from friendship. In Family Number Two, all the members had access to each other, and where one could not provide, the others would. Sammy knew that he could go to his house, the house of his grandmother, his aunts or even a woman referred to by his father as "Auntie Sue." John told me that "Auntie Sue, she's a real nice lady. Sometimes when I came home from school, she'd say, "Your mama ain't here, but I got a nice supper waitin' for you." Sometimes she was harder on me than my own mama. . . . Whereas mama would say, 'John, make sure you clean up your mess behind yourself.', and she'd just leave. Auntie Sue, she won't be standing right over me, but I knew she'd be somewhere watching me. Sometimes I'd try to sneak away, but I knew she'd catch me and say, 'Oh, no you don't do that. Get back there and clean up your mess 'fore I get this dish rag to you.' I used to get so mad at her, but I'm glad she was that strict with me."

These options are not alternatives to any rule holding that members will say that the mother is neglecting her "duties" because the child has to go to another member's house for food or whatever. What may be referred to as an alternative behavior in the nuclear family is embedded in the rules of the black family. In Family Number Three the availability of a member as well as his or her ability to provide is the determining factor. They rely on each other for the maintenance and functioning of the family. Betty said, speaking of Cynthia, "It's like this, anything I ask her for, if she's got it, I know I can get it. Anything I ask her to do, if she can do it she will. All of us are working at different times. We don't have to worry about our kids eating or getting to school on time. I do the same for her. We all pitch in and help each other out. These are the kind of things you expect your kinfolks to do."[13]

Whether the family is poor or self supporting, who provides for other members and the options available to each member is not confined to the status of the person who provides the services. I asked Steve (the young man that works for Mr. Smith) of Family Number Four about his relationship to the Smiths and he said, "We're very close, they are all very close to me. It's the same as my second family. I never really knew my daddy. Mr. Smith is the same as a daddy and Mrs. Smith is the same as a mama to me. They treat me the same way they treat

Ronald. Mr. Smith is sending both of us to college. He buys my clothes and my books and lets me work in his shop to have some money to pay for my food and stuff like that."

Bertha talked of Annie Mae who provided for her while she was growing up. She was raised by her grandmother. Ronald was raised by his grandmother and aunt. Members are constantly coming to the Smith's house to live; there they are provided with services they would receive if they were at their own houses. As Ronald said, "One of my mama's younger brothers stayed with us for three years. He and I was more like brothers than he was my uncle. I went to school up there with my grandmama. . . . My grandmama didn't want me to leave, and I didn't want to leave here when it came time for me to live with my mama and daddy. That's why I spend all my summers with them and every time I get a chance I'm up there with them."

In the nuclear family the rules are explicit. Father provides, protects, and has the authority over his family (Schneider 1968). He and only he is supposed to perform in these capacities (Parsons 1965). The mother nurses and takes care of the child, and she is responsible for housekeeping.[14] Where other people perform in these capacities, you no longer have a nuclear family, that is, a "broken home," or the parents are failing in their duties; therefore, he is not a good father and she is not a good mother (Schneider 1968).

Members of the nuclear family are defined in terms of blood and marriage, whereas informants describing members of the black family do so in terms of qualities of social behavior. See Appendixes B, C, D, E for descriptions of attributes of certain members in the black family. Appendix F lists the attributes of a person who is not related by blood or marriage, but who is said to be the same as, in this case, "mama." Since membership in the family is predicated on the relationship and one's performance, it is not difficult to see how people who are not related by blood or marriage can become members of a family by possessing certain attributes.

Although I have used categories (mama, daddy, sister, brother) the description of the attributes—the qualities of the attributes—is important. For example, a male or female can possess any of these qualities and attributes. Thus, the black family incorporates people who are not related by blood and members who provide services that are not determined on the basis of their sex. As a consequence, a second category of people is established. These are people who become members because of their social relationships to other members instead of a biological or physical relationship.[15] Anthropologists have long recognized the differences between the physical person and the social person. Malinowski (1930), Radcliffe-Brown (1950), Goodenough (1970), Carroll (1970), and Stack (1974) are some of the social scientists who have called our attention to the importance of these two categories of people and their relationship to members of the family. Appendix G illustrates an example of the social contrasted to the physical (related by blood) person.[16] The black family differs from the nuclear family by incorporating social members based on their ability to perform rather than what sex to which they belong.

In the black family, sex roles and gender distinction in terms of a division of labor are not predicated on biological or marital connections. Therefore, the rules that govern the nuclear family become even more obscure if applied to the black family. Activities are performed to maintain the family by whoever is available to do the work, regardless of sex. Doing house chores is not looked down on as "effeminate" or "demeaning."[17]

In Family Number Three, Johnny said, "I have seen my wife give birth to both of my children. I have just tried to sit there 'cause the nurses held me back. If my wife can go through that, I can go through eight hours a day and come home, do the cooking and washing and cleaning up the house—that's nothing—I've done it all my life."

In Family Number Two, Ola May's brother told me, "My wife left me and four small children just because I had to do six months on the county farm for taking a cow and selling the meat so that my family could eat. If I hadn't known what I did, I don't know how I coulda made it, but I did. I cared for my children. I raised them all the way until they was grown. I cooked, sewed, washed clothes. I did everything until my children got to the age where they could help me out. My mama used to tell me, 'You never know how your life's gonna turn, it's best you be prepared.' "

When I was in Lina, talking to Clara and her husband Larry, Larry told me, "Well, me and my wife, what we try to do is, if I get off work before she do, I start cooking, I clean up the house and I go and wash with my two oldest children. I don't have no certain things to do. I know I work and when I get off from work, if I'm tired 'caused I've had a long day, she'll cook and do such and such. So, I don't have no special things to do. I try to help out anyway I can. 'Cause before I married, I stayed by myself. For five years I took care of the little house I was staying in by myself."

Terry, of Family Number One, told me, "I often do kitchen chores. I often get up in the morning and cook my breakfast, and when my wife was sick, I took care of my daughter. Not so much from having to do it, but rather from being able to do it. Now I may spend all damned day in the kitchen, but we were brought up that somebody would come by to make sure that the kids are fed. I used to bathe my daughter, but I would call a friend to come by and comb her hair—it's just that simple."

In Family Number Four, all the members took pride in saying how well they were able to cook, iron, wash and clean up, with the exception of Mr. Smith. He turned to Bertha and said, "That's what I married her for. If one day I come in here and there's no food—I'll get it for myself that time—but then I'll be getting me another wife. I did all those things you talked about before I got married, but I'll be damned if I do them now. Now, I'm not saying I couldn't do them, I'm saying that I won't do them."

Then Ronald said to him, "Oh! Come on daddy! What about that time when mama had to go and see about grandmama?

Who cooked for you then? And when I came home from school the house was clean and we both took turns cooking."

"Well, that was different. Even so, I ate out during the week and sometimes Steve brought me over some food his mam cooked."

Domestic or wage-earning work is not clearly defined within the realm of black work. Outside employment creates a need for household management that falls on the nonworking members. The necessity for all members to learn how to take care of the home and themselves becomes important. If by chance the male is without work and the female has to work she is not expected to do house chores. The male or the children will wash, iron, cook, and clean house. It is the very structure of the black family that equips members to perform these chores whenever needed, and this need not be limited to the wife being ill or not present.[18] This is not to say that males are *supposed* to do household chores, per se, but its implications are that certain tasks must be performed, and that whoever is in the position to perform them is expected to do so.

It is rare for someone to be told specifically to observe a task such as cooking, washing and ironing, cleaning the house so that he or she will be able to perform such tasks when needed. The members, as they are growing up, basically observe others doing these tasks and then attempt to do so. Of course when such tasks are being performed and done incorrectly, the member will be shown by experienced members how to do them correctly. For example, in Family Number Three, Betty said, "I came home from work one day and my kids met me at the door, saying 'Mama! We got a surprise for you.' I was surprised all right. There was flour from one end of the house to the other. It was such a mess. And sitting on the table was this thing they called a cake. Honey! I'm telling you, I was so tickled I like to die. I tried to stop laughing, 'cause they tried, but I just couldn't help myself. The only way I could stop laughing was to think of the mess they had made and pretend to get mad. They asked me to try it. I didn't have the heart to tell them no, I didn't want to disappoint my children, so I went ahead and tried it. It was like a rock. I thought I would never get it down. They stood 'round me waiting for me to say something. I told them it was good. . . . That Saturday, I decided to bake a cake and I called them in and showed them a few things they did wrong. Honey! Now that oldest boy of mine, he can cook better than me."

Therefore, what would be called an exception or an alternative to the rules in the nuclear family is as much a part of the rule as other behavior in the black family. As a consequence, one can understand the nuclear family through its rules. All one has to do is come up with the set of rules that govern "ideal" behavior that is supposed to take place (Schneider 1968). Any other behavior can then be lumped into a package and called "alternative behavior." I am not saying that alternatives do not appear where there are rules—the very nature of rules is that they provide alternatives. The point here is that one should not exclude behavior simply because it does not appear to fit into some particular set of rules. Behavior that cannot be accounted for may not be the fault of the rules; it may be that the researcher conveniently labeled it as "alternative."

This is impossible to do for the black family for two reasons: (1) it is impossible to come up with a set of rules that will account for all behavior in all contexts, and (2) what may be acceptable behavior in one given context at one time, may not be acceptable at another context and another time. This may simply be a matter of distinguishing between *general* rules and *transformation* rules. Nevertheless, the point being made is *ideal* behavior versus *real* behavior, and that if one is talking about ideal behavior—which is presumably what American culture is based on, thus the nuclear family—there is no problem in describing what rules are. However, where a family structure is based more on real behavior, then the approach to an analysis of rules must occur at a different level, one capable of including both real and ideal behavior while at the same time distinguishing between rules and their alternatives.

Thus, the idea of jural rules is theoretically unproductive for explaining the black family. What is expected from a given person at a given time depends on the context of interaction and the person's ability to perform at the time, who else may be present and available, and so forth. How is it possible to account for all contexts under which certain behavior will or should occur? If you were to ask a member of the black family, "What happens if X does so-and-so?," informants almost always say, "It depends. . . ."

There are so many possibilities that it would be fruitless to attempt to account for all situations and contexts in which they may occur. Response to so-called "proper" behavior depends on the context in which the behavior is meaningful. If there are rules to be considered, *they are rules by which people encode and decipher messages about themselves, that is, rules by which information is put together, not jural rules.*

Once a difference to the approach of rules between the two family types is understood, their other differences become clearer. With this consideration in mind, I feel that what has been referred to as the black family can best be represented by what I now will refer to as the Black Domestic Unit (BDU).[19] The term domestic is not new in its application to family types; it has been used by Radcliffe-Brown (1950), Fortes (1958), and Bohannan (1957) to name a few. Its application to the black family is not new either. Of those social scientists who have used it, Nancy Gonzalez (1970) and Carol Stack (1974) have employed the term most effectively in discussing the "black family." Nancy Gonzalez effectively applied the term to Afro-Americans in her attempt to define matrifocality. Carol Stack also used the term in her study of the black urban poor. Although Gonzalez and Stack presented a deeper understanding of certain aspects of the black family, what they meant by domestic unit in reference to household and family differs from my usage.

Gonzalez refers to the household as a domestic unit.[20] I see the household as being only part of the domestic unit. This domestic unit according to Gonzalez is a "cooperative group" of people who work together in a "given *residential* structure." Here she implies a single residence; however, I would add that several residential dwellings may be involved in a single domestic unit. Nevertheless, Gonzalez's concept of a domestic unit paved the way for Stack's implementation of more concise evidence as proof of the model. Therefore, Stack was able to see the wider implication of black family lifestyle in her definition of a domestic unit.[21] For example, she recognized the importance of nonbiological people being a part of the domestic unit once they met certain qualifications. Stack stated that the domestic unit contained "durable network of kin and non-kin who interact daily, providing domestic needs of children and assuring their survival" (Stack 1974:31). I have incorporated some of Gonzalez and Stack's ideas and concepts, but added further dimensions in hope of providing an even better understanding of what I refer to as the BDU.

The major difference between my presentation and those of Gonzalez and Stack is that they are talking about the black "poor" and the black "lower class," while I am talking about the black family in general. I have also departed from previously held universals about the family and refused to view data that do not conform to the norms of the nuclear family as being irrelevant. For example, people who were not connected to the family by blood or marriage are treated by some as "fictive" kin. I evaluated the data that I acquired from my fieldwork and, in my opinion, these people referred to as fictive kin are as much a part of the BDU in every respect as the people who are related by blood and marriage. Since they are not treated differently from other members of the BDU, there was no reason or justification for me to treat them as being different.

The major criterion for who is a member of the BDU, as opposed to who is not, is his or her identification as a member by those who are members and him- or herself. There are certain clues that will assist the researcher in considering membership in the BDU where there is doubt. For example, if one is in prescribed contact (whether it is daily or not) and has continual interaction with other members in the unit, then he or she is usually considered a member. If one performs necessary tasks for the maintenance of the unit such that his or her absence would jeopardize the existence of the unit, then he or she is considered a member of the BDU. If one's relationship with others in the BDU is perceived as that of a "kin" and is referred to as such, then he or she would be considered a member of the unit by others and by himself or herself. Therefore, frequency of interaction, performance of tasks, and personal relationships (regardless where a member resides) combine to form the criteria of eligibility for membership in the BDU.

Where Gonzalez refers to household, I refer to it as "activity clusters."[22] Specific activities, shared only by certain members, cannot be viewed as necessarily separating them from the unit as a whole.[23] Instead, these activities between certain members must be viewed in terms of the various clusters of relationships that are shared among all members. It is this consideration that gives rise to the terms: *BDU* and *activity clusters*.[24] Activity clusters are smaller groups of people; however, they make up a network of the wider organizational structure of the BDU.[25] A person may belong to several of these clusters simultaneously. These activity clusters create a home base where a member may go to receive immediate assistance. They act as an "effective" group to which a person can go for food and other basic necessities.

The members in the person's activity cluster are immediately accessible to him or her. The members may not be connected to the person through blood or marriage. Witness in Family Number One: Peggy and Terry could go to Jim and Phillis's house for services that were not available to them at home. In Family Number Two, when he came home from school Sammy could go to his grandmother's house, to either of his aunts, to Sue's house, or to other members of his unit. In Family Number Three, every member was providing or receiving daily services from other members of the unit. If Betty did not feel like cooking when she got off from work she would simply go by Johnny's house. If Cynthia had not cooked before she left for work she knew that her husband and daughter could eat at any of the member's homes. Even in Family Number Four, Steve knew that he could go to the Smith's house for food and assistance, Ronald could go to his godmother's house, Bertha could go to Annie Mae's house and Mr. Smith, well, he did not go by anybody's house so whatever he desired would have to be brought to him.

Even though the person is aware that other persons in his activity cluster can provide for him, he learns whom he can "count on" when these people of his cluster cannot or do not provide. These clusters form an orderly network system that prevents a person from becoming confused or frustrated in the face of "too many possibilities" as some social scientists would suggest.[26]

In conclusion, black kinship structure is composed of activity clusters. These activity clusters combine to form the BDU. The interaction taking place between members in these clusters is based on relationships, whether they are formed through blood, marriage, or friendship.[27] Maintaining relationships within the BDU is predicated on one's ability to perform in one's roles. Relationships are often seen as "good" or "bad" relationships. For example, a member may say, "We have a good relationship" or "We have a bad relationship," referring to a person's ability or inability to perform in his or her roles. Thus, the BDU contains a wide range of people, related by blood, marriage, and friendship, who may or may not reside in the immediate area. These members work collectively for the maintenance and survival of the unit as a whole.[28]

Appendixes B–F represent attributes of certain family members as described to me by informants across the United States; they include the four families of study.

Appendix B
Attributes of Mama

Someone:
   who is with you all the way
   who takes care of you
   who cares about you from the heart
   who is always concerned about you
   who gives you advice and you listen to
   you'd do anything for
   you come to with your problems
   you'd do anything for, any time
   you'd tell anything
   you have a closeness with
   you can turn to
   who gives you what you need
   who is concerned about your welfare
   who can punish you when you do wrong
   who is always there when you need her
   who raises you
   who keeps in touch with you
   who shows you that she loves you
   whom you love, respect, obey, confide in, trust, and support
   who guides you
   who is demanding, forceful, and has authority over you

Appendix C
Attributes of Daddy

Someone:
   you love and obey
   you'd help if he needed you
   who respects his family
   who gives his children whatever help he can

who takes care of his family
who punishes you
who supports you
who gives advice to you
who is concerned about you
who watches over you
who guides you
who protects you
you go to when you have special problems
who sees that there is food for the children

Appendix D
Attributes of Sister

Someone:
   you protect (if male is speaking)
   you keep informed about guys
   you can relate to
   you talk to about girl problems
   you'd do anything for if she asked you
   you'd try to stop from getting involved with the wrong guy
   you respect
   you love
   you confide in
   you do things with—together (if female is speaking)
   you help when you can
   who helps you when she can
   to help guide you
   to help mama around the house
   who has respect for the family
   who gives you advice when she can

Appendix E
Attributes of Brother

Someone:
    you help in any way you can
    you share your life with
    who takes up for you
    who understands you
    who believes in you
    who goes out of his way for you
    who helps protect you
    who makes sure I'm going out with the right guys (if female
      is speaking)
    who is closer than a friend
    you can relate to
    who is like a close friend in a way
    who is truthful
    who keeps me out of trouble
    whom you have confidence in
    you respect
    you believe in
    you know you can always call on him
    I can rely on
    who gives you advice

Appendix F
Attributes of a Person Who
Is the Same as a Mama

Someone:
    who is the same as another mama
    who takes the place of a mama

who can punish you

who will talk to you and try to understand you

who financially supports you

you would help whenever she needed you

you do for because you want to

whom you are attached to the same way and sometimes more
   than my mama

who cares about you more than your own mama

who never gets mad at you

you can always go to her house and eat

who doesn't try to control you so much

who cares about you more than your own mama

who is very close to you

who treats you the same as a real mama

who treats you like you are her daughter

you can confide in

you can respect

you can trust

you can love

you feel at ease around

who still listens and understands you

who's closer than a lot of my family

you'd do for the same as my mama

who gives you advice

you can rely on

who's an all-around person

Appendix G
The Social and Physical Person

"The kinship term father . . . refers to the *socially recognized
genitor*. 'Daddy,' which informants themselves put in quota-
tions by intonation, refers to an essential kin such as the man
who raised a child" (Stack 1974:157). The two distinctions
presented here require more explanation if one is to fully understand their importance.

Genitor (father)	Social (father)
Father	Father
Daddy	Daddy
The man who raised me	The man who raised me
The man who took care of me	The man who took care of me
The person responsible for my birth	

In other words, the first four expressions may be applied to the "physical" father as well as to the "social" father. Only the last expression that is used for genitor distinguishes the physical from the social person. The expression *for my birth* is of little meaning in the BDU. The expressions *took care of* or *raised me* are of paramount importance. This person or persons may be male or female, related by blood, marriage, or friendship. Therefore, one should consider only the expression "The person responsible for my birth" if interested in demonstrating the differences between any biological or nonbiological person. If one considers the physical person as being connected by blood, then one can use this same analogy to apply to all members of the BDU, whether the person is related or unrelated by blood and/or marriage.

1. See, for example, Schulz (1968), Hannerz (1969), Gonzalez (1970), Ladner (1971), Staples (1971), Hill (1972), Schneider and Smith (1973), Stack (1974), Gutman (1976), and Scanzoni (1977).

2. "We contend that the lower-class has a perfectly coherent and well-organized family system which differs from middle-class family structure whereas middle-class norms attach positive value to the nuclear family as an independent entity, lower-class norms stress different patterns of solidarity, and lack the emphasis upon nuclear isolation. Since we do not question the fact that all Americans share the same kinship system, including the concept of the family" (Schneider and Smith 1973:4).

3. ". . . studies tended to reinforce populace stereotype of the lower-class black family—particularly the black family in poverty—as deviant, matriarchal, and broken. Given the prevailing academic biases, it is not surprising that few attempts have been made to view black families as they actually are, recognizing the interpretations black people have of their own cultural patterns" (Stack 1974:22).

4. Raab and Selznick (1959) typify the attitudes responsible for the injustice I speak of when they state, "In every respect Negro families suffer greater instability. Not only divorce, separation, and desertion . . . make normal family life among Negroes extremely precarious. . . . The mother or grandmother was as a rule the head of the household into which the adult Negro male was often only superficially integrated" (Raab and Selznick 1959:321–22).

5. Extensive analyses have been presented on the idea of matri-

focality by Fortes (1958), Randolph (1964), Cleaver (1968), Gonzalez (1970), Stack (1970, 1974), Davis (1971), Ladner (1971), and Staples (1971).

6. Davis (1946), Rodman (1965), Lewis (1966), Schneider and Smith (1973), Ladner (1971), and Stack (1974) are a few social scientists who have talked about values in relationship to the black family.

7. "Lower-class has often been associated with blacks. Prior to the middle and late '60's very little fieldwork had been done on lower-class non-blacks. Frazier (1939) did a study on the black family and it was his study of the black family that gave insight on the poor. Therefore, black meant poor, poor was equated with poverty and through time poverty with lower-class. However, no empirical studies had been made to analyze these four distinctions. The four distinctions and their features of this society (black, poor, poverty, and lower-class) was used by Frazier and those writers after him if they represented the 'truth' " (Valentine 1968).

8. For a detailed account of the "culture of poverty," see Oscar Lewis's Introduction to his work *La Vida* (1966).

9. Roger Keesing (1970) has presented a thorough explanation of rules and regulations in an analysis of role in his work, "Toward a Model of Role Analysis."

10. Meyer Fortes (1969) presents a complete analysis of the concept of jural rules in his work, *Kinship and the Social Order: The Legacy of Lewis Henry Morgan.*

11. See Ward Goodenough "Rethinking Status and Role."

12. Schneider (1968), Murdock (1949), Parsons (1954), and Raab and Selznick (1959) have advanced this idea about the nuclear family.

13. Betty's boyfriend Louis is also an important person for providing services to members of her household. Schulz (1968) and Ladner (1971) have also noted the intricate part the boyfriend plays in the black family. Schulz states, "The importance of the boyfriend's role becomes apparent when one realizes that four of the five women . . . now heading households receives support from boyfriends" (136–44).

14. Schneider (1968) has presented a complete analysis of the "mother" role in the nuclear family.

15. Radcliffe-Brown (1950), Roger Brown (1965), and Carol Stack (1974) have presented arguments concerning the idea of role and person; for example, the "physical" and the "social" persons roles.

16. Radcliffe-Brown (1950) noted that "Kinship therefore results

from the recognition of a social relationship between parents and children, which is not the same as the physical relation, and may not coincide with it" (4).

17. "It is a strength when family members can 'fill in' and assume each other's roles as needed. For example, a father can function as a 'mother' and children can temporarily be 'parents' to the father and mother" (Hill 1972:17).

18. According to Hill (1972), "In many two-parent Black families, especially those with working wives, occasions often arise that require the wife to act as the 'father' or the husband as the 'mother.' " (17).

19. I have used the term Black Domestic Unit (BDU) because it best describes the people, their grouping, their behavior toward one another and the households in which they live. That is, their interaction and, most important, their relationships and the idea of performance. Let me add that this is an *etic* term. The people do not refer to themselves as a BDU. Their terms can range from "family" to "part of the family" and many other terms to denote members of their unit.

20. For Gonzalez (1970), the domestic unit is "A cooperative group which maintains the participants in a given *residential* structure, even though the contribution of any one individual may be part-time . . . the fact that individuals have simultaneous loyalties to more than one such grouping may be important in understanding the social structure as a whole . . . men, particularly, tend to be placed in positions in which potential conflict between households develops upon them, thus putting strain upon the individual in his role in one or both units" (232).

21. Stack (1974) defines the domestic unit by stating that "The poor adopt a variety of tactics in order to survive. They immerse themselves in a domestic circle of kinfolk who will help them. To maintain a stable number of people who share reciprocal obligations, at appropriate stages in the life cycle people establish socially recognized kin ties. Friends may be incorporated into one's domestic circle: if they satisfy one another's expectations, they may be called kin—cousins, sisters, brothers, daddies" (29–30).

22. The term "activity cluster" was introduced by Radcliffe-Brown (1950), who also is credited with the term "domestic unit" to some degree in its present application. It has been successfully used by Gonzalez (1970) and Stack (1974) in describing behaviors similar to those that I refer to in the BDU; however, my usage must be understood within the context of the behavior I describe, not the broader usage of the term by others.

23. "It became clear that the 'household' and its group composition was not a meaningful unit to isolate for analysis of family life in The Flats. A resident in The Flats who eats in one's household may sleep in another, and contribute resources to yet another. He may consider himself a member of all three households" (Stack 1974:31).

24. "Personal kindreds overlap to form clusters of individuals who can each bring others into the domestic network. Participants in domestic networks in The Flats move quite often and hold loyalties share mutually conceived domestic responsibilities. Children may be cared for by their parents or by other participants in their parents' domestic network, or they may be transferred back and forth from the household of their mother to the household of other close familial kin" (Stack 1974:39).

25. By activity cluster I am not necessarily referring to a group of people living in close proximity. Instead, I am referring to a group of people *sharing* common interests and *working together* to assure the functioning and maintenance of one another *collectively*, rather than individually. They provide material as well as spiritual supportive needs.

26. Stack (1974) also reports that "The family network is diffused over several kin-based households, and fluctuations in household composition do not significantly affect cooperative familial arrangements" (31).

27. For a complete analysis of friendship and its importance to family membership, see "The Nature of Nurture" by Mac Marshall. Ladner (1971) and Stack (1974) have also reported the importance of friendship in the relationship of members of the black family.

28. For a thorough bibliography on most of the literature written about the black family, see: *The Black Family In The United States: A Selected Bibliography of Annotated Books, Articles, and Dissertations on Black Families in America,* by Lenwood G. Davis, 1978, Greenwood Press, Westport, Conn., and *Afro-American Folk Culture,* by John F. Szwed and Roger D. Abrahams, 1978, A Publication of the Institute for the Study of Human Issues, Philadelphia.

BIBLIOGRAPHY

Abrahams, Rogers (1963) *Deep Down in the Jungle: Negro Narrative Folklore from the Streets of Philadelphia.* Folklore Association, Hatboro, Pa.

Banfield, E. C. & L. F. (1958) *Moral Basis of a Backward Society.* Free Press, New York.

Bernard, Jessie (1966) *Marriage and Family Among Negroes.* Prentice-Hall, Englewood Cliffs, N.J.

Billingsley, Andrew (1968) *Black Families in White America.* Prentice-Hall, Englewood Cliffs, N.J.

Bohannan, Paul (1957) "An Alternate Residence Classification," in *Marriage, Family, and Residence.* Eds., Bohannan and Middleton, 1968. The Natural History Press, New York.

Bott, Elizabeth (1955) "Urban Families: Conjugal Roles and Social Networks," in *Sociology of The Family.* Ed., M. Anderson. Penguin Books Ltd., England.

Brown, Roger (1965) *Social Psychology.* The Free Press, New York.

Buchler, Ira R. & Selby, Henry A. (1968) *Kinship and Social Organization: An Introduction to Theory and Method.* The Macmillan Co., New York.

Carroll, Vern, ed. (1970) *Adoption in Eastern Oceania.* University of Hawaii Press, Honolulu.

Cleaver, Eldridge (1968) *Soul on Ice.* Delta Books, New York.

Davenport, William (1961) "The Family System of Jamaica," in *Marriage, Family, and Residence.* Eds., Bohannan and Middleton, 1968. The Natural History Press, New York.

Davis, Angela (1971) "The Myth of the Black Matriarch," in *MS*. Ed., Francis Klagsburn, 1973. Warner, New York.

Davis, Allison (1946) "The Motivation of the Underprivileged Workers," in *Industry and Society*. Ed., W. F. Whyte. McGraw-Hill, New York.

Diggs, Irene (1973) "Black Man Runs Family." *New York Times*, March 11, 1973, p. 30.

Drake, St. Clair and Cayton, Horace (1945) *Black Metropolis: A Study of Negro Life in a Northern City*. Harcourt Brace, New York.

Du Bois, W. E. B., ed. (1909) *The Negro American Family*. M.I.T. Press, Cambridge, Mass.

Fortes, Meyer (1958) Introduction in *The Development Cycle in Domestic Groups*. Ed., Jack Goody. Cambridge Press, Cambridge, Mass.

——— (1969) *Kinship and the Social Order: The Legacy of Lewis Henry Morgan*. Aldine Publishing Co., Chicago.

Fox, Robin (1967) *Kinship and Marriage*. Penguin Books Ltd., Harmondworth, Middlesex, England.

Frazier, Franklin E. (1939) *The Negro Family in the United States*. The University of Chicago Press, Chicago.

Gonzalez, Nancie (1969) *Black Carib Household Structure: A Study of Migration and Modernization*. University of Washington Press, Seattle.

——— (1970) "Toward a Definition of Matrifocality," in *Afro-American Anthropology*. Eds., Whitten, Jr., and Szwed. The Free Press, New York.

Goodenough, Ward (1965) "Rethinking Status and Role," in *In the Relevance of Models for Social Anthropology*. Ed., M. Banton. Tavistock Press, London.

——— (1970) *Description and Comparison in Cultural Anthropology*. Aldine Publishing Co., Chicago.

Gough, Kathleen (1959) "The Naya and the Definition of Marriage," *Journal of the Royal Anthropological Institute of Great Britain*, 89:23–24.

Gutman, Herbert G. (1976) *The Black Family in Slavery and Freedom, 1750–1925*. Pantheon Books, New York.

Haley, Alex (1976) *Roots: The Saga of an American Family*. Doubleday, New York.

Hannerz, Ulf (1969) *Soulside: Inquires into Ghetto Culture and Community*. Columbia University Press, New York.

——— (1970) "What Ghetto Males Are Like: Another Look," in

Afro-American Anthropology. Eds., Whitten, Jr., and Szwed. The Free Press, New York.

Herskovits, Melvin (1958) *The Myth of the Negro Past*. Beacon Press, Boston.

Hill, Robert (1972) *The Strengths of Black Families*. Emerson Hall Publishers, New York.

Johnson, Charles S. (1934) *Shadow of the Plantation*. The University of Chicago Press, Chicago.

———— (1941) *Growing Up in the Black Belt*. 1967. Schocken Books, New York.

Keesing, Roger (1970) "Toward a Model of Role Analysis," in *A Handbook of Method in Cultural Anthropology*, Eds., Raoul Naroll and Ronald Cohen. Columbia University Press, New York.

Keil, Charles (1966) *Urban Blues*. The University of Chicago Press, Chicago.

Kluckhohn et al. (1952) "Values and Values-Orientations in the Theory of Action," in *Toward A General Theory of Action*, Eds., Parsons and Shils. Harvard University Press, Cambridge.

Ladner, Joyce (1971) *Tomorrow's Tomorrow: The Black Woman*. Doubleday, New York.

Leach, E. R., *Rethinking Anthropology*. London School of Economics, The Athlone Press, London.

Lévi-Strauss, Claude (1969) *The Elementary Structures of Kinship*. Beacon Press, Boston.

Lewis, Hylan (1965) "The Family: Resources for Change," in *The Moynihan Report: The Politics of Controversy*. Eds., Rainwater and Yancy. Cambridge Press, Cambridge, Mass.

———— (1967) "To Fulfill These Rights." Ibid.

———— (1971) "Courtship, Marriage, and the Family," in *The Black Family*. Ed., Robert Staples. Wadsworth Publishing Co., Belmont, Calif.

Lewis, Oscar (1966) *La Vida*. Vintage Books, New York.

Libow, Elliot (1967) *Tally's Corner: A Study of Negro Street Corner Men*. Little, Brown and Co., Boston.

Linton, Ralph (1937) "One Hundred Percent American," in *Every Man His Way*. Ed., Alan Dunes, 1968. Prentice-Hall, Englewood Cliffs, N.J.

Malinowski, Bronislaw (1915) "The Native of Mailu," in *Transactions of the Royal Society of South Australia*, 39:494–707. In Sahlins, "The Relevance of Models for Social Anthropology," *ASA*, Monograph 1, 1965.

—— (1930) "Parenthood—The Basis of Social Structure," in *The New Generation*. Eds., V. F. Calverston and Samuel Schmalhausen. Macauley, New York.

Marshall, Mac (1977) "The Nature of Nurture," *American Ethnologist* (4), November 1977.

Mead, Margaret (1962) *Male and Female*. New American Library, New York.

Merton, Robert (1967) "Discrimination and the American Creed," in *The Study of Society*. Ed., Peter I. Rose. Random House, New York.

Moynihan, Daniel P. (1965) "The Negro Family: The Case for National Action." Department of Labor, Washington, D.C.

Murdock, George (1949) *Social Structure*. Macmillan, New York.

Myrdal, Gunnar (1944) *An American Dilemma: The Negro Problem and Modern Democracy*. Harper and Row, New York.

Parsons, Talcott (1954) "The Kinship System of the Contemporary United States," in *Essays in Sociological Theory*. Ed., Parsons. The Free Press, New York.

—— (1965) "The Normal American Family," in *Family in Transition*. Eds., Skolnick and Skolnick. Little, Brown and Co., Boston.

Pinkney, Alphonso (1969) *Black Americans*. Prentice-Hall, Englewood Cliffs, N.J.

Raab, Earl and Selznick, Gertrude (1959) *Major Social Problems*. Harper and Row, New York.

Radcliffe-Brown, A. R. and Forde, Daryll, eds. (1950) *African Systems of Kinship and Marriage*. Oxford University Press, London.

Randolph, Richard (1964) "The Matrifocal Family as a Category," *American Anthropology*, 66 (3), Part I, June 1964.

Rappaport, A. (1963) *Kinship and Social Organization*. Eds., Buchler and Selby, 1968. The Macmillan Co., New York.

Reed, Evelyn (1972) "In Defense of Engels on the Matriarchy," in *Feminism and Socialism*. Ed., Linda Jenness. Pathfinder Press, New York.

Rodman, Hyman (1965) "The Lower-class Value Stretch," Reprint from *Social Forces*, December 1963. University of North Carolina Press, N. C.

Sahlins, Marshall (1965) "The Relevance of Models for Social Anthropology," in *ASA*, Monograph 1, 1965.

Scanzoni, John H. (1977) *The Black Family in Modern Society: Patterns of Stability and Security*. The University of Chicago Press, Chicago.

Schneider, David (1968) *American Kinship: A Cultural Account.* Prentice-Hall, Englewood Cliffs, N.J.

Schneider, David and Smith, Raymond (1973) *Class Differences and Sex Roles in American Kinship and Family Structure.* Prentice-Hall, Englewood Cliffs, N.J.

Schulz, David A. (1969) *Coming Up Black: Patterns of Ghetto Socialization.* Prentice-Hall, Englewood Cliffs, N.J.

———— (1968) "The Role of the Boyfriend," in *The Black Family: Essays and Studies.* Ed., Robert Staples, 1971. Wadsworth Publishing Co., Belmont, Calif.

Stack, Carol B. (1970) "The Kinship of Viola Jackson: Residence and Family Organization of an Urban Black American Family," in *Afro-American Anthropology.* Eds., Whitten, Jr., and Szwed. The Free Press, New York.

———— (1974) *All Our Kin: Strategies for Survival in a Black Community.* Harper and Row, New York.

Staples, Robert (1970) "The Myth of the Black Matriarchy," in *The Black Scholar.* January–February, 1970.

———— (1973) "The Myth of the Important Black Male," in *Contemporary Thought: The Best from The Black Scholar.* Eds. Robert Chrisman and Nathan Hare. The Bobbs-Merrill Co., New York.

————, ed. (1971) *The Black Family: Essays and Studies.* Wadsworth Publishing Co., Belmont, Calif.

Valentine, Charles A. (1968) *Culture and Poverty: Critiques and Counter-Proposals.* The University of Chicago Press, Chicago.

Whitten, Jr., Norman and Szwed, John F., eds. (1970) *Afro-American Anthropology: Contemporary Perspectives.* The Free Press, New York.